The San Francisco Civic Center

The San Francisco Civic Center

A History of the Design,
Controversies, and Realization
of a City Beautiful Masterpiece

James W. Haas

UNIVERSITY OF NEVADA PRESS   *Reno & Las Vegas*

University of Nevada Press | Reno, Nevada 89557 USA
www.unpress.nevada.edu
Copyright © 2019 by University of Nevada Press
All rights reserved
Cover photograph by John W. Bare @JBinSF
Cover design by Matt Strelecki

LIBRARY OF CONGRESS CATALOGING-IN-PUBLICATION DATA

Names: Haas, James W., author. | Feinstein, Dianne, 1933– writer of foreword.
Title: The San Francisco Civic Center : a history of the design,
    controversies, and realization of a City Beautiful masterpiece / James W.
    Haas ; foreword by Dianne Feinstein.
Description: Reno ; Las Vegas : University of Nevada Press, [2019]. |
    Includes bibliographical references.
Identifiers: LCCN 2018041290 (print) | LCCN 2018047400 (ebook) | ISBN
    9781948908146 (ebook) | ISBN 9781948908153 (cloth : alk. paper)
Subjects: LCSH: Civic Center (San Francisco, Calif.)—History. | Civic
    centers—California—San Francisco—History. | Urban
    beautification—California—San Francisco—History. | Civic
    centers—United States—History.
Classification: LCC F869.S36 (ebook) | LCC F869.S36 C594 2019 (print) | DDC
    979.4/61—dc23
LC record available at https://lccn.loc.gov/2018041290

The paper used in this book meets the requirements of American National Standard for
Information Sciences — Permanence of Paper for Printed Library Materials, ANSI/NISO
Z39.48-1992 (R2002).

FIRST PRINTING

Manufactured in the United States of America

CONTENTS

FOREWORD

by Senator Dianne Feinstein

From its very beginning, San Francisco's Civic Center has been a vibrant and bustling urban hub that has required shrewd leadership, dedication, and vision to maintain. Although its revitalization has presented challenges over the years, one thing is clear to San Franciscans and visitors alike: Our city's Civic Center is a unique and beautiful treasure that must be preserved, enhanced, and celebrated. In *The San Francisco Civic Center: A History of the Design, Controversies, and Realization of a City Beautiful Masterpiece*, Jim Haas explores the area's fascinating history, major challenges to improvement projects over the years, and the importance of continued efforts to ensure its completed revitalization.

Ever since I first met Jim Haas during my earliest days on the San Francisco Board of Supervisors, he has demonstrated a consistent and admirable commitment to the well-being of our city. While his advocacy and leadership over the years has proven essential to a number of projects and issues, Jim will long be remembered for his thirty-year commitment to the completion and improvement of the city's Civic Center.

In *The San Francisco Civic Center*, Jim takes his record of service to the city to a higher level by bringing to light the unique history of the Civic Center. By doing so, he helps us not only to understand how the Civic Center came to be, but also to grasp its significance and central place in San Francisco's past, present, and future.

This book recounts the story of how Mayor James Rolph's groundbreaking leadership in the first quarter of the twentieth century enabled the Civic Center to become a reality. By demonstrating the influence of the City Beautiful movement on San Francisco's early planning, this book clarifies major pieces of San Francisco architectural and civic history, including the singular role of John Galen Howard, the original designer of the Civic Center, and of Arthur Brown Jr., the architect of City Hall, the War Memorial buildings and the Federal Office Building, as well as the numerous other important histories attached to the Civic Center's origins. In the century that has followed Mayor Rolph's initial efforts to build the Civic Center, there has been no shortage of disputes and controversies surrounding the site's development and upkeep: from lack of funding and bureaucratic neglect, to the inevitable evolution in architectural taste and civic priorities.

I began my career as mayor at a tumultuous time—just after the assassination of my predecessor, George Moscone. It took time to stabilize the city and address its numerous needs. With Jim's help, I realized that the Civic Center was also in need of attention, and devoted my last three years in office in developing a plan and program to complete the Civic Center with a new main public library and a court house as well as converting the old main library into a home for the world-class Asian Art Museum. Although it gives me great pride to see that all those important buildings have been completed, efforts are still ongoing to make the Civic Center a useful and welcoming public space for all San Franciscans.

The beautification of cities has never been a frill. The quality and condition of a city's municipal structures and public spaces are core elements in creating community. As this important book demonstrates, San Francisco's Civic Center—designed according to the progressive reform ideas from the City Beautiful movement that sought to inspire community engagement through conscientious urban planning—was built around this very goal.

Before his passing, the late mayor Edwin Lee launched a major initiative to improve the Civic Center public realm. Investment in the care of our public spaces is essential to the continued vitality of our beautiful city. Although it will only be possible through meticulous planning, hard work, and the help of many passionate people, I have faith that we will someday see the completed revitalization of San Francisco's Civic Center. This book will help people understand and appreciate what a magnificent treasure we in San Francisco have with our Civic Center and why we must continue to work to preserve and enhance it.

I urge everyone to read it.

— Senator Dianne Feinstein

PREFACE

My involvement with the development of the San Francisco Civic Center began in fall 1984, when Marjorie Stern, a great advocate for the public library, asked me to join her campaign to build a new main library on Marshall Square. The old main library had numerous problems, and a major effort had begun to encourage the city to back the construction of a new library building in the Civic Center area. The project would require a tremendous amount of money, and Dianne Feinstein, who was then mayor, was reluctant at first to get behind the effort. At the time, all of the Civic Center buildings and plaza had suffered from decades of neglect and were badly in need of attention. To help overcome Mayor Feinstein's reluctance to endorse the library project, I encouraged her by letter to view the library as part of a larger effort toward making major improvements to all of the Civic Center. Eventually, as she and her staff studied the situation, this tactic would prove effective, and in December of 1987, Mayor Feinstein announced an area development plan for the Civic Center, a plan which included a new library.

Once Feinstein offered her support for a new library—funding for which the voters initially approved in 1988 and which would open in 1996—I went on to advocate for improving the rest of the Civic Center through the implementation of Feinstein's area plan. As part of those efforts, I began to research the Civic Center's background because I often needed to write articles and make presentations to support improvements. However, during those research efforts, I quickly discovered that public information about the Civic Center and City Hall was limited, antiquated, and frequently inaccurate. As a result, I needed to look for more useful sources. The late Joan E. Draper's PhD thesis, "The San Francisco Civic Center: Architecture, Planning, and Politics," is the most comprehensive, and perhaps the only, discussion extant of civic centers in general and of the San Francisco Civic Center in particular.[1] However, it was written more than forty years ago and has never been published. In 2006, Jeffrey T. Tilman published *Arthur Brown Jr.: Progressive Classicist*, a biography of the architect who designed four Civic Center buildings: City Hall, the War Memorial Opera House and Veterans Building, and the federal office building at 50 United Nations Plaza.[2] Tilman's work was a great source of information on Brown's long life, and also describes these buildings and their development in great detail.

As useful as both of these resources were, I found that the only way I would be able to construct a whole story of the San Francisco Civic Center that included local political developments was to scour primary sources. The electronic age has made this task much easier than before, with digitized documents including, most importantly, newspapers. For example, James Rolph, who was elected mayor of San Francisco in 1911 and who would later become governor of California, played a leading role in the Civic Center story. However, no one has written about Rolph's life or work in a way that covers the time period of his first election or his work during the Panama-Pacific International Exposition—critical moments in the Civic Center's history. Thus, I had to put together that story from primary material. In addition, much of the existing information played down or even ignored the role of the prominent architect and planner John Galen Howard as the original planner. Since Howard was the person largely responsible for the design of the Civic Center complex, I have taken pains to highlight his unique contribution.

I approached this history as a researcher determined to dig deeply to uncover essential facts on which to base a complete and accurate record. However, as time passed, and my years of involvement with the area's development became decades, I found myself an actor in the story as well as a chronicler. I had originally contemplated recruiting a graduate student to work with me or perhaps write the history as his or her PhD thesis. But after consulting Bay Area and national academic sources, I was unable to locate such a scholar. I realized that if the story were to be told, I would have to tell it myself, so I have devoted the last eight years to the project. Not being a professional or trained writer, my efforts were sometimes inefficient, but I strove to be thorough. My approach to this history has been guided by Martin Gilbert, a well-known British historian and the official biographer of Winston Churchill, who wrote, "I am not a theoretical historian, seeking to guide the reader to general conclusions. I'm quite content to be a narrative chronicler, a slave of the facts." I examined many archives, including the papers of Daniel Burnham at the Art Institute of Chicago, Rolph at the California Historical Society, and James Duval Phelan at the Bancroft Library at the University of California, Berkeley. I also reviewed a century of newspaper articles on the internet.

Several earlier projects that I did on San Francisco history gave me the confidence to undertake and complete an in-depth study on the history of the Civic Center. In 2008, Charles Fracchia, the founding president of the San Francisco Museum and Historical Society and the editor of its journal, *The Argonaut*, encouraged me to write a biography of the largely forgotten Edward Robeson Taylor, mayor of San Francisco from 1907 to 1910.[3] We anticipated that his biography would be short; however, his life was so diverse and interesting that the article appeared in two long installments. I also ended up curating an exhibit on Mayor

Taylor's interesting life for the San Francisco History Center at the main library. Later, I produced three articles on the Civic Center for *The Argonaut* about the Civic Center's origins, the design and construction of City Hall and other core buildings from 1911 to 1919, and the center's mid-twentieth-century development. Those articles have been revised and became the basis for this book.[4]

My longtime friend and colleague, the late professor Kevin Starr, the eminent California historian, steadfastly encouraged me, as he had done with so many starting writers, to complete the book project and was most helpful with suggestions about how to develop it into a book and get it published. Before his passing, he had planned to write one of his insightful introductions to the book, which we will unfortunately miss.

In my more than thirty years' experience advocating for completing and improving San Francisco's Civic Center, I have absorbed its magnificent ambitions and have dealt with the stark reality associated with trying to convince people to support this historical landmark. City officials and the public have frequently shown a lack of interest in, and even indifference to, the area and its history, and that pains me. Their reluctance to invest in revitalizing the center as a whole, despite attention paid to particular buildings—such as City Hall and the Opera House—has been unfortunate, especially considering the extraordinary prominence that the Civic Center has within San Francisco's urban design and architectural history.

I have had a life-long passion for public affairs and history. My interest in these subjects was first instilled in me during my years as an undergraduate at Stanford, and then later during my studies for a law degree at Colombia University. However, it never occurred to me at that time that I would devote more than half of my adult life to the restoration, completion, and enhancement of the nation's most magnificent municipal architectural treasure, the San Francisco Civic Center. It has been a long, often frustrating and very humbling experience. But after so many years of this work for the Civic Center, I am proud of the success that has been achieved.

I hope this book will help people understand the architectural and social philosophies that inspired the Civic Center's great building designs and the reasons behind their construction. I also hope people will be inspired to appreciate more fully the idea that the Civic Center as a whole is more important than each individual building. I also wish to stimulate greater appreciation of this incredible monumental civic area so that people will feel it belongs to them and will want to spend more time enjoying it in the future. I am happy to herewith share its story with the people of San Francisco and everyone who loves this vibrant city.

Introduction

The San Francisco Civic Center is a grouping of monumental publicly owned buildings that are clustered between Market, McAllister, Hayes, and Franklin Streets about two miles up Market Street from the Ferry Building. The area today contains thirteen government office and cultural buildings, among them City Hall, the main branch of the San Francisco Public Library, the Asian Art Museum, the War Memorial Opera House and Veterans Building, Davies Symphony Hall, Department of Public Health, the Supreme Court and State offices, the Bill Graham Civic Auditorium, the federal office building at United Nations Plaza, and the headquarters for the city's Public Utilities Commission. It is located in the nerve center of San Francisco's major streets grid with the domed City Hall anchoring the area. The area is classified as a historic district on the National Register of Historic Places. It has been the central site of San Francisco's government for more than a century, and the civic and architectural philosophies undergirding its design have been a driving force in San Francisco's urban design since the time the 1906 earthquake forever altered San Francisco's city planning. Because of its long and central history in San Francisco, and its extraordinary architectural heritage, the Civic Center has been discussed as a possible candidate for consideration as a UNESCO World Heritage site.

Despite this remarkable history, the Civic Center in San Francisco and its status as the grandest collection of monumental municipal buildings in the United States suffers from a lack of appreciation among the public, specifically relating to its original design philosophy and its intended function within San Francisco's municipal and civic cultures—ultimately drawing limited global or local interest. Promotion of the city in the media, advertising, and posters at the airport shows pictures of well-known San Francisco places such as Coit Tower, the Golden Gate Bridge, and the Transamerica Pyramid. Rarely is the Civic Center and its imperial City Hall included. The goal of this book is to provide readers with an understanding of the background of the Civic Center that will elevate the public appreciation of this unique place.

The concept of a "civic center," a grand central seat of local democratic government, is a major component in town and city planning in the United States. However, even though many cities today lavish funds on building or enhancing these centers of municipal and public activity, city officials and the general public often have limited knowledge of the origins of the city planning or architectural concepts underpinning the civic center idea. The San Francisco Civic Center, originally planned in 1912, is one of the most complete civic centers contemplated by any American city. It is often considered in both design and materials one of the finest achievements of the American reformist City Beautiful movement, an influential urban planning and landscape movement that began near the end of the nineteenth century. After one hundred years, those urban design concepts which inspired its original construction still guide the city's efforts to add to and improve the Civic Center in the spirit of the original plan set down in 1912 by its designer, John Galen Howard.

The centerpiece of San Francisco's Civic Center is the magnificent domed City Hall, about which the architectural critic Henry Hope Reed Jr. wrote, "In the just quality of ornament, in the play of space, in the total overwhelming effect, the San Francisco City Hall is the best that American art has produced."[1] The Civic Center complex is a stunning manifestation of the confident spirit of one of the nation's most dynamic and creative cities.

The San Francisco Civic Center, like many great monumental city spaces and architectural works around the world, is a work in progress. As so frequently occurs in San Francisco history, the Civic Center's story is characterized by great inspiration and leadership, but also by controversy, feuds, inaction, negativity, and failures. Nevertheless, it is a paradox that, for all of its grandeur and despite the extraordinary effort it took to build, the San Francisco Civic Center not only fails to garner significant public attention, but very little has been written about it. *The San Francisco Civic Center: A History of the Design, Controversies, and Realization of a City Beautiful Masterpiece* addresses this gap by telling the 150-year story of San Francisco's city halls and its surrounding Civic Center, providing answers to many important unanswered (and frequently unasked) questions about this historic site. For example, where did the idea of a municipal and arts center first come from? How did it become central to the urban planning initiatives in San Francisco in the early twentieth century? Why was it built, and by whom? How did the City Hall fit in the plan?

In what ways has the site held onto its founders' vision throughout the past century amid heated public debates about the site's function and achievement? What is its current status and its future?

Although this book focuses on San Francisco, it also discusses related national trends in city planning and the architectural and art movements that influenced those trends. The first chapter examines the origins of the City Beautiful movement and how the civic center concept grew from it and how it was implemented in American cities. Subsequent chapters discuss how these ideas arrived in San Francisco and how they endured as a defining architectural philosophy in the development and improvement of the Civic Center for decades.

In the United States, the major event that launched the City Beautiful movement was the World's Columbian Exposition in Chicago in 1893. This Exposition was a landmark event in American urban design. With its elaborate landscape and architectural creations, the Exposition introduced a vast number of Americans to the idea of a well-organized and beautiful planned urban space and helped stimulate interest in what would become the City Beautiful movement. In the first years of the twentieth century, a number of cities, including Washington, DC, Cleveland, Chicago, and San Francisco, undertook major city planning projects, while Seattle, Denver, and Dallas began large-scale park and parkway beautification projects. The City Beautiful movement fostered the concept of groups of public buildings that became known as "civic centers." Seventy-two American cities engaged in civic center planning from 1902 to 1920, but construction was only undertaken on a few of those centers, and, of those, most were only partially built.[2]

Although City Beautiful was a homegrown American movement, it was also influenced by the neoclassical styles emanating from the École des Beaux-Arts in Paris as well as German engineering and municipal administration. From a political standpoint, the movement was tightly connected to the progressive reformist ideas prevailing in the United States near the end of the nineteenth century and that were a reaction to the excesses of post—Civil War industrialization and the resulting Gilded Age of flaunted wealth, self-interest, and corruption. Seeking changes across civic and economic sectors, reformers called for honest and efficient government, healthy and safe living and working conditions, and services for the poor and needy. The nation's cities, in particular, suffered from poor sanitation, tenement housing, and weak and corrupt governments. Anxious urban middle- and upper-class residents of cities and towns attempted to bring order and, in their view, rectitude to disparate populations through such reform measures as Sunday schools, the Young Men's Christian Association (YMCA), set-tlement houses and other charitable institutions, Prohibition and other anti-vice efforts, as well as kindergartens and playgrounds. The City Beautiful movement was a culmination of this broader progressive social agenda prevailing through the later part of the nineteenth century.[3]

Rather than exhort or coerce urban dwellers to conform to a model of good citizenship and behavior, City Beautiful reformers took an indirect approach. If cities were rebuilt with tree-lined boulevards, grand parks, clean water systems, and palatial public buildings (libraries, schools, opera houses, and government offices) open to all, they hoped that people would respond by adapting positively to the healthier, uplifting environment. To bring about these changes, reformers needed experts to prepare grand city plans, something that led to the establishment of the planning and landscape architecture professions. Additionally, the reformers knew cities would need honest and forward-thinking governments, so campaigns were organized around the country to replace the boss-dominated mayors with new ones who would help advance the new reformist ideas. These political efforts were often helped along by "muckraking" journalists, such as Lincoln Steffens and Ray Stannard Baker, who exposed many corrupt political bosses and city officials. President Theodore Roosevelt was also active in sup-porting good government at the state and local level.

But City Beautiful proponents were not only concerned with the idea of integrating and controlling new and growing urban poor populations; they were also motivated by the optimistic belief that good planning and beauty could help city residents reach other more personal goals, such as better lives for their families and the rest of the community. Many proponents of City Beautiful values were competitive businessmen who wanted to help their cit-ies prosper. The World's Columbian Exposition in Chicago in 1893 had been organized by such advocates.

Progressive and City Beautiful values were channeled to San Francisco by James D. Phelan, who served as mayor from 1896 to 1901. After he retired as mayor, Phelan would become a major proponent for the City Beautiful ideas and urban planning. San Francisco's urban development in the nineteenth cen-tury had been haphazard and the city suffered from a lack of effective public investment and oversight. In the years just before the 1906 earthquake, Phelan recruited Daniel H. Burnham of Chicago—the most influential City Beautiful planner in the United States—to prepare a comprehensive city plan for San Francisco. Although Burnham's plan did in fact include a proposal for a civic center, and despite the tremendous need for development after the earthquake, for a number of reasons, the city would not go on to develop that plan. But it was an important precursor, and it helped lay the groundwork for such a project in the future. It would not be until Congress, in February 1911, backed San Francisco to host the Panama-Pacific International Exposition of 1915 that the city would be galvanized to proceed with construction of a new city hall (the old one had been destroyed in the 1906 earthquake)—and to build it within a monumental civic center.

The development of City Hall and Civic Center in the years surrounding the 1915 Exposition would be led by Mayor James Rolph Jr., a progressively minded mayor first elected in 1911 who was also backed by the city's business community and who had been voted into office by an overwhelming margin. Rolph had the leadership and energy to make building a civic center and new city hall the first priority of his new administration. He recruited John Galen Howard, the most prominent architect in the San Francisco Bay Area, to design the civic center complex and oversee construction of three monumental public buildings including City Hall, the Exposition Auditorium (now known as the Bill Graham Civic Auditorium), and a new main library around a huge landscaped plaza—all based on City Beautiful design values—to be ready by the time the Exposition opened in 1915. Construction on the Civic Center would continue apace in the years following the Panama-Pacific International Exposition and during his five terms as mayor, Rolph pushed for the construction of additional Civic Center buildings.

After World War II, new public attitudes in San Francisco began to disparage old City Beautiful ideals, and people began to view City Hall and the other Civic Center buildings as overbearing and undemocratic, designed with foreign-influenced architecture. The modernist attitude—whose aesthetic priorities were far different from the neoclassical ones which had defined the Civic Center's design—had become pervasive in the city, but city government inertia and fiscal restraint spared the existing complex of then eight buildings from demolition or drastic change. By the early 1970s, the historic preservation movement had taken hold in San Francisco, and eventually the Civic Center was placed on the National Register of Historic Places and made a city landmark, thus protecting its original Civic Center plan and City Beautiful design values. But these designations did not automatically lead to new improvements to the area, nor enhance the Civic Center with any additional buildings.

There would not be a focused effort to enhance the Civic Center more fully until the administration of Dianne Feinstein in the 1980s. Mayor Feinstein, reacting to pressure to build a new public library on the vacant block at Larkin and Fulton Streets, organized and published in 1987 a comprehensive development plan for the area that strongly underscored the original civic center concept. This plan would become the road map for further development and improvements.

The timing of the creation of this comprehensive development plan would turn out to be oddly fortuitous. Two years later, when the Loma Prieta earthquake damaged all of the Civic Center buildings, San Franciscans responded by voting for hundreds of millions of dollars in bonds to restore the buildings to their original designs and conditions. In addition, a new library was financed and built, along with a courthouse and, recently, an office building for the San Francisco Public Utilities Commission. The old library was converted into the Asian Art Museum, bringing the total number of grand public buildings in the area to thirteen.

Although a billion and a half dollars would be spent on structures during this major renovation of the Civic Center buildings, little or no attention was given to exterior public areas, and the empty plaza remained a wasteland and the surrounding streets, rough. Area agencies and institutions were so charged with fulfilling their own missions that they gave little attention to the surrounding environment, even though it adversely affected their activities. Citywide planning and preservation groups likewise paid no attention to the problem. When Gavin Newsom was elected mayor in 2004, he recognized the need for a renewed focus on the plaza and surrounding area and authorized a new Community Benefit District designation for the area. In 2014, for the first time since Feinstein's 1987 plan, Mayor Edwin Lee included in the planning department budget funds to undertake a Public Realm Plan for the Civic Center, more than one hundred years after the complex had begun.

The Civic Center's long journey is a both a story of perseverance and dysfunction. The record shows that the Civic Center was, despite being at the heart of the city government's operations, frequently underfunded and overlooked by the community and by city officials. But it is also true that moments of great leadership, tremendous creativity, and courage among San Francisco's residents, architects, and officials enabled the San Francisco Civic Center to be built and become the extraordinary urban center that it is today.

The American Civic Center: Origin and History

Between 1903 and 1920 some seventy-two cities and towns around the country prepared plans to construct a civic center, a new architectural and urban design concept that was becoming popular in city planning at the time. Some of these plans were developed in conjunction with large parks or comprehensive plans; most were sponsored by chambers of commerce or private civic improvements groups. Many studies were conducted by municipal planning bodies or other public agencies, and a few were prepared or sponsored by local individuals or architects. However, of the seventy-two cities and towns that investigated civic centers and prepared plans, only seven attempted to implement them.[1] Some of those that were implemented were only partially developed, and of those municipalities that did fully develop them, only one succeeded in building a civic center according to the original plans—San Francisco. Through unique circumstances and opportunities as will be described later in the book, San Francisco was able to build a civic center and city hall of imperial pretensions.

The origin of the idea of a civic center in America is found in the City Beautiful movement, the leading urban reform initiative in America of the first decade of the twentieth century.

William H. Wilson, the noted City Beautiful expert, describes it as follows:

The heyday of the City Beautiful movement . . . [saw] middle- and upper-middle class Americans attempt[ing] to refashion their cities into beautiful, functional entities. Their effort involved a cultural agenda, a middle-class environmentalism, and aesthetics expressed as beauty, order, system, and harmony. The ideal found physical realization in urban design, public and semi-public buildings, civic centers, park and boulevard systems . . . the tokens of the improved environment. So were ordinary street improvements, including good paving, attractive furniture such as lampposts, and carefully selected and maintained trees. The goal beyond the tangibles was to influence the heart, mind, and purse of the citizen. Physical change and institutional reformation would persuade urban dwellers to become more imbued with civic patriotism and better disposed toward community needs. Beautiful surrounding[s] would enhance worker productivity and urban economics.[2]

The underpinnings of the City Beautiful movement were heavily influenced by the work of Frederick Law Olmsted, one of the nineteenth century's most pioneering landscape architects. Olmsted was the designer of many of the most celebrated urban parks in America, including Central Park in New York City, and his design vision of planned, detailed landscapes featuring extensive natural areas alongside man-made constructions was highly influential within the City Beautiful movement. Olmsted developed his broader design vision on Central Park where, in 1858, he had been appointed superintendent of construction and where he would work for the following two decades. Although he

From the Chicago World's Columbian Exposition in 1893: The "Court of Honor" looking east toward Lake Michigan, with the Manufactures Building on the left and the Agriculture Building on the right. Source: Courtesy of Avery Architectural and Fine Arts Library, Columbia University.

intended the park to welcome all people, Olmsted's vision was one that strongly appealed to middle-class aesthetics and his work at Central Park was so successful that it would lead to invitations to design other major parks in New York City and other cities around the country. Universities, asylums, and private real estate developers also requested his landscape-planning consultation. Olmsted would establish the first landscape architecture firm in the United States, eventually including his son Frederick Law Olmsted Jr., and John C. Olmsted, his stepson. Mount Royal Park in Montreal, the Back Bay Fens in Boston, and the Stanford University campus are among his achievements. In essence, Olmsted reestablished city planning in America and created the profession of landscape architecture, which spurred the growth of park and parkway design projects around the country. Olmsted's designs for the 1893 World's Columbian Exposition in Chicago, in particular, would play a pivotal role in inspiring urban planners and reformers around the United States, and the Exposition would become the key inspiration for the City Beautiful movement which would sweep the country in the coming years.

The World's Columbian Exposition in Chicago

Queen Victoria and Prince Albert began the tradition of world expositions with the Great Exhibition of 1851 in London's Crystal Palace, an event intended to display the current achievements of industry, agriculture, and the arts of that prosperous time in England's history. In 1876 the United States celebrated its centennial by holding the first US world exposition in Philadelphia. As the century neared its close, American cities vigorously competed to host a world exposition in 1893 to commemorate the 400th anniversary of Columbus's discovery of America. Chicago, backed by a committee of businessmen, won the competition. When the committee moved to hire someone to help locate and develop the site for the exposition, the committee immediately asked Olmsted, who had also previously prepared a major planning report for the Chicago South Park Board of Commissioners in 1870 to transform nearly a thousand acres of land six miles south of the city center on Lake Michigan into functional parks.[3] However, in October 1871, the Great Chicago Fire destroyed much of the city as well as the materials Olmsted had prepared for the South Park project. Those park projects immediately became a low priority and were never built, thus the land became available as the site for the Exposition two decades later.

To help locate the buildings on the Exposition grounds, the committee also asked the prominent Chicago architect Daniel Hudson Burnham to join Olmsted as consulting architect. By fall, they had prepared a plan to develop the marsh along the lakefront into the Exposition's centerpiece: an architectural court of grand buildings enclosing a basin of water with access to Lake Michigan. A canal from the basin would lead to a series of irregularly shaped lagoons, the largest of which contained a natural wooded island. State and foreign pavilions and museums accessible by boat would ring the lagoons' shorelines. The plan also addressed the practical concerns of water, power, and sewage. Olmsted and Burnham suggested creating a commercial and entertainment zone on the wide strip of land extending away from the Exposition site, which would become famous as "The Midway." Theirs was a remarkable plan, with both a formal urban setting for major buildings and a less formal one for the extensive Exposition grounds.[4]

In the interest of efficiency, the Chicago committee agreed that the consulting architect and landscape architect should select all other designers for the Exposition buildings. In addition to selecting five Chicago firms, Olmsted and Burnham invited some of the most prominent architects in the country to participate in the Exposition's planning. Burnham traveled east to secure participation from several well-known New York firms, which he obtained on their conditions that all buildings share a common cornice height and that major buildings would be in the neoclassical style. The New York architects believed that a collection of neoclassical buildings would be a striking new vision. This was a significant departure from the Romanesque style that had dominated architecture for the previous twenty years. As Burnham and the architects got further into the building design, they agreed that the primary color would be white, giving rise to the "White City," as the Exposition became known.[5] The group of colossal classical white buildings around the basin became known as the "Court of Honor."

Twenty-seven million rural and urban Americans, out of the total US population of sixty-five million, visited the Exposition. Word about the Exposition radiated throughout the country. Olmsted traveled to many states in the first half of 1893, and he wrote to Burnham on June 20, "Everywhere I have found indications that people are planning to go to it. In country papers accounts of visits are now appearing adapted to increase the desire to see it. Clergymen who have been to the Fair are referring to it in their sermons."[6] Eventually, visitors came in droves and were dazzled by clean and orderly grounds, grand and stately buildings, and creative water use and landscaping.[7] In the evenings, the grounds were illuminated by electric lights, which had been recently commercialized by Thomas Edison. The notions of good sanitation, city planning, public administration, landscaping, and civic beauty as practiced at the fair became part of middle- and upper-class progressivism. The world's fair also turned an American version of neoclassical architecture into the country's dominant style.

Millions of visitors returned to their hometowns and shared their experiences. Several of the Exposition's New York architects and artists were so enthusiastic about what they experienced in Chicago that they organized the Municipal Art Society in 1893 to convince New York City to provide "sculptural and pictorial decorations for public buildings and parks." (The organization exists today.) Cities, such as Kansas City, that had begun park and parkway projects before the Exposition proceeded with renewed enthusiasm.[8] However, this national momentum would be interrupted in mid-1893 when the United States suffered a financial panic and entered an economic depression caused by dropping grain prices, runs on banks, and railroad and business bankruptcies. This led to lower wages and labor strikes, such as the violent Pullman strike of 1894. As a result of the depressed economy and public despair that would last for almost five years, few communities were willing to take on massive planning and beautification projects. Nevertheless, excitement for these artistic and urban reform ideas was not lost and it would blossom in the decade ahead. The impact of the 1893 Exposition on city planning in the United States would be a major factor in the future development of the civic center.

City Beautiful and City Planning

As the country recovered from the depression of the 1890s and entered what is known as the Progressive Era, numerous "improvement" societies were founded in cities and towns across the nation to advocate for everything from public works projects such as better sanitation systems to beautification projects such as billboard removal. National organizations—such as the American Park and Outdoor Association, and the National Municipal League—were established to support local groups, promote municipal improvements, and improve the operation of local government.[9]

The first time that the words "The City Beautiful" actually appeared in print was in *Municipal Affairs*, a publication started in 1897 by a group of reformers to circulate articles about planning and beautification when the December 1899 issue displayed the words *The City Beautiful* across the cover in bold type. Artists and writers had been toying with the notion, based on the Arts and Crafts movement in England, but this was the first time the phrase appeared in print.[10]

The phrase would start to appear in numerous works in the years ahead. In mid-1899, Charles Mulford Robinson, a young journalist who had visited the Columbian Exposition, discussed the "City Beautiful" in a three-part series of articles called the "Improvement of Cities" for the *Atlantic Monthly*. Impressed with his work, *Harper's* magazine sent him overseas to write a series on municipal improvements in Europe which would lead him to publish in 1901 the influential work in city planning called *The Improvement of Towns and Cities; Or, The Practical Basis of Civic Aesthetics*, a book-length "handbook" that sold out within months and was revised and republished several times. In this work, Robinson advocated for readers to take a comprehensive view of city problems, stressing the inseparability of beauty and utility. The book endorsed the civic design concepts of grouped public buildings, formal spatial settings, public statuary, and well-designed street furniture. Robinson wrote three more books on cities and planning and became a consultant who prepared planning reports for nearly two dozen American cities.

As the new century arrived, the United States saw the first large-scale actualization of the kind of civic design project that the City Beautiful advocates had been championing. In 1900 Americans celebrated the centennial of the District of Columbia as the nation's capital, an event which prompted Congress and Washingtonians to examine the current conditions and the changes affecting Pierre Charles L'Enfant's original 1791 district plan. L'Enfant's open Capitol Mall had become filled in with a rail yard and station, cattle pens and industrial buildings. The American Institute of Architects, which held its national convention in Washington, DC, in December of that same year, called upon Senator James McMillan, the powerful chairman of the Committee on the District of Columbia, to take leadership in addressing these conditions. McMillian responded to the AIA's request and arranged for the Senate to authorize a three-person commission to study the district's park system, including the mall. He appointed the prominent New York architect Charles Follen McKim, who had been one of the architects of the Chicago Exposition, Frederick Law Olmsted Jr., and, as chairman, Daniel Burnham, giving Burnham a second opportunity to make grand civic plan. A year later, Burnham and his colleagues released what was called the McMillan Plan. It boldly redefined the area around the Capitol with a masterfully designed park and boulevard system in a way that City Beautiful supporters around the country saw as the realization of what they had been advocating. The proposal included a parkway in Rock Creek, a tidal pool at the foot of the Mall at the Potomac, and a new bridge across the river. Burnham's proposal to solve the railroad station problem was to construct a huge union station north of the Capitol, for which he received the commission from several railroads. The plan created a sensation when the drawings and model were publicly exhibited at the Corcoran Gallery of Art in January 1902. Montgomery Schuyler, the most prominent architectural critic of the day, praised it for showing the public "the all-importance to a city of having a plan."[11] Burnham pushed the City Beautiful notion further by publishing an article in the February 1902 issue of *Century*

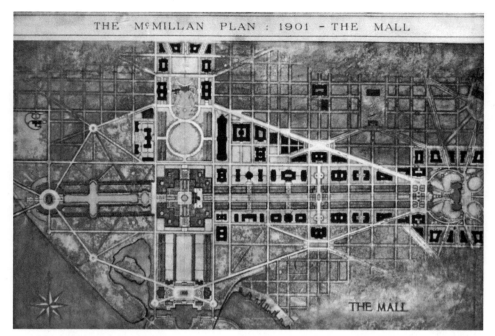

THE McMILLAN PLAN : 1901 - THE MALL

THE MALL

Plan for the US Capitol and Mall in Washington, DC, prepared by the McMillan Commission in 1902.
Source: Courtesy the National Capitol Planning Commission.

Magazine entitled "White City and Capital City," in which he related the lessons learned from the Chicago Exposition about the value of beauty and harmony and urged other cities to create similar plans.

Many other cities did, indeed, follow suit. Seattle citizens had a strong interest in creating parks and playfields, and so in 1902 they engaged John Charles Olmsted, of Olmsted Brothers, to develop a string of interconnected park- and waterways. A few years later Portland, Oregon, and Spokane, Washington, asked him to prepare similar plans. In 1905, Denver citizens invited Robinson to prepare a plan to develop a parkway system. Later that year, Robinson would also design one for Honolulu. Burnham's complex and massive plans for Union Station in Washington, DC, would also stimulate nearly a dozen similar large union stations around the country, of which Burnham designed several. In 1909 Burnham published his massive *Plan of Chicago*, which was the largest City Beautiful plan undertaken.

The first major civic planning project in the United States that was closest to being a "civic center" occurred in Cleveland. After visiting the Chicago Exposition in 1893, a group of Cleveland citizens and architects had begun to conceive of a group of essential public buildings inspired by the Exposition's "Court of Honor." However, they made little progress until 1901, when Cleveland elected a dynamic reform mayor, Tom L. Johnson. He campaigned

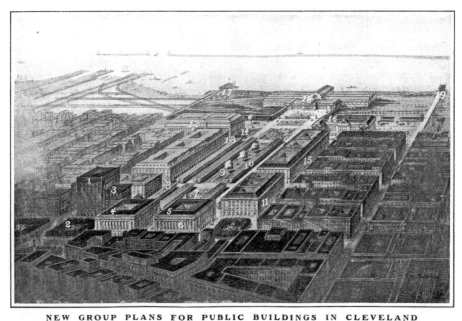

NEW GROUP PLANS FOR PUBLIC BUILDINGS IN CLEVELAND

For a description of the new plans for public buildings in Cleveland the reader is referred to an article on the opposite page. The Federal Building, of which Mr. Arnold W. Brunner is the architect, is now under way, and the corner-stone will be laid about June 1. In the drawing Fig. 1 is the present Society for Savings Bank; 2, Public Square; 3, Chamber of Commerce; 4, Federal Building, including Post-office, Custom-house, and Court-house; 5 and 6, Proposed Library; 7, 8, 9, 10, 13, and 14, The Mall; 11 and 15, Proposed buildings on land along Bond Street to be acquired by the city; 12, Proposed County Court-house; 16, Proposed City Hall; 18, Proposed Union Railroad Station; 17 and 19, Proposed Recreation Piers

The Cleveland Group Plan facing Lake Erie with the twin Federal and Public Library buildings forefront, 1903. Source: Harper's Magazine, XLVIII, April 23, 1906, p.624–626.

on a platform that included building a "Group Plan" to inspire civic pride through good architecture and landscaping. In 1902 Johnson convinced the Ohio legislature to create a three-person commission and a way to finance the project. At Johnson's suggestion, Governor George Nash appointed Daniel Burnham; John Carrère, of the prominent New York architecture firm of Carrère and Hastings; and Arnold Brunner, also of New York, who had already received the commission from the US government to design a federal courthouse and post office in Cleveland.[12] These three members of Cleveland's Group Plan commission worked diligently on the project for a year and issued their report in November 1903, calling for six to eight monumental neoclassical buildings set around a rectangular plaza extending south from Lake Erie, slightly northeast of the existing business district. Herbert Croly, the well-known architectural critic and reformer, wrote about the plan in *Architectural Record in 1907*, "There is no other city in the country where local aspiration towards cleanliness, comeliness and wholesomeness of municipal life has received abler and more varied expression."[13] Although work was slow to start and Cleveland would ultimately only partially complete the number of buildings in its original plan, the plan itself received much attention around the country.

While civic leaders in cities and towns across the country were considering new municipal plans inspired by the values of City Beautiful, the movement's leading practitioners and proponents were producing a steady stream of books and articles on design, planning, and social reform. During this time, the term "civic center" was coined by the former congressman John DeWitt Warner, the president of the Municipal Art Society of New York, in the March 1902 issue of *Municipal Affairs.* DeWitt used the term in an article where he presented a survey of European city public building groupings to demonstrate that it was a concept with an existing tradition, and he went on in the article to discuss proposals for building similar groupings in several American cities. In 1903, Robinson published his second book, *Modern Civic Art: Or, The City Made Beautiful*, in which he turned his attention to the municipal geography, arguing that cities should have a number of focal points, including an administrative center where public life could take place. He recommended grouping public buildings to lend the governmental process convenience, cooperation, and dignity. He warned against locating major buildings along streets, whether on one side or lining both sides, since such an arrangement would not highlight the buildings' scale and relative importance and would lose the opportunity for perspective.[14] "The buildings are best located around the edge of a square or plaza with new buildings in harmony with each other as in the Court of Honor," he wrote.[15] As a paean to this idea, he wrote, "The municipality, in this representation of the mightiness of its total business, seems a more majestic thing and one better worth the devotion and service of its citizens."[16] Robinson's book and Burnham's Cleveland Group Plan inspired additional publications proposing that civic centers could make government and politics more honest; reduce the chaos of urban life through good planning; and harmoniously, orderly, and symmetrically arrange buildings. They could also provide the public opportunities for enlightenment and self-improvement in libraries, concert halls, and museums. For civic center proponents, planned landscape and architecture were not an exercise in grandiosity but a way to mold and improve civic character, increase opportunity for citizens, and build better communities.

In the first two decades of the twentieth century, civic center planning studies and reports proliferated across some seventy-two cities and towns. In most cases, consultants drew up these plans and reports. Many were drawn up by the era's leading planners: Edward Bennett, who had been a partner of Burnham, created eight. John Nolen, one of the first graduates of the newly established Harvard School of Landscape Architecture, also created eight plans. Robinson devised six; Frederick Law Olmsted Jr., five. In some cases, the plans were prepared by prominent architects, such as Cass Gilbert, Carrère, or Brunner.[17] Local planners and architects crafted most of the remaining schemes.

Some cities commissioned civic center reports, but then took a completely contrary course. Rather than acquire blocks of private land to house low-rise monumental buildings, Oakland, California, and New York each decided to construct a single high-rise building to house all government activities. New York's Municipal Building, just east of the historic City Hall built in 1811, is a richly decorated forty-story tower designed by the prominent New York firm McKim, Mead, and White and built between 1909 and 1914.

Many civic center reports were detached from pressing local needs and therefore could be considered a bit utopian. As a result, they also often raised opposition from existing property owners and taxpayer groups concerned about funding the improvements since building a civic center required taking over and converting many blocks of central city land. For example, in Kansas City in 1907, in an effort to counter a fear that the area in front of the city's huge new Union Station would become populated by saloons and other low-class businesses, the construction of a civic center was proposed. But the plan was widely attacked because it was seen as wiping out good business property and being ruinously expensive. Kansas City would eventually abandon the proposals for the civic center, and after World War I, the city bought the station property for a park and war memorial. On a terrace opposite the railroad station, the city built the Liberty Memorial, a 217-foot-high stone monument to commemorate the Great War's fallen soldiers.[18]

One of the few complete civic centers to be built in the United States is in Denver. Although it took approximately a hundred years to build and went through numerous changes to its design over that time, it is nevertheless a development deeply rooted in the City Beautiful movement. The first civic center plan proposed in Denver was drawn by Robinson. The plan included the city acquiring seven or eight blocks of business properties near the existing state capitol building to accommodate a new library, auditorium, and headquarters for the chamber of commerce. Although the city's mayor, Robert W. Speer, strongly endorsed the project, many property owners and businessmen were against it, and when the project was presented to voters in 1907, it lost by a substantial margin.[19] Nevertheless, the idea of building a civic center persisted in Denver, and subsequent city administrations invited and entertained numerous other design proposals from many of the era's notable architects and designers including Frederick Law Olmsted Jr., and Frederick MacMonnies, a sculptor who had been commissioned to design a monument to Colorado pioneers as part of a civic center plan.[20] Eventually, when Speer was elected again in 1916, he hired Bennett to synthesize the many proposals that had been made over the prior decade. Voters would eventually approve that plan, and construction would start in 1919 on land the city had already acquired for the project. Among the first buildings was an amphitheater with a colonnade backdrop on one side, and a Colonnade of Civic Benefactors on the other. In 1932, a long-discussed neoclassical City and County Building was built and then after World War II, the Denver Public Library constructed a new building to add to the civic center.[21] In 1971, the Denver Art Museum opened its striking North Building, designed by Gio Ponti, in the civic center area. In 2002, the city built a large municipal office building near the City and County Building, and in 2006, it added the "Hamilton Building" to the Art Museum, a structure designed by the architect Daniel Libeskind. Today, Denver's civic center meets most of the definitions of the idea as the civic center had originally been conceived. However, because of its very long and winding design and construction history, the complex generally lacks the architectural uniformity for which City Beautiful planners had earlier advocated.

Among the dozens of cities and towns which explored the possibility of building civic centers and prepared plans, with the exception of San Francisco, none succeeded in building them according to the original plans, and many of those that were begun were only partially developed. While civic center planning did not always lead to a large number of projects, those planning exercises in civic center and City Beautiful projects pushed communities to create public-planning bodies and engage professional planners, thus making land development subject to public policies and process, an important step in the evolution away from the laissez-faire urban development of the past.

City Practical and the Evolution of the Civic Center

The City Beautiful movement gave rise to ambitions of urban reform through well-considered city planning, and it brought into its fold people with varied interests and skills, such as engineers, housing reformers, and social activists. Over time, however, as the movement evolved, many of these people became critical of City Beautiful movement, charging that it was too focused on aesthetics. Benjamin Marsh, a New York housing-reform advocate, wrote that the poor were confined in "their squalid, confining surroundings [and could not] view the architectural perfection and experience the aesthetic delights of remote improvements."[22] This dramatic change of attitude among some of the movement's earlier practitioners and advocates came to a head at the First National Conference on City Planning convened in Washington, DC, in May 1909. Robert Anderson Pope, a landscape architect, argued that City Beautiful encouraged the view that the primary goal of city planning was to beautify by building expensive and often inaccessible improvements made available to a small portion of the

Front view of Calabasas, California, Civic Center, 2008. Photographer: Peter Aaron/Otto for Robert A.M. Stern Architects. Source: Courtesy of Robert A.M. Stern Architects, LLP.

community—the wealthy and leisure classes. He went on to say that cities had "rushed to plan showy civic centers at gigantic cost inspired by civic vanity" when nearby there existed "unbelievable congestion with its hideous brood of evil: filth, disease, degeneracy, pauperism, and crime." These new planners called for cities to establish strong planning commissions that would complete surveys, collect data, prepare comprehensive strategies, limit industrial activity by zoning, and locate parks in crowded districts. These revisionist views also appeared at the annual meeting of the American Institute of Architects in December 1909, where the prominent architect Cass Gilbert said "personally I detest the phrase 'City Beautiful'" and asserted that he would "absolutely suppress" it. He called for "the city useful, the city practical, the city livable, the city sensible, or any other title . . . but we want a city well done and a city that can be lived in." His audience of the architectural elite responded with "widespread and hearty applause."[23] City Practical became the slogan of the new national urban agenda.

As the City Beautiful movement faded in the coming years from the American consciousness, the idea of the civic center did not. However, the means to build them eluded urban planners for many years. In the years following World War I, the cost of materials and land increased to the point that it became prohibitive for a community to develop a civic center, even if it desired to do so. Later, after World War II, an explosion of newly designed and constructed suburban towns and the new federal redevelopment program supporting slum clearance prompted some communities to again consider building civic centers to give them focus.

Since the 1950s, a number of towns and cities around the country have developed facilities which they have called civic centers, albeit on a smaller scale than those in the largest cities and for narrower purposes, sometimes developing only a single building to serve as space for public activity. In 1979 the Greater Des Moines Civic Center opened only as a performing arts center, and similar facilities have been built in Atlanta and Oklahoma City. Savannah, Georgia; Memphis, Tennessee; and Hartford, Connecticut have arenas as their civic centers to accommodate sports events and circuses, making them primarily entertainment and commercial venues; nevertheless, they were designed to be central points where the public could meet for civic activities.

Some new cities have sought to revive the original civic center concept. Calabasas, a wealthy new Los Angeles suburb, needed a permanent city hall, so its citizens proposed a civic center to serve as the core of this community, including a city hall, public library, and amphitheater. Architect Robert A. M. Stern was engaged to design the complex in a mix of Mediterranean and mission revival styles to give it prominence. The Calabasas Civic Center was completed in 2008 at a cost of $42 million, proving that citizens are still willing to tax themselves to give their community a civic heart.

Victorian City Hall
and Early City Planning
in San Francisco

In an article published in the *San Francisco Chronicle* on December 30, 1894, about a year after the Exposition in Chicago, A. Page Brown, one of San Francisco's most prominent architects, expressed his views on the city's planning and architecture. He called the existing buildings "possibly the most uninteresting collection of wooden structures ever erected" and presciently suggested that "sweeping fire, accompanied by an earthquake, would accomplish great good if it could occur without the loss of life." He also bemoaned city streets laid out "with little attention paid to artistic or architecture effects." At the time, San Francisco's buildings were largely made of wood and the city's rapid growth over the second half of the nineteenth century had led to a haphazard development of the streets and neighborhoods.

Brown called for new buildings that were subject to "rational limitations" and constructed of sturdier materials, such as brick and stone. Instead of gasworks and other nuisances lining the Bay front, he suggested there be "a boulevard and quays flanked by public buildings." He called for a proper park around the City Hall—a building which was nearing completion after decades of stop-and-start construction—"which would lend dignity to the present structure and provide a breathing space for the City."

Brown's musings on San Francisco urban design reflected the tremendous effect the World's Columbian Exposition of 1893 had on national opinion regarding cities and their design. Brown had designed the Exposition's California State Pavilion, and Michael Henry (M.H.) de Young, publisher of the *San Francisco Chronicle*, had been vice president of the Exposition's national commission. Themes derived from the Columbian Exposition would have a large influence on San Francisco's planning and its recurring discussions about a new city hall and a civic center. However, to understand the context of the need for urban reform and a new city plan in San Francisco, it's important to understand the city's efforts to build a city hall during the second half of the nineteenth century: That building's faulty structure, scandalous administrative oversight, and poor location in the city's grid would drive the urban design reforms in the early twentieth century, ultimately resulting in a civic center.

By the late 1860s, San Francisco dominated the West Coast. The city had grown from an instant gold rush town into a thriving port. The census of 1870 recorded 149,473 residents living in neighborhoods radiating in all directions from the early settlement around Portsmouth Square. Banking, commerce, and manufacturing flourished, fueled in part by gold and silver bonanzas in California and Nevada. Visitors stayed in grand hotels, such as the Baldwin Hotel and the Palace Hotel. Most of San Francisco's citizens eagerly anticipated the completion of the transcontinental railroad, which would promote further prosperity.

Shortly after California became a state, the San Francisco civic leaders realized that they needed a building out of which to run the city. In 1852 they purchased an imposing four-story masonry building on Portsmouth Square that had served as the Jenny Lind Theatre for $200,000. After some modifications,

San Francisco's first City Hall, formerly the Jenny Lind Theatre, 1865.
Source: Courtesy of San Francisco History Center, San Francisco Public Library.

it became the first City Hall. Nevertheless, despite the booming population, San Francisco had a weak government, with the terms of many elected officials and the mayor limited to only two years. The Consolidation Act passed by the California legislature in 1856 abolished the existing municipal government and created a combined city and county with limited powers, including an inability to incur debt and the need for state approval for significant actions. The primary objective of successive city administrations and politicians of all persuasions was to limit government expense and keep taxes low.

When an earthquake on October 21, 1868, significantly damaged that first City Hall, city leaders debated about whether or not to repair the old building, demolish it and build a new one on the same site, or start fresh at a different location. Mayor Frank McCoppin and other leaders advocated building a new structure large enough to accommodate all municipal offices and imposing enough to reflect their aspirations that San Francisco become the most important city on the West Coast.

On December 31, 1868, a California grand jury issued a report on public buildings calling for a new city hall building, suggesting Yerba Buena Park as a suitable site.[1] Yerba Buena Park was located in an area that had previously been a cemetery—called Yerba Buena Cemetery. That cemetery had been created eighteen years earlier, in March 1850, when the city had set aside fifteen acres bounded by Market, Larkin, and McAllister Streets for a municipally operated cemetery. Some 7,000 bodies were buried there during its first years. However, the location of the cemetery was generally considered inconvenient, unattractive, and poorly maintained. As the growing city began to encroach on its boundaries, in May 1854 the city sold some 320 acres farther west to real estate developers as a site for the new and larger Lone Mountain Cemetery.

Although the poor still used Yerba Buena Cemetery for burials rather than the new more fashionable cemeteries in the western parts of the peninsula, a proposal was made in 1860 to close Yerba Buena Cemetery and use the land for a public park. Although the decision was eventually made to establish Yerba Buena Park, the city had no money to develop the park, so the area would consist mainly of empty sandlots for many years.

By the beginning of 1870, about two years after the first City Hall in the old Jenny Lind Theatre building had been damaged by the earthquake, major support began to grow for the construction a new city hall at Yerba Buena Park. At the time, no one was aware that underground streams on the property would make it potentially unstable as was discovered in the 1906 earthquake. Legislation was introduced in the California State Assembly on March 12, 1870, to authorize construction of a new city hall financed through the sale of lots. The main concern was on funding, not urban design. The governor appointed a board to oversee the project, and it was given three years (until April 1874) to complete the work at a cost "not to exceed $1,500,000." No taxpayer funds were proposed for the project. The scheme called for subdividing the portion of Yerba Buena Park parallel to Market Street into ninety-nine lots 25 feet wide and 100 feet deep, half of them facing onto Market Street and the other half facing onto City Hall Avenue, a new street parallel to Market on which the new city hall would face. Rows of lots would be divided in the center by a 200-foot-wide Park Street, which would connect the new building to Market Street. The ninety-nine lots would be sold at auction to generate construction funds.[2]

The legislature approved this novel scheme on April 4, 1870, and Governor Henry Haight appointed the first commissioners: P. H. Canavan, a member of the San Francisco Board of Supervisors; Joseph Eastland, of the San Francisco Gas Company; and Charles McLane, of Wells Fargo and Company.[3] The commissioners quickly prepared specifications describing the city's needs and in June published a competition brochure that was delivered to architects around the country. Twenty submissions were received by November 15, 1870, and exhibited to the public. Soon afterward, cost estimates were prepared for a short list of proposals. On February 11, 1871, the commissioners announced that Laver, Fuller and Co. of New York had prepared the winning design.

The son of an English solicitor, Augustus Laver had apprenticed to an architect on the Isle of Wight and then had worked in several architecture offices until he was qualified to practice and be a member of the Royal Institute of British Architects. In 1858 he emigrated to Canada and started a practice with an older architect, Thomas Stent, in Ottawa, which had just been designated the capital of the Dominion of Canada. Among Laver's notable projects before the San Francisco City Hall were two governmental office buildings that he designed in Ottawa, and the New York State capitol building in Albany, which he was working on when the San Francisco City Hall project was awarded.[4]

Laver's plan called for a four-story building with a full basement in the Second Empire style then popular for American civic buildings, such as the new city halls in Philadelphia and Baltimore, as well as the State, War, and Navy Building in Washington, DC (now the Eisenhower Executive Office Building) next to the White House. In accordance with the style, Laver included a mansard roof and a 453-foot tower above a curved grand entrance facing down short Park Street onto Eighth Street. The building was laid out on an irregular plan, extending from the main entrance to the three corners of the triangular lot in a "W" configuration. The walls were faced with extremely tall columns.

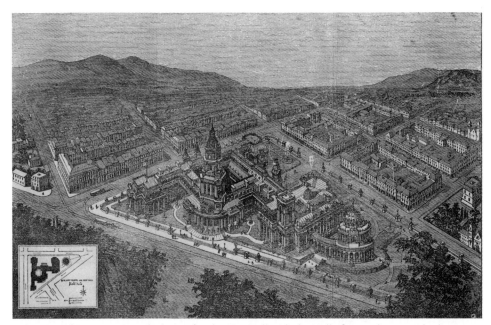

A drawing of Augustus Laver's design for the City Hall with the Hall of Recorders attached as approved by the City Hall commissioners.

Source: Courtesy of San Francisco History Center, San Francisco Public Library.

However, the board requested plan modifications: Two proposed wings on McAllister Street and a fourth floor with a mansard roof should be removed to reduce costs, and a Hall of Records designed by the local firm Patton and Jordan should be added.[5] Laver, who had traveled from New York for the competition, agreed to these terms, adjusting the plans to connect the domed, circular Hall of Records to the east wing of the building by a curving arcaded corridor.

From the start of the project, however, there was evidence of managerial problems and administrative dysfunction. For example, while Laver was in New York at work on the complex design, the commissioners contracted for the excavation of the basement level and foundation work in March 1871. This reflected the commissioners' early policy decision that they, not the architect, would control the schedule and expenses. They also decided to divide the city hall project into parts and seek separate bids for each rather than issue a single construction-and-materials contract. Consequently, specifications and cost estimates for the entire project were not available until work was well under way, and by then costs were significantly out of control. In general, this reflected how little experience the officials had with city planning and large-scale municipal development.

Moreover, the commissioners were not proactive in auctioning off the ninety-nine parcels adjacent to the City Hall block to raise funds for the project, despite the fact that the contracts had already been issued. When the parcels were all finally sold, the net proceeds amounted to only \$953,900 (of which 25 percent was paid immediately in cash), not the projected \$1.5 million.[6] At this time, California was suffering from the nation's post–Civil War recession, which was magnified within the state by the new transcontinental railroad and subsequent heavy influx of cheap goods and migrant labor. The slow economy delayed development of the lots that had been sold, and some buyers defaulted on their lots, which then had to be resold. As a result, it would not be until much later in the 1890s that structures began to even be developed along the Market Street frontage. When they were finally built, the resulting architecture of the area was a hodgepodge of one- and two-story commercial buildings, some with a saloon or restaurant in the basement.

Despite the grand architectural goals for City Hall, the construction for the building had begun with little consideration for how it would fit into the city's grid or how its placement would leave it obscured from view by the buildings around it. This lack of conscientious urban design or civic beautification efforts by the San Francisco government—whose primary objective had been to keep taxes low—created a notably inelegant setting for the grand City Hall.

In fact, one of the only efforts to create adornment in the area around the building, which was otherwise crammed between other structures, came from a private citizen named James Lick, California's richest man at the time. Upon his death in 1876, Lick bequeathed to the city \$100,000 to commission and install in front of the new City Hall a sculptural monument to commemorate California pioneers. The city created a small park out of Park Street in which to locate the monument and eventually called the park Marshall Square, after James Marshall, who had discovered gold in California. Frank Happersberger, a local sculptor, designed the huge five-section monument, which was cast in metal, assembled locally, and finally installed in November 1894.

The ever-increasing costs of the project were a major issue, something that inevitably led to political controversy. When Laver finally submitted a complete set of building specifications in December 1873, he estimated the cost would be \$1.7 million, more than the budgeted \$1.5 million. Governor Newton Booth was not happy with the news, and he asked the state legislature to create a committee to investigate the affairs of the commission in charge of San Francisco's City Hall. Convened in late December 1873,[7] the committee found that work on the building was good but that the commissioners, although honest and well intentioned, were inexperienced, negligent, and not up to the task of supervising a major construction project. As a result, the San Francisco Board of Supervisors then engaged the architects John P. Gaynor and David Farquharson to review Laver's cost estimates; in a report dated January 31, 1874, they projected a cost of whopping $4,108,060 for the entire project. These two reports upset everyone, and desperately in search of a solution, the legislature voted on March 30, 1874 to abolish the board of City Hall commissioners and turn over its responsibilities to the city government.[8] Laver was then fired, and one of assistants, Edward A. Hatherton, became the project's new architect. But this new arrangement didn't resolve the oversight and management problems, and the city and state continued to struggle to construct San Francisco's City Hall. As the costs mounted in the coming years, the state legislature voted in 1876 to allow the city to raise taxes to help pay for the costs along with reestablishing a new Board of City Hall Commissioners composed of the mayor, city attorney, and city auditor.[9] The Hall of Records was completed in 1877, and sections of the main building began to be finished and occupied starting the following year. In 1882, special tax funds expired and work slowly stopped, so Hatherton resigned. A five-year hiatus set in until 1887, when the legislature gave all state municipalities the power to impose a special ad valorem tax on property to finance public buildings.[10]

As construction resumed, more controversies would follow: The city reinstated Laver as supervising architect and decided to pursue a mansard roof on the fourth floor as originally conceived in Laver's design. However, the city balked at building the 453-foot central square clock tower that Laver had also originally planned, even though the foundations and structure were already in place. Laver refused to change his design, and so in April 1889 the city fired him

San Francisco's second City Hall under construction, circa 1880.
Source: Courtesy of San Francisco History Center, San Francisco Public Library.

for a second time.[11] Instead the city would later build a round, shorter domed tower, which would not be completed until 1896.

By 1890 the building's landscaping was complete, and the building and grounds began to appear finished. However, in true San Francisco fashion, scandal—albeit a faux scandal—could not be avoided, and on June 6, 1890, the *San Francisco Chronicle* published the first of a series of articles exposing alleged fraud associated with City Hall construction, which charged that the building's walls were filled with rubble rather than constructed of solid brick. The charges were based on the testimony of a bricklayer, George R. Hanks, who had opened walls for inspection by Mayor Edward Pond and a *Chronicle* reporter, causing sand and chunks of brick to fall out. The mayor exclaimed to the reporter, "I could hardly believe that such a thing could have happened. . . I will summon a meeting of the City Hall Commissioners tomorrow and have two or three experts go over every part of these walls." Hanks told the mayor that he worked for the contractor McCarty, Rellet and McCann up to a week before, when he was discharged.[12] The following day, Mayor Pond, Commissioner George Flournoy Jr., the newly appointed inspectors John A. Wright and John McCarthy, and several members of the grand jury assembled in City Hall to test more walls. After a number of boring tests, only the walls Hanks identified were found to be defective. Robert Higgins, a master mason working on the building, approached the group to say that he had worked with Hanks before and knew that he had served time at San Quentin Prison for burglary. Other workmen spoke up to say that Hanks had lied about being a member of the bricklayers union and added that they would sign affidavits stating that Hanks had invited them to install "rotten" work in return for money he would receive for selling the story to the newspapers. The contractors McCarty, Rellet and McCann pleaded innocence about the defective work and announced that they would repair any defective walls.[13]

The commissioners and the grand jury met frequently during the next several weeks, hearing expert reports, contractor testimony, and Hanks's assertions that the accusations against him were lies. In the end, Wright concluded that most of the completed work was up to standard and followed specifications and that the defective work had not been done fraudulently by contractors but still needed to be replaced.[14] The grand jury presented its report on July 23, 1890, concluding that Hanks was responsible for putting rubble in the walls.[15] No documentation has been found showing whether or not Hanks was indicted for the misdeed. Pressed by this scandal, the City Hall commissioners engaged three assistant supervisors to help oversee construction. It appears that Mr. Hanks's charade didn't get much further than its launch by the *San Francisco Chronicle*.

However, the story of the rubble in the walls has lived on to show that the City Hall project was riddled with fraud and corruption.

After a change of city administration in January 1891, the City Hall commission, now chaired by Mayor George Sanderson, found that the building was in poor condition, but they found no evidence of fraud or graft. They did, however, commission a report that found several other remarkable issues: that the foundation and "building [was] with a roof that did not shelter, elevators which would not elevate, water-closets that ran dry and failed to comply with the regulations of the Board of Health, a nuisance to ears, nose and eyes, reeking in filth, harboring vermin and breeding disease. In the basement, under the Mayor's office, a foul and filthy pool had been accumulating for years, and allowed to stay there, dispensing malaria and disease to those having business in the office of the city's Chief Magistrate."[16] Nevertheless, by the end of the fiscal year, the commissioners told the public in enthusiastic terms about all of the corrective measures that they had taken to resolve problems and restore the building to a high standard of care.

Despite the problems with the construction, rumors of corruption, the need for numerous architects, and cost overruns, City Hall finally contained nearly all of the city departments—two decades after the completion date that had originally been set. Nevertheless, the site was still under construction and the issue of the tower and fourth floor remained unresolved. In January 1893, the commissioners made Frank T. Shea the City Hall architect and gave him the task of finishing the building. Shea had studied architecture in Chicago and Paris and worked as a draftsman and practicing architect for ten years. He was thirty-two years old at the time of his appointment. (He later became known as the "Church Architect" after he designed several churches for the Catholic Archdiocese of San Francisco after the earthquake.) Shea rejected Laver's clock-tower design and prepared plans for a more fashionable neoclassical dome tower, which was put out to bid in May 1894.[17] He had the tricky task of installing a round tower on the previously constructed square foundation and superstructure. Laver brought a lawsuit to enjoin construction of the dome tower, alleging it "would be greatly out of harmony with the other parts of the building already completed and materially detract from its architectural beauty." The matter ended up in the California Supreme Court in November 1895, which found for the city.[18] By this time, the tower was nearly complete, but, inexplicably, the diagonal bracing called for in the plans was never installed. Shea also abandoned the fourth floor with the mansard roof.

When complete, the dome tower was 335 feet high, 118 feet shorter than the proposed Laver tower. On July 12, 1897, James Duval Phelan, who had just been

The old City Hall looking west with the Hall of Records in the foreground surrounded by small commercial buildings and other unattractive structures, early 1906.

Source: Courtesy of the San Francisco History Center, San Francisco Public Library.

elected mayor that year, oversaw ceremonies celebrating the finished building.[19] The project's final cost was \$5,723,794. It would take another two years to install a proper roof and finish innumerable details. The City Hall commission turned over the building and its records to the board of supervisors and went out of business on June 31, 1899, nearly thirty years after the idea of a new city hall had been conceived.

The story of this City Hall reveals the extensive municipal management problems associated with the early history of San Francisco city planning. San Francisco finally had a grand City Hall in a hybrid architectural style, even if its creation had been overseen by eight different architects.[20] The building was an imposing structure, but because of the utter lack of meaningful urban planning, it had numerous other drawbacks. For example, with the exception of a narrow opening onto Market Street, the building was screened on all sides by common low-rise commercial and residential structures, hardly suitable for a building of such cost and that was supposed to symbolize the city's greatness.

Considering that it had taken far longer to build City Hall than had been anticipated, and the construction had cost nearly four times the original estimate, some historians and commentators view the construction process and building as scandalous. But a comparison with other major public buildings from this time would suggest that other cities also suffered from enormous administrative and planning problems. The Philadelphia City Hall, for example, also suffered from decades-long construction, cost overruns, and oversight by multiple architects. The Philadelphia City Hall also suffered from outright graft and corruption. The record in San Francisco shows no such blatant activity. The principal weaknesses in the City Hall commission's efforts were that laypeople oversaw a huge project without adequate professional staff to supervise the work and that the commission decided to design and construct the building piecemeal, using many different architects and contractors. Engineer and historian Stephen Tobriner wrote that City Hall "was a proverbial disaster waiting to happen."[21]

In spite of the building's problems, when it was finally finished, San Franciscans were generally pleased with the results. Tragically, however, it would be a temporary pleasure, because just under a decade after Phelan oversaw ceremonies celebrating the building's completion, the 1906 earthquake would devastate the structure, and force the city to reconsider once again how to build a city hall for a booming West-Coast metropolis.

The history of the construction of San Francisco's City Hall is a reflection of the urgent need for reforms and better municipal administration and planning. It also provides some perspective on why a number of influential individuals in the city were so motivated to embrace the progressive urban reform ideals that were sweeping the nation at the turn of the century. The Chicago Exposition, which allowed so many people to see what conscientious urban planning and development might mean, and which took place right at the end of the nearly two decades of controversy and problematic construction with San Francisco's City Hall, was especially resonant among a number of prominent San Francisco citizens. As a result, in the years following the debacle of the construction of City Hall, a number of people would begin to agitate for new approaches to planning in San Francisco and several major efforts were made to encourage the city to move in more progressive directions, much of which would be inspired by the City Beautiful movement and the Chicago Exposition.

California and the Chicago Exposition:
The City Beautiful Comes
to San Francisco

The World's Columbian Exposition in Chicago in 1893 would be an inspiring event for many of California's architects, politicians, and businessmen. Many of them had been involved in the development of California's State Pavilion. When Chicago received the designation from Congress to hold this world's fair and put out the call to the states to participate, California had eagerly responded. Governor Henry H. Markham asked the legislature to appropriate $300,000 for a state pavilion and authorize counties to contribute funds if they so wished. Among the seven people Markham appointed as commissioners to the California World's Fair Commission were individuals who would later play critical roles in San Francisco's city and architectural planning including Irving M. Scott, the president of San Francisco's Union Iron Works, who served as president of the commission, and James Duval Phelan, a San Francisco banker and future mayor of the city, who served as vice president. The seven California State commissioners joined two other Californians appointed by the president of the United States to the National World's Fair Commission, William Forsyth of Fresno, and M. H. de Young, publisher of the *San Francisco Chronicle*, who served as the national commission's vice president.[1] These Californians were heavily involved with the world's fair, spending extensive time in Chicago and promoting the Exposition throughout the state.

The California Pavilion was intended to showcase the state's products, particularly agricultural goods. Scott, Phelan, and two other commissioners visited Frederick Law Olmsted at his home in Brookline, Massachusetts, to obtain his support for a 2½-acre site for the pavilion on the lake in the fairgrounds.[2] To design the pavilion, they selected architect A. Page Brown, who during the 1880s worked at the New York architecture firm McKim, Mead, and White, which designed many buildings at the Exposition. Brown prepared plans for

The California Building in mission revival style was located at the northwest end of the Exposition Grounds at the Chicago World's Columbian Exposition in 1893.
Source: Courtesy of the Chicago History Museum Archive.

a huge three-story mission revival structure to maximize display space. It became the second-largest state pavilion and attracted much attention, as the Californians had hoped. Tens of thousands of Californians from all walks of life visited the Exposition.

Among those for whom the Chicago Exposition would prove particularly inspiring was Phoebe Apperson Hearst, philanthropist and mother of publisher William Randolph Hearst. Hearst came with a delegation of women from San Francisco and stayed for twelve days, becoming strongly influenced by what she saw and learned about the plan and buildings of the Exposition.[3] Hearst had previously developed a philanthropic interest in the University of California, initially focusing on scholarships for women students. But after her visit to the Chicago Exposition, she became acquainted with Bay Area architect Bernard Maybeck, who would go on to advise her about architecture and planning and also encourage her interest in improving the Berkeley campus. This would result in Hearst's announcement in October 1896 that she was underwriting an international competition to choose an architect to prepare a master plan for the growing school's campus, a project that would in turn be an important catalyst in San Francisco's planning.

M. H. de Young was so carried away by his experiences at the 1893 Exposition that, shortly after it opened, he proposed organizing the California Midwinter International Exposition (also called the Midwinter Fair) in San Francisco as an adjunct to the Columbian Exposition, in which would be displayed exhibits from the Chicago World's Fair. By August 1893, he had moved quickly to assemble a committee of prominent supporters, including Phelan, and obtained approvals to use 200 acres of Golden Gate Park. The fair's design was entrusted to Leopold Bonet, a French artist de Young had met in Chicago. Opening in January of 1894, the Midwinter Fair entertained and educated two million visitors during the next six months. The design for the fair included an elongated oval-shaped plaza that Bonet had designed—which is now the Golden Gate Park Music Concourse—surrounded by five pavilion buildings. An Eiffel Tower–influenced illuminated structure was built in the center. De Young wanted to differentiate his exposition from the one in Chicago by avoiding a uniform architectural style, so he suggested that buildings be designed in a variety of "exotic" styles.[4] A. Page Brown was commissioned to create two buildings, one of Byzantine Gothic and the other of Moorish design. The other buildings were designed in Egyptian, oriental, and mission revival styles. De Young's objective for the Midwinter Fair was to promote California, stimulate economic activity since the country was in a depression, and give the public a good time—not to make a grand urban design statement. His fair would also make a profit.

On the other hand, James Phelan, whose involvement during the Chicago Exposition had also been extensive, would come away from the event with even larger-scale and longer-term ambitions. After Irving Scott became ill, the task of overseeing construction of the California Pavilion had fallen to Phelan. Phelan spent time in Chicago before and during the Exposition as the California commissioner, where he became acquainted with Daniel Hudson Burnham and other reform-minded people, attended assemblies and lectures, and became familiar with the most modern and progressive thinking of the day. Phelan was interested in implementing in San Francisco the progressive reform measures that were gaining momentum at this time, and upon his return he became a leader in such efforts. Phelan and his colleagues wanted to repeal the 1856 legislation providing San Francisco with limited government controlled by the legislature and bring home rule to San Francisco through a locally adopted charter, rid the city's politics of bossism and graft, and create an honest and efficient government. In 1896, Phelan ran for mayor, advocating for reform and talking about the need to beautify the city. Quoting Pericles and Plato in a speech on September 1, 1896, at the opening of the annual Mechanics' Institute industrial fair, he talked about beauty instilling civic pride in the people.[5] When he was elected, he immediately threw himself into a grueling campaign for a new city charter, which would be endorsed by the voters in May 1898. He was reelected in November and began to reorganize city government under the new charter.

City Beautiful and City Planning in San Francisco

The national discussion about practical and aesthetic municipal improvements resonated in San Francisco. A number of artists and architects had established the Guild of Arts and Crafts in 1894, modeled after the Municipal Art Society in New York.[6] The initial members included the architects A. Page Brown, Albert Pissis, and Willis Polk (subsequently Burnham's West Coast representative); the painters William Keith and Arthur Mathews; and the artist Bruce Porter. The guild petitioned the charter reform committee to have the "Board of Public Works foster artistic feeling in the development of the City." Although after several years personality clashes prompted the organization to disband, the aesthetic and civic motivations of the guild resounded with the spirit of the times.

Elsewhere in the Bay Area, influences of the reformist ideas and the Chicago Exposition were also evident. After the initial announcement in 1896, Hearst's international competition for a new design for the UC Berkeley campus was organized. Regent J. B. Reinstein, who became Hearst's close adviser on the project, hoped that the new plan would produce "stately and glorious buildings which shall rival the dreams of the builders of the Columbian Exposition."[7] Bernard Maybeck would oversee much of the competition's administration and set up a complex selection process that would span several years.

Phelan, meanwhile, who became mayor of San Francisco in 1897, was interested in developing a new plan for the city also based on the artistic and social ideas displayed in Chicago, and he followed the University of California master plan competition closely. In October 1898, when eleven semifinalists were invited to California to visit the Berkeley site, Phelan graciously hosted a dinner on December 3, 1898, at the Bohemian Club for the architects and jury, along with university and city officials. Barely a week before, he had announced the appointment of eight prominent businessmen, architects, and artists to a committee to look into preparing "a comprehensive plan for the artistic improvement of the City of San Francisco," and that night at the dinner, Phelan stunned guests by announcing that Hearst shared his belief that San Francisco should have a comprehensive plan and that she would fund the competition to choose architects to prepare one. Phelan spoke grandiosely about a plan to give San Francisco the aura of Georges-Eugène Haussmann's Paris.[8] Hearst was actually in Paris at the time Phelan hosted the dinner, but she had designated as her representative university regent Reinstein who confirmed Hearst's intentions.[9]

San Francisco Mayor James D. Phelan addressing an outdoor gathering, circa 1905.
Source: Courtesy of San Francisco History Center, San Francisco Public Library.

Over the next two years, as the Berkeley competition process ground on, Phelan maintained periodic communication with Hearst and Reinstein and hosted additional social events for the competition. On September 7, 1899, three years after it had begun, the jury of the Berkeley competition announced that out of four finalists that had been selected, the Parisian Émile Bénard had won first prize. The decision aroused great public interest, and that night his drawings were installed at the Ferry Building for public viewing. However, despite Phelan's initial interest in the Berkeley competition, and despite being in contact with Hearst and Reinstein, the project would ultimately not materialize and there were no additional public announcements from Phelan about a competition for a San Francisco master plan, nor was there any further word about the committee he had assembled.

Although Phelan's efforts while mayor to create a new city plan never got started, others were inspired to pursue urban planning ideas. On October 8, 1899, the *San Francisco Examiner* published a full-page article describing a plan for the area around the City Hall that had been drawn by a young architect named Bernard J.S. Cahill. Born in London in 1866 and educated at the University of London and the South Kensington School of Art (now the Royal College of Art), Cahill had immigrated to the United States, arriving in

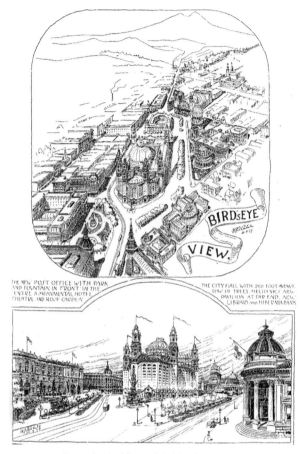

Drawings of B. J. S. Cahill's proposed plan for beautifying Market Street.
From California Architect & Building News, October 1899.

62

Drawings of B. J. S. Cahill's proposed plan for beautifying Market Street around the old City Hall.
Source: California Architect & Building News, October 1899, p. 110.

San Francisco in 1888 where he had taken up a position as a draftsman with a local architecture firm and eventually became a partner. His works in San Francisco from this time included a crematorium for the newly established Cypress Lawn Memorial Park and a columbarium off of Geary Street for the Independent Order of Odd Fellows in 1897. However, Cahill was also interested in city planning, and he had submitted a proposal to the International Competition for the Phoebe A. Hearst Architectural Plan for the University of California, one of only three entries from the Bay Area out of 105 submissions worldwide. Although Cahill did not make the cut, he evidently possessed a great deal of self-confidence and continued to push forward on his other planning designs, such as the plan that was published in the *Examiner*. He described in the article how he had recently visited Paris and Vienna and how that had influenced him when he developed his ideas for improving San Francisco's Market Street. He had also shown his ideas to many prominent San Franciscans, including Mayor Phelan.

Although Cahill's plan was not a proposal for a civic center (it would still be a year or more before the term *civic center* would be coined), his plan represented a notable exercise in urban design, and despite only focusing on a small portion of San Francisco, its publication in the *Examiner* generated immediate interest. The plan addressed long-standing tawdry conditions around City Hall by calling for the city to purchase (by condemnation, if necessary) small parcels on both sides of Market Street from McAllister and Sixth Streets to Larkin and Ninth Streets. Market Street itself would be divided and traffic lanes moved north and south to create a large oval-shaped parcel in the middle for a hotel and theater.[10] In this design, City Hall would now face Market Street, as would the new US courthouse and post office on Seventh Street.

However, the plan also had problems. Although Cahill claimed that the city could make a profit buying and selling land to accomplish the project, there were legal impediments. First, California law would not allow a municipality to take property by eminent domain and then sell it to private parties. Second, financing the acquisition, clearing a large amount of property, and then re-building Market Street would require a large sum of money, which would probably have to be authorized by voters in a bond election. Third, some property owners in the area had development plans of their own for their parcels and expressed opposition.

At the time, Phelan was heavily involved in a bond election campaign to pay for new schools, sewers, a city hospital, and a Golden Gate Park panhandle extension to Van Ness Avenue (a particular cause of his). He did not have the time or interest to take on Cahill's scheme. Moreover, Phelan's opportunities in office to bring about large-scale civic projects were curtailed by legal setbacks and diminishing political support. Although the voters approved the bonds Phelan had requested, the California Supreme Court in 1900 voided them on a legal technicality. In 1901, a divisive labor dispute broke out between the Teamsters' Union and nonunion workers. Phelan upset the unions by allowing police to intervene and protect strikebreakers. He also upset business interests by refusing to ask the governor to send the National Guard to San Francisco to break up the strike. As a result, Phelan found himself with little support on both sides, which greatly diminished his chances of winning reelection. He left office having accomplished many reforms but without having been able to accomplish the larger city planning and beautification projects he had hoped to pursue.

As an outgrowth of the divisive strike, a newly created Union Labor Party was organized and won the election in 1901 with its candidate for mayor, Eugene Schmitz. Schmitz's victory had been orchestrated by Abraham Ruef, a young and ambitious lawyer who had previously dabbled in local Republican politics. Ruef had realized that labor activists organizing the new party were naive and inexperienced, and he convinced his friend Schmitz, president of the Musicians Union, handsome leader of a popular band, and a Roman Catholic, to run for mayor. Schmitz was a political blank slate who was happy to leave issues to Ruef, who fashioned a platform that accommodated labor concerns but still appealed to small businessmen. But it included no grand plans of civic improvement, and in general, keeping government expenditures and taxes low was a primary campaign theme.

After leaving office, Phelan continued to participate in major planning events and exhibitions, something that would deepen his interactions with national reform and planning discussions and help him connect with other prominent personalities involved in such projects. In 1904, for example, the Louisiana Purchase Exposition was held in St. Louis, and Phelan agreed to join and chair committees to organize participation by California and San Francisco. During that experience, Phelan saw how the city's citizens had mobilized to support urban reform. Founded three years earlier in 1901 in anticipation of the Exposition, the Civic Improvement League of St. Louis had 2,000 members by 1903, championing billboard control, health and sanitation measures, parks, and beautification.[11] In 1904, some 1,740 such improvement organizations existed in the United States. The fact that San Francisco had few such organizations would not have been lost on Phelan.

The Burnham Plan for San Francisco

In the years just prior to San Francisco's 1906 earthquake and fire—an event that would profoundly alter the urban landscape as well as the political context for any future planning—a major effort had been undertaken to develop a new city plan for San Francisco. Although frozen out of San Francisco government after leaving office, Phelan was still motivated by the idea of developing grand civic planning projects in the city, and along with his reformer business and professional colleagues, he still had financial resources that could be used to help influence public opinion on such projects. In May 1903, Phelan reached out to Burnham to inquire whether he would be interested in creating a comprehensive plan for San Francisco based on Burnham's work with the

Chicago Exposition, and in Cleveland and Washington, DC. On October 27, 1903, Burnham wrote to Polk, his representative in San Francisco: "Making the plan for San Francisco would be the most delightful occupation possible."[12] He indicated to Phelan that he would only ask for reimbursement of expenses on the project, as he had done for the Cleveland plan.

In addition to Phelan, other notable individuals were advocating for a more reformist and bold approach to civic development in San Francisco. Allan Pollok, a prominent businessman and manager of the soon-to-be-open grand St. Francis Hotel on Union Square, went public with his concerns about San Francisco in a front-page interview in the January 4, 1904, *San Francisco Bulletin.* "San Francisco has been asleep while Southern California, which offers nothing like the inducements we have within our grasp to lay before visitors, has taken possession of the tourist and the wealthy from the East looking for new homes," Pollok said. San Franciscans lack civic spirit, he added, and have made "no effort to take advantage of the city's natural beauty and provided no allurements to the tourist and people looking to move to San Francisco." He advocated organizing a committee of public-spirited men to work for the welfare of the city. He concluded with a quote from Pericles: "Above all, let us ever consider beauty in its relation to utility." Pollok was a reformer who would later become a city supervisor in 1907.

A few days after the publication of Pollok's interview in the newspaper, Phelan invited twenty or so prominent business and professional men to attend a meeting at the Merchants Exchange Building on January 15, 1904, to "discuss a plan for the improvement of San Francisco."[13] During the meeting, many individual city improvement projects were discussed, but Phelan won the group over to his view that the primary need was a single overall development plan. He said that he had been in touch with Burnham, who was willing to prepare such a plan. Familiar with Burnham's work—Burnham had already designed several of the San Francisco's major office buildings—the group agreed. It formed the Association for the Improvement and Adornment of San Francisco (AIASF) and elected Phelan as president. The organization decided that membership should be open to anyone who was genuinely interested in improving the city, and, by April, three hundred businessmen had paid their fee to become members. Phelan extended a formal invitation to Burnham to prepare a plan. In response, Burnham and his wife arrived in San Francisco on May 1, 1904, for a two-week stay to explore the city and discuss the plan proposal.

The AIASF honored Burnham at an elegant dinner at the new St. Francis Hotel on May 4, where Burnham spoke about the "possibilities of enhancing the beauty of the city" and generated a great deal of excitement among those in attendance.[14] Two days later, he appeared before two hundred people invited from the city's business, artistic, and improvement groups, including the California Club and the Outdoor Art League, two civic groups run by women. He appealed to the attendees, saying, "Whatever may be my ideas, I can accomplish little or nothing without the people of San Francisco. Your suggestions must start the general scheme in operation and must furnish the basis on which I must work." The response was enthusiastic. Even the conservative *San Francisco Chronicle* endorsed his efforts, although it warned that what counted was the execution of a plan.

Burnham returned to Chicago in late May, but kept up a stream of correspondence about the San Francisco plan with AIASF, Phelan, and others, encouraging them to send him their ideas. Through Polk, he expressed his desire to have a temporary cottage and workroom constructed on top of Twin Peaks. "Being up there we can constantly see the city and everything else and this will be of great value to us." He told Polk that he did not want to work in a downtown office: he wanted to be "where the influence around me will stimulate Golden Gate Thoughts."[15]

To do much of the actual work on the plan, Burnham selected Edward Bennett, a young architect working in Burnham's office at the time who would later rise to national prominence as a renowned city planner and oversee future projects in San Francisco. The son of a master of a clipper ship, Bennett had been born in Bristol, England, in 1874 and was educated in Bristol schools before

Daniel Burnham standing outside the temporary cabin built on Twin Peaks as a work studio for him and Edward Bennett, 1904. Source: Courtesy of the Chicago Art Institute.

coming to San Francisco in 1890. After trying his hand at ranching, he found employment in the architecture office of Robert White. To learn more about the profession and about design, he participated in architect Bernard Maybeck's Berkeley Saturday seminars on design where he became friends with other participants who would become leading Bay Area architects including Julia Morgan, the first woman to be granted an architect's license in California, and Arthur Brown Jr, the architect of the new City Hall. Maybeck had been impressed with Bennett's talent and arranged for him to study at the École des Beaux-Arts in Paris with a stipend provided by Hearst. In 1901 Bennett received his École *diplôme*, a major achievement for a student from the United States. After working a brief stint in the offices of the prominent New York architect George B. Post, Bennett was recommended to Burnham by W. Peirce Anderson, who was Bennett's friend from the École des Beaux-Arts and a D. H. Burnham and Co. design partner. Burnham immediately liked Bennett and later wrote that he had a "deep and reverent spirit" and was a "poet with his feet on the ground." Bennett was the perfect person to take to San Francisco; he had lived there before and had friendships with key Bay Area architects.

In September of 1904, Burnham returned to San Francisco with Bennett and set up operations in the Twin Peaks cottage, often using it as a residence. Leaving Bennett in charge to begin work on the plan, Burnham left San Francisco on October 13, 1904.

In the meantime, Thomas McCaleb, secretary of the AIASF, solicited suggestions from a wide range of people on issues to be addressed by Burnham and Bennett. The city's long disregard for urban planning had led to serious shortcomings in the infrastructure and street layout. Numerous issues needed attention, most significantly, the area around City Hall, which was widely considered unappealing, difficult to access, and largely problematic as the site of the city's major municipal functions.

Among those who submitted ideas during this time was Cahill, the local architect whose ambitions had led him in 1899 to publish a design for a plan he made for San Francisco in the *Examiner*.

According to an article Cahill wrote for the publication *The Architect and Engineer of California and the Pacific Coast* in 1918, McCaleb wrote to Cahill asking for a copy of his 1899 plan.[16] There is no record of Cahill participating in any of the AIASF private or public meetings or discussions prior to that request. However, motivated by McCaleb's communication, Cahill also decided to design a new plan, specifically focused on the blocks around City Hall. The new plan he produced was supported by detailed drawings that showed the City Hall blocks as the starting line and then moved west on Grove and McAllister

Streets. He proposed developing a new modern auditorium on the block where the existing, but decrepit, Mechanics' Institute Pavilion was located, as well as building a new public library on the block bounded by Van Ness Avenue and Fulton, Polk, and Grove Streets (Block 67). He suggested devoting two blocks between Grove and McAllister Streets to a large plaza facing City Hall and then filling in the block to the west (next to the proposed library) and the one to the north (opposite the auditorium) with more grand buildings. Cahill also proposed turning Fulton Street into a parkway from City Hall to Alamo Square Park, which would be extended two blocks farther in stages to connect with the Golden Gate Park panhandle.

Cahill submitted his plan to the AIASF, which sent a copy to Burnham at his Chicago office. Although Burnham would later offer praise to Cahill for his assistance, Burnham did not use Cahill's proposals in his own plan. Cahill had also been a professional acquaintance of Bennett, and he brought his plan to Bennett in the Twin Peaks cottage where he was working. But Bennett was uninterested. Cahill also contacted Phelan about his plan, but Phelan, who was in New York at the time, noted that he desired the extension of the city's panhandle to continue eastward along Oak and Fell Streets to Van Ness Avenue and Market Street, something that would not work in Cahill's plan. In general, despite Cahill's active efforts to be involved in the broader planning projects at this time and in the coming years, his ideas were not considered seriously by Burnham or Phelan. Cahill would later feel rejected by this, and he would develop a long-term resentment toward Burnham and the others associated with San Francisco's planning in the coming years. His motto became *Delenda est Chicago,* a variation of Cato's famous vow in the Punic Wars, *Carthago delenda est* (Carthage must be destroyed). He vowed to "destroy faith in this Chicago imposition."[17] Cahill's animus toward Burnham and anything with which he was involved was permanent. Burnham, however, who was probably unaware of Cahill's anger, in his *Report on a Plan for San Francisco* acknowledged Cahill's assistance on the project and indicated that Cahill's civic center plan influenced his thinking on the report's civic center recommendations.

Although the plan that Burnham and Bennett would design at this time would never be developed in San Francisco—among other reasons, all planning projects would be greatly affected by the earthquake in 1906—it would become a major precursor to later civic development in the city, particularly because it included a proposal for a civic center. This plan, nevertheless, was Burnham's first attempt at what he called a comprehensive plan, which primarily dealt with physical development—roads, parks, and the treatment of hills—but also contained comments on a wide variety of subjects, including economic development, air pollution, subways, the water supply, health facilities, and, of course, arts and municipal adornment.

Burnham submitted his nearly 200-page *Report on a Plan for San Francisco* to the AIASF on September 15, 1905, almost a year to the day from when he started. In the introduction, he wrote, "The scope of this report is general . . . . It is not to be supposed that all the work indicated can or ought to be carried out at once. Or even in the near future. A plan beautiful and comprehensive enough for San Francisco can only be executed by degrees, as the growth of the community demands and as its financial ability allows."

In the opening section, "General Theory of the City," Burnham wrote that an examination of major European cities showed that they contained concentric ring roads intersected by diagonal boulevards.[18] For San Francisco, he thus proposed an Outer Boulevard at the edge of the landmass, approximately following the coastline around the city and invading the Presidio. The innermost and smallest ring would focus on the intersection of Market Street and Van Ness Avenue, which Burnham called the "civic center." However, the civic center that Burnham proposed in this plan was not presented as a grouping of public buildings, as he had proposed for Cleveland. San Francisco, he felt, was too large for this. "No central Place will be adequate for the grouping of public buildings," he wrote. Instead, around the Market–Van Ness "civic center," a number of subcenters would develop at the intersections of the radial arteries, at each of which would be a public *Place* that would contain buildings for "administration, education, amusements and shopping of the finer order." Burnham's "civic center" in this report would differ from the civic center San Francisco would eventually build years later. But the same City Beautiful ideals would inform both projects. As Burnham wrote, the civic center is the "real being of the city proper; all else should contribute to its honor and maintenance. In its national character it guarantees the city's relation to the country and its civic character to its citizens."

In Burnham's plan, the first ring would consist of a widened Fulton Street from City Hall to Gough Street, with a diagonal to Octavia Street, across Market Street to Fourteenth Street, and then another diagonal to Eighth Street and back to City Hall. At Market and Van Ness Avenue, nine diagonal streets and boulevards crossing the ring would convene in a huge semicircular *Place*. As Phelan desired, the panhandle would be extended from where it was terminating—on Scott Street one block wide between Oak and Fell Streets—becoming a 150-foot-wide boulevard as it approached the focal *Place*. It would then extend across Market in a southeasterly direction to South Beach. Eleventh Street would be widened and reoriented from Bryant Street, where a great railroad station would

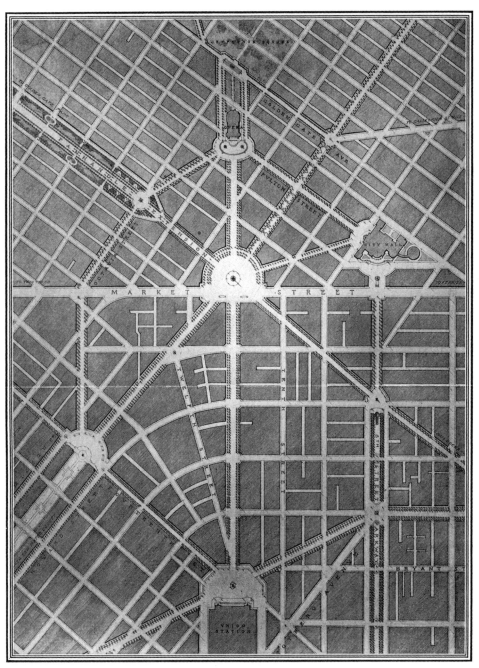

PLAN OF CIVIC CENTER

Burnham's Plan for San Francisco showing the configuration of the Civic Center with the train station at the bottom and the opera house at the top. The old City Hall stands at the right middle, 1905.

Source: Courtesy of San Francisco History Center, San Francisco Public Library.

be located, and extend northwest through the grand *Place* to Gough and Fulton Streets, where a new opera house would be constructed.

Around this same time, there was an effort underway to find a new location for the city's public library. Since 1888 the public library had been located in various rooms in City Hall, which was considered an inadequate arrangement. Library trustees sought a block for a freestanding building to house the growing institution. Influential trustees, including former mayor Phelan and Edward Robeson Taylor, the dean of Hastings College of the Law and a future mayor, secured a commitment of $750,000 for the project from Andrew Carnegie. In December 1904, they had selected the block along Van Ness Avenue and Hayes, Franklin, and Fell Streets (Block 73). Cahill mounted an opposition to moving the library to that block—as it would undermine his civic center plan which he was still hoping would gain traction. But the library trustees went ahead and selected that block, as Burnham had also approved of this choice and incorporated into his plan.[19]

Burnham's report called the section on the "civic center" with its public *Place* the most important location in the plan and suggested that its design should be "vigorous if it is to hold its own and dominate the exaggerated skyline of its surroundings." The report recommended expanding the open space around City Hall by acquiring twenty to twenty-five feet of private property along McAllister Street and City Hall Avenue, the short street running in front of City Hall. In this new semicircular space, Burnham recommended erecting a colonnade or arcade with pavilions flanking City Hall Square (later, Marshall Square) at Market Street. "This treatment would, in some measure, extend the architectural effect of the civic center around the City Hall and impose a sense of order in its vicinity."[20] A cornice line eighty feet from street level was recommended for all buildings in the civic center area.[21]

The AIASF presented Burnham's San Francisco Plan to the board of supervisors at a special meeting on the afternoon of September 27, 1905, with Mayor Schmitz in the presiding chair. With Phelan in Paris, William Greer Harrison, the AIASF vice president, presented the plan to the city by exclaiming that this was "the greatest day in the history of the city." He promised that Phelan and the AIASF would work with "energy and enthusiasm" to see that the plan was implemented. The mayor responded by saying that it gave him "real pleasure to accept the plan on behalf of the city." He even went as far as to suggest the city would begin considerations to start work on the plan's Outer Boulevard and the Panhandle Parkway.[22] Despite the mayor's show of enthusiasm, such outward expressions of harmony and goodwill between the AIASF and Schmitz lacked sincerity. In general, the reformist businessmen led by Phelan had developed a

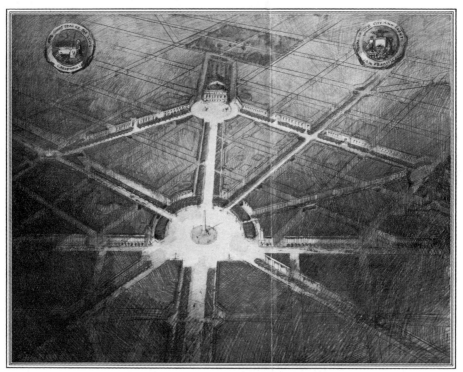

VIEW OF CIVIC CENTER, LOOKING FROM THE SOUTH SIDE OF MARKET STREET

Daniel Burnham's Plan for San Francisco showing a more detailed representation of the enormous *Place* at Van Ness and Market, 1905. Source: Courtesy of San Francisco History Center, San Francisco Public Library.

strong distrust of the Schmitz administration and felt that most of its appointees were incompetent, if not corrupt. That evening the AIASF held a banquet at the St. Francis Hotel. Harrison again acted as spokesman and welcomed everyone as "neophytes in the temple of beauty, a temple within whose doors no discord should enter." Further expressions of goodwill followed, and Mayor Schmitz responded with a toast to "the new San Francisco." Then the whole assembly stood and drank to the health of the absent Burnham. Two days later, McCaleb wrote to Burnham: "The plan has met with both expert and popular success in the community. All classes are pledged to see that its principal features are carried out as soon as possible."[23]

Despite the optimism in McCaleb's words, he would have known any immediate implementation of the plan was unlikely. While preparing his plan, Burnham had consulted with few people, if anyone, from the Schmitz administration. Also, at this time the political season was underway, and campaigns for the offices of mayor and supervisors were in full force. Almost to a man, the reformers opposed Schmitz's reelection. Fremont Older, the editor of the

San Francisco Bulletin and a reformer, ran front-page articles accusing Schmitz and Ruef of corruption. For the previous four years, the majority of the board of supervisors had been composed of reformers who had kept a watchful eye on Schmitz and Ruef. At the November election, Schmitz was reelected, and his Union Labor Party candidates swept all seats on the board of supervisors, meaning any implementation of Burnham's plan would be even more unlikely. These were men of modest backgrounds chosen personally by Ruef so that they would he beholden to him and Ruef would make no room for the Burnham Plan unless he could see a way to profit from it.

In spite of political maneuvering and underlying ill will between them, both Phelan's AIASF and Schmitz and Ruef's supporters saw public relations value in promoting the Burnham Plan. The AIASF felt that success depended on broad public understanding and support. The board of supervisors appropriated $3,000 for printing the report, and Burnham designed and edited the final document. The illustrations reflected Burnham's passion for neoclassical architecture and had a baroque feel that some found difficult to absorb. The AIASF members spoke at association and club meetings, with Phelan taking the message to the most prominent organizations. At a joint meeting before the women of the Outdoor Art League and the California Club on January 16, 1906, Phelan and the poet, ornithologist, and architectural writer Charles Keller Reed discussed the plan's practical and aesthetic aspects.[24] In March 1906 the *San Francisco Bulletin* and the *San Francisco Chronicle* published laudatory editorials supporting the plan.[25]

The plan's most significant positive critique was made by the national progressive reformer Herbert Croly, the editor of *The Architectural Record*. In the June 1906 issue, he argued that Burnham's plan was of national significance, since San Francisco would be one of the three or four most important American cities and the home of finance, industry, and intellectual life in the West. With the implementation of Burnham's beautification recommendations, along with the city's physical advantages of water and hills, San Francisco would become a major tourist destination. The biggest obstacle to achieving the plan, he felt, was the need for "the community, acting with the fullest and most definite determination, to make San Francisco a great city." Croly endorsed virtually all of Burnham's individual proposals, particularly that of the civic center. "Everybody who knows the city will understand that it constitutes an ingenious and complete means of connecting by broad thoroughfares [the city's] several main divisions."[26]

The publicity about Burnham and his plan also caught the attention of Oakland, where progressive Frank Mott had recently been elected mayor. Mott was pro-growth and eager to have Oakland be also recognized as a major city. He approached Burnham to see if he would do a plan for Oakland as well. In a letter to Councilman Benjamin Pendleton dated July 31, 1905, Burnham wrote, "the possibility of planning for Oakland allures me as nothing else could. . . . It is a little glimpse of paradise you offer, but I must turn my face away from it."[27] Undeterred, they contacted Charles Mulford Robinson, who had recently taken on work as a planning consultant and had completed a city plan for Syracuse, New York. He accepted and submitted a twenty-page report to Oakland in May 1906. Robinson focused on the city's parks and ways to improve and expand them.

Burnham's report—copies of which, ready for distribution to the public, were finally delivered to City Hall on April 17, 1906[28]—would play a major role in allowing the civic center concept to take hold in San Francisco. The activities surrounding the plan over the previous two years had caused San Franciscans to ponder the state of the city, its economic position, competition from other emerging West Coast cities, and its quality of life. Many people had seen the actual plan or discussed it, and many had reacted favorably to its proposals.

However, Burnham's plans for the new San Francisco would suddenly became moot because the day following the delivery of the report to City Hall, San Francisco experienced a catastrophe that would challenge its very survival.

The 1906 Earthquake's Aftermath: Catastrophe, Disarray, and Indecision

Early in the morning of April 18, 1906, the earth's Pacific Coast tectonic plates violently lurched, causing a 270-mile rip in the San Andreas Fault. Waves of energy radiated from the center of the quake, shaking coastal California in bursts, the first lasting 45 seconds and the second, 25 seconds.

In San Francisco, the shaking was most violent along the shoreline and on areas of landfill. Movement at City Hall was intense because the ground was sandy and water ran beneath the building. City Hall, whose design and construction were flawed, suffered severely. Officer E. J. Plume, on duty in the building's police station, made this report.

> As the earthquake progressed, the noise from outside became deafening. I could hear the massive pillars that uphold the cornices and cupola of City Hall cracking with reports like cannons, then falling like thunder. Huge stones and lumps of masonry came crashing down outside our doors; the large chandelier swung to and fro, then fell from the ceiling with a bang. In an instant the room was full of dust as well as soot and smoke from the fireplace. It seemed to be reeling like a cabin of a ship in a gale. Feeling sure that the building could never survive such shocks, and expecting . . . to be buried under a mass of ruins, I shouted to [my fellow officers] to get out.[1]

The steel superstructure of the dome tower held firm, although the dome shifted 8¼ inches out of plumb. The dome's roof, lantern, and rooftop statue survived the shaking, but the tower's masonry cladding rained down on the main building, bombarding the roof and exterior façades, which were greatly weakened by the quake. The building's cornices moved outward, causing the tremendous freestanding columns to crack and fall. Much of the debris landed on the Larkin Street side of the building. The Hall of Records, detached and located on the eastern side of City Hall, survived with little damage, as did the McAllister Street corner of the building. The building as a whole was ruined and could no longer serve as the seat of local government.[2]

The low-rising Mechanic's Pavillion was among the notable buildings destroyed that surrounded City Hall and it covered the block bounded by Larkin, Hayes, Polk, and Grove Streets. Adjacent to City Hall, the two large structures were a civic center prototype, with the pavilion serving as the city's meeting and convention hall.

The Mechanics' Institute—which had first purchased the property next to City Hall in 1881 and which had erected the pavilion at the site—was an adult education establishment, or "craftsman's college," one of hundreds located throughout Great Britain and the English-speaking world. The Mechanics' Institute in San Francisco had been organized in 1855 by a diverse group of businessmen, including a sawmill owner, a contract carpenter, and a coffee roaster.[3]

Before the site near City Hall, the Mechanics' Institute had maintained pavilions at several other locations in the city. By 1874, it had leased a large lot at Eighth and Mission Streets and commissioned David Farquharson, the most prominent architect of the day, to design what was essentially a two-story wooden box to cover the half-acre site. The new pavilion accommodated hundreds of displays, a bandstand, and gardens. The second floor was devoted to an art show highlighting works by the cream of California's landscape painters.[4] Later, when the landowner wanted his lot back, the Mechanics' Institute purchased a vacant block at Larkin and Grove Streets across from the new City Hall in 1881 for $175,000. For another $165,000, the Mechanics' Institute dismantled its existing wooden pavilion and reassembled it on the new site. Farquharson was asked to design faux-marble baroque façades for the east and west ends of the building to give it a grander appearance.[5]

At this pavilion, industrial fairs were held throughout the 1880s and 1890s, but the huge building was primarily used for trade shows, civic and athletic events, convocations, gospel gatherings, symphony and operatic concerts, dances, and memorial services. A throng of 10,000 people filled the pavilion on May 13, 1903, to hear President Theodore Roosevelt give a speech advocating expansive US leadership in world affairs.[6] However, the pavilion was probably best known for hosting major prizefights at a time when San Francisco had become the epicenter of American boxing.

In the hours immediately following the earthquake in 1906, the Mechanics' Pavilion served as a makeshift emergency hospital. At the time of the earthquake, the building was closed, and only the janitor, M. G. Buckley, was on site.

As he recalled, he was surveying the outside of the building after the shaking had stopped when he saw an ambulance arrive at the Central Emergency Hospital, which was located across the street in the basement of City Hall. The hospital had been partially covered in rubble and was unusable. The victim in the ambulance was the fire chief, Dennis T. Sullivan, who had been buried by falling bricks and scalded by a burst radiator pipe. As the driver was about to move on, Buckley opened a large door on the side of the pavilion and beckoned him to enter. Shortly thereafter, doctors and nurses set up a temporary hospital inside. Within an hour, hundreds of injured and wounded people flocked to the improvised medical facility.[7]

However, fires ignited by the earthquake in several areas of the city were quickly spreading. One of them, the "Ham and Eggs" fire in Hayes Valley, moved eastward and reached the Mechanics' Pavilion at about eleven a.m., causing the roof to catch fire, and forcing people caring for the injured to rush them out of the building and move them to the Presidio and other safer locations in the western part of the city

The destruction of the Mechanics' Pavilion put an end to the institute's exhibitions and events on this block, and the site would remain undeveloped until it would become the location of a new auditorium constructed for the 1915 Panama Pacific International Exposition and subsequently given to the City to be an integral part of the Civic Center.

As the fire moved on from the pavilion, it crossed Larkin Street to the ruined shell of City Hall, where it burned for three days, consuming most of the building's furniture and city records. The charred City Hall, with its tall dome supported by an exposed steel superstructure against a vast landscape of ashes, became a monumental sign of the destruction that had befallen the city.

Mayor Schmitz led the city through three days of firestorms. Within hours of the earthquake, he established a Committee of Fifty, consisting of the city's most prominent men, to deal with the disaster and plan relief efforts. To restart the city government, they searched for usable office space in neighborhoods west of the fire zone. Franklin Hall at Fillmore and Bush Streets became the mayor's headquarters, and the police and other departments were installed nearby, at Lowell High School on Sutter and Gough Streets. The courts, sheriff, and district attorney settled at the Sherith Israel synagogue at California and Webster Streets.[8]

These locations were inevitably temporary and indicative of the extraordinary work of rebuilding that the city government faced. The earthquake and fire brought the previously thriving and booming metropolis of San Francisco to its knees. The city would be confronted with a need for rebuilding and development on an unprecedented scale, something that would require leadership and com-munity agreement to be able to move forward, something which would be found lacking in the subsequent five years.

Rebuilding With an Eye Toward City Beautiful

The massive destruction ultimately represented a major turning point in the history of San Francisco city planning. In addition to requiring rebuilding of structures in many districts. It also brought a renewed energy to long-standing efforts by city planning activists, politicians, and business leaders to develop and improve the city's overall design, particularly in the replacement of the de-stroyed municipal buildings.

Many people saw the devastation in the center of the city as a singular oppor-tunity to implement the Burnham Plan. On April 29, 1906, James Phelan said, "This is a magnificent opportunity for beautifying San Francisco, and I believe that the property owners will gladly cooperate. . . . I am sure that the City will rise from its ashes greater, better, and more beautiful."[9]

At the April 30 meeting of the Committee of Fifty, University of California Regent J. B. Reinstein suggested that Mayor Schmitz appoint a separate re-construction committee to focus on planning and rebuilding the city.[10] The mayor asked Abraham Ruef to organize the committee, and on May 5 the mayor announced its formation, along with twenty-five subcommittees. One of those subcommittees was focused on the Burnham Plan whose members included Phelan; Reinstein; John Galen Howard, professor of architecture at the University of California; and Willis Polk, head of the San Francisco office of D. H. Burnham and Co. Ruef also appointed himself a member of several key committees.[11]

In early 1906 Burnham and his wife had been touring extensively through Europe. When they learned of the San Francisco disaster, they immediately booked passage home. Upon arriving in Chicago on May 1, 1906, Burnham found that he was being heralded in California and elsewhere as the oracle who would shape San Francisco's reconstruction.

Reacting to exuberant expectations for the prospects of the implementation of Burnham's plan, the San Francisco Chronicle cautioned, "We must not lose our heads. We may allow visions of the beautiful to dance before our eyes, but we must not permit them to control our actions." Schmitz chimed in with an admonition against a reconstruction plan of "an extravagant scale." He asked his new committee for suggestions that were "practical, not theoretical." Howard responded by asserting that the Burnham Plan was "admirably conceived . . . and based on sound principles." He stressed the practical aspects of the plan, including "provisions for taking care of traffic and for making each part of the City accessible."[12]

Burnham's much-anticipated arrival in San Francisco occurred on May 14. He was greeted enthusiastically by Phelan and others from the AIASF, as well as by Mayor Schmitz and Ruef. His colleague Polk hosted him at his apartment on Buchanan Street, which was in an area that had not been damaged by the earthquake and fire. Although his presence made everyone more confident, Burnham told people that he was not in San Francisco to implement his plan, but to be an adviser primarily to the streets, parks, and boulevards subcommittee, which was concerned with reconstructing the burned district with wider streets to improve traffic flow and fire prevention. At a public meeting on May 15, Burnham told the subcommittee which Ruef chaired, "Utility is the main thing to consider in laying out streets. Adornment will come later and will take care of itself." He submitted a plan based on his previous work showing Montgomery, Geary, and other streets widened and the addition of several new diagonal streets, including one extending southeast to the Bay from the Market-Van Ness Place that he had proposed in his original Plan for San Francisco, and a second street leading to his proposed railroad station at Bryant and Eighth Streets. The new post-earthquake plan, however, omitted the grand ring roads. Street planning progressed well throughout the week with support from all the participants. On May 21, Ruef submitted this street plan to the meeting of the board of supervisors, where Burnham gave his assurances that it was not a beautification plan, but one designed to relieve congestion and facilitate transportation. The board endorsed it unanimously. In a show of actual community solidarity caused by the disaster, Mayor Schmitz exclaimed, "The adoption of this plan makes it certain beyond all cavil or doubt that the men of San Francisco are in earnest in their determination to rebuild the city, and to rebuild it on a grander scale than before." Delighted, Burnham returned to Chicago.[13]

Years of Disarray and Indecision

Despite the unanimous vote of adoption by the board of supervisors, Burnham's streets plan had dissenters, notably M. H. de Young, who was not only the conservative publisher of the *San Francisco Chronicle* but also a downtown property owner. For several weeks, de Young ran editorials depicting Burnham's streets plan as part of an unnecessary beautification scheme and warning about the ruinous costs of reorganizing streets when the priority should be rebuilding the city in its existing form. In addition, de Young actively organized property owners in the downtown and Union Square areas into groups to oppose street changes. By late May, the *San Francisco Chronicle* had begun to characterize

Burnham's streets plan in articles and editorials as the "cobwebby" plan. The publishers of the *San Francisco Bulletin* and *San Francisco Call* also chimed in with editorials warning against actions that would delay rebuilding the city.[14]

An underlying problem with Burnham's streets plan was that, under San Francisco's current charter and the California Constitution, the city did not have the power to undertake many of the proposed changes. To solve that problem in light of the disaster and speed up implementation, Ruef prepared state legislation endorsed by the committee for reconstruction. Not only did Ruef control city government, but he also had major influence with the legislature in Sacramento. Governor George Pardee called a special session of the legislature to deal with the San Francisco earthquake, and Ruef introduced his legislation on June 2, 1906. The *San Francisco Chronicle*, property owner groups, and labor and civic leaders testified against it, but Ruef outmaneuvered them, and it was approved on June 11.[15] Much of the legislation had to be on the November ballot as constitutional amendments, which would delay any implementation of the streets plan.

Although controversy over the streets plan and beautification was heating up, the reconstruction committee's work continued, incorporating ideas that went beyond just Burnham's streets plan and that reflected the grand urban design approaches that City Beautiful had introduced into the American planning lexicon over the prior years. The reconstruction committee's subcommittee on municipal buildings issued a report calling for establishing a government center along each side of Van Ness Avenue, from Market Street to Hayes Street, with six municipal buildings, including an administration building or city hall, a new public library, and possibly state and federal office buildings. Although this proposal did not follow Burnham's pre-earthquake plan with its widely dispersed set of public buildings situated around a grand plaza at Van Ness and Market, the proposal was indeed for a "civic center" in the accepted sense of a tight grouping of public buildings. The report proposed to partially pay for the new buildings by selling off property where the old City Hall was located. Committee members assumed that the old structure was unsafe and would need to be demolished, although no official finding had yet been made about the building's condition. However, the committee's final report concluded with the statement, "Such a group of buildings would present something in the form of magnificence not seen in American cities. . . . It would make San Francisco distinctive among the world's great cities." The larger reconstruction committee adopted this report with little discussion on June 16, 1906,[16] a remarkable indication that many of the city's business and public leaders had already accepted the idea that a great city should have a civic center.

US Senator Francis Newlands of Nevada, who had interests in the Palace Hotel and other downtown properties, became concerned about the drift in reconstruction plans being proposed by San Francisco's committees and felt that stronger leadership was necessary than was currently in place. Thus, he wrote to Burnham on July 12 inquiring whether he would come back to San Francisco and take charge of a commission and oversee full-time the reconstruction and implementation of the Burnham Plan. Burnham was flattered by the offer, but he would have had to drastically uproot his professional and family life in Chicago to accept. Despite receiving repeated pleas to oversee the work, Burnham declined and the city committee would move forward without him.

Pressed to make a determination of what to do with the wrecked City Hall, the board of supervisors created a four-person panel of building experts, including the well-known architect William Curlett, to examine the structure and report their findings to the mayor and board. On September 4, 1906, they reported that they had found the Hall of Records little damaged, and they estimated that with an expenditure of $110,000, it could be made functional. The board accepted this recommendation, and the recorder eventually reoccupied the structure in June 1907. With regard to City Hall itself, the panel found the Larkin Street wing and the City Hall Avenue façade virtually destroyed, the dome and tower stable, and the northeast wing on McAllister Street repairable.[17] The board of supervisors agreed to remove debris and repair the McAllister Street section, which was later reoccupied in July 1907 and became the shabby offices for the mayor, auditor, and the department of elections. The tower superstructure and dome were left to loom over the city for several more years. Some citizens regarded the relic lightheartedly and covered it in decorative lights during the Christmas holidays.

Despite the great need for robust action after the earthquake, city officials found themselves meeting obstacles to moving forward—frequently involving their own administrative dysfunction. For example, the supervisors proposed constructing a temporary municipal building on the block at Van Ness Avenue and Hayes, Franklin, and Fell Streets, only to be confronted by the fact that this property had been purchased by the trustees of the public library in 1905. Nevertheless, moving quickly, the board of public works engaged architect Frank Shea to develop plans with a budget not to exceed $50,000. But the library trustees, led by Phelan, Edward Robeson Taylor, Reuben Hills, and other prominent men, protested strongly that this block was not city property, but under the jurisdiction of the library trustees, and was already designated as the site for a new public library. They were unable to convince the supervisors and mayor to change their minds, so they filed a lawsuit to stop the city from constructing a building on the block. On October 10, 1906, the Superior Court found in favor of

The old City Hall from the Larkin Street perspective shortly after the 1906 earthquake and fire, showing the destruction and damage to various parts of the building. The bulk of the falling debris landed on the Larkin Street side, causing additional damage to the lower parts of the structure. Source: Courtesy of SFMTA Photo Archive | sfmta.com/photo U00831.

The Hall of Records rehabilitated and in use by city staff after June of 1907.

Source: Courtesy of California Historical Society, [No. 69} CHS2015.1990.

the library trustees, forcing the city to continue to rent space wherever it could.[18] Additionally, that same month, any effort at the implementation of Burnham's streets plan was suddenly and dramatically overshadowed by the indictment of Mayor Schmitz and political boss Ruef for graft. They faced charges of extorting funds from the owners of so-called French restaurants (places of prostitution). This was the beginning of a public uproar that continued for many months while Schmitz and Ruef attempted to defend themselves.

Further eroding momentum for the streets plan, on November 6, 1906, California and San Francisco voters soundly rejected (58,042 to 35,649 and 7,940 to 4,128, respectively) Ruef's constitutional amendments. The city government was further crippled by the indictment of Police Chief Jeremiah Dinan for bribery and extortion on November 15. Later, on March 18, 1907, sixteen of the eighteen elected members of the board of supervisors confessed to having received bribes through Ruef from the Home Telephone Company and other utilities, streetcar companies, and people seeking favors from the city. These board members were granted immunity in return for their cooperation in the trials of Schmitz and Ruef and in other actions the prosecution might demand.

These indictments sharply divided the city, making it nearly impossible to accomplish major planning or rebuilding. Instead, business and real estate leaders quickly followed their own interests and began to rebuild in a manner as close as possible to what had existed before the earthquake, driven by the economic imperative of getting things back to normal. During the three years after the earthquake, private parties constructed 20,500 buildings, of which 19,000 were wood-frame structures that were vulnerable to fire like the pre-earthquake wooden structures that had contributed to the devastating blazes. During the same period, the public sector constructed virtually no buildings.

Ruef pleaded guilty on May 15, 1907. Mayor Schmitz refused to withdraw his plea of "not guilty," went to trial, and was found guilty by a jury on June 15. On July 7, Judge Frank Dunne sentenced Schmitz to five years in San Quentin Prison, which meant that the office of mayor was officially vacant. The prosecutors had to find a suitable replacement quickly. After searching for several days, they recruited the sixty-eight-year-old physician and lawyer Edward Robeson Taylor, the dean of Hastings College of the Law. Under pressure from the prosecutors, the board of supervisors elected Taylor as mayor in the evening of July 16.

Taylor faced Herculean tasks. The first was to recruit sixteen new, competent members for the board of supervisors, a police chief, and many other city officials. He was also immediately confronted with an outbreak of bubonic plague and a violent transit strike. He then had to run for the mayor's office in

November, which he won, despite opposition from several labor leaders. And yet, his greatest task as mayor remained: to rebuild the city's devastated streets, sewers, schools, police and fire stations, and other critical infrastructure.

Taylor recruited the young architect Newton Tharp to oversee this development effort, appointing him city architect on October 23, 1907. Tharp had grown up in Petaluma, California, and studied art and architecture, first in Chicago and then in Paris. He returned to the United States and worked as a draftsman in architectural firms in New York, Chicago, and Los Angeles before settling in San Francisco. After his appointment, Tharp threw himself into the job as city architect. In May 1908 he presented to voters six bond measures totaling $18.2 million to start the reconstruction of city buildings, all of which would pass by large margins.

One of the major issues Mayor Taylor's new board of supervisors were confronting was the future of the damaged City Hall. On March 30, 1908, they approved a "select committee" of six supervisors to consider the subject, and shortly thereafter they appropriated $2,500 to finance the city architect's study of the matter. Tharp issued his report on May 25, finding that, although the building's basements and foundation were in good shape, the fire had destroyed the structural integrity of City Hall. The earthquake had sheared the rivets on the dome's support columns, requiring that the dome be dismantled and rebuilt. Tharp gave the committee three choices and their costs: reconstruct and rehabilitate the building for $3 to $4 million; demolish and rebuild it using the existing foundations for $4.5 million; or start anew with a fresh modern design for $5.2 million. The supervisors appointed an advisory committee of three prominent architects—Albert Pissis, James Reid, and Howard—to review Tharp's report. After their review, the architects concluded that the best alternative was to build anew according to current best practices.[19] On October 5, 1908, the board of supervisors passed a resolution finding the old City Hall unsafe and appropriating $50,000 for its demolition, while keeping the Hall of Records and the McAllister Street structure in use. The demolition began in January 1909 and took six months to complete, leaving the foundation for a future determination.

With the demolition of City Hall under way, the building committee of the board of supervisors, chaired by Supervisor Loring P. Rixford, a trained architect, grappled with replacing it. They considered commissioning a private firm to build a new city hall that the city would lease permanently, but were advised by the city attorney that such an approach was prohibited by law. They gave serious attention to building a new city hall on the existing foundations of the old building. However, most of the supervisors were progressive thinkers long associated with Phelan's reform and improvement efforts and therefore they favored moving the location to the Van Ness Avenue and Market Street location outlined in the Burnham Plan. In the meantime, Polk, as Burnham's local representative, made revisions to Burnham's earlier plan, taking into account the demolition of the old City Hall. His plan abandoned Burnham's massive civic center and called for a tight group of public buildings including a city hall, courthouse, library, state and federal buildings, and a grand auditorium facing a semicircular plaza opening on Market Street and bisected by Van Ness Avenue and Oak Street. He proposed locating the city's railroad station on the opposite side of Market from the new plaza.

In April 1909 Burnham stopped in San Francisco for a few days during a West Coast business trip. On April 14, Mayor Taylor hosted a meeting with Burnham and city officials to discuss the civic center proposal as proposed in Polk's revision to Burnham's earlier plan. Burnham argued that implementing this plan and spending money on making the city more attractive would add to the prosperity of all citizens by attracting tourists and visitors. Phelan also spoke in favor of Burnham's view of building a city hall in a new location near Van Ness and Market Streets as in Polk's proposal. Responding to these exhortations, the supervisors' building committee met that afternoon and recommended a bond measure to cover the $4.3 million cost of acquiring property around Van Ness and Market Streets and $4 million for constructing a new city hall at that location.[20] To make the bond issue more palatable to city voters, the supervisors added funds to create six new neighborhood parks and construct a new San Francisco Polytechnic High School. Fifteen of the eighteen supervisors voted to place the bonds on the ballot at a special election to be held in June 1909.[21] Burnham learned of the board's approval of these bond issues on his return to Chicago and sent a telegram to his friends and colleagues in San Francisco stating, "If this improvement [Polk's plan] be determined upon, it will attract attention to San Francisco from all quarters of the globe. It will stimulate real estate in and around the city. It will be the best thing ever done by an American city to make of itself a magnet attracting from every quarter those men and fortunes which bring lasting prosperity to a great commercial center."[22]

Not all San Franciscans, however, shared his rosy view of a civic center's beneficial effect, while some others were effectively unavailable to support the project. Mayor Taylor, harassed by a variety of political opponents, often for petty matters and now seventy years old, was growing tired of his mayoral duties, and by May 1909 he had made up his mind not to run for another term. He was therefore unwilling to take on causes such as the civic center bonds and only made halfhearted speeches in favor of them.

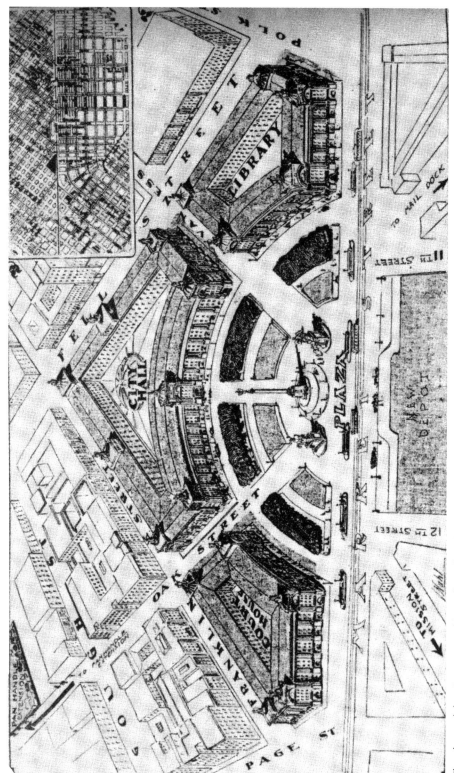

The plan and drawing prepared by Willis Polk with Daniel Burnham's endorsement for a Civic Center at Van Ness and Market Streets. This plan was the basis for the unsuccessful 1909 bond election. Source: Image scan courtesy of the author.

Meanwhile, Tharp, the city's architect, who was a strong advocate for the civic center, died in May 1909, when he suffered a heart attack while visiting New York to examine the newest designs in hospital construction. Tharp had designed thirty-four new school buildings, a hall of justice, and a new modern hospital, among other structures. At the time of his death, sixty draftsmen worked in his office. They had completed the plans for six schools, including Commerce High School on Grove Street between Van Ness Avenue and Polk Street, which would open in December 1910, but which would very soon thereafter be moved in a feat of remarkable engineering to accommodate the new Civic Center.[23]

The death of Tharp deprived supporters of a credible advocate for the civic center program. Still, the reformers labored on, and Phelan, Polk, and a number of the supervisors campaigned before many community and civic groups. The *San Francisco Examiner, San Francisco Call,* and *San Francisco Bulletin* all endorsed the bonds.

But the dissenters to the plan were also vociferous in their opposition. M. H. de Young and the *San Francisco Chronicle* were relentlessly hostile to any program other than the construction of a new city hall on the old site for the least expenditure possible. They argued that the city, still recovering from disaster, could not afford a large bond issue for any purpose.[24] The San Francisco Labor Council opposed the bonds, arguing that the city needed a reliable source of water as its first priority.[25] In spite of the inclusion of a number of neighborhood parks in the bond issue, a variety of neighborhood improvement associations and small property owners also opposed the bonds. Cahill also weighed in against the bonds saying that the Polk and Burnham Van Ness–Market scheme was an extravagance that the city could ill afford, a comment reflective of his hostility to anything involving Burnham.[26]

Despite the controversial bonds, on June 22, 1909, only one-third of city voters participated. Only the bonds for the new San Francisco Polytechnic High School received the necessary two-thirds margin. The civic center bonds received 55 percent of the vote, while the park bonds received more than 60 percent.

Civic center proponents were deeply disappointed by the defeat. The *San Francisco Bulletin* editorialized that de Young was a "traitor to his city." Phelan said that the public had not been well-informed about the merits of the project and stated that the AIASF would raise funds for another campaign.[27]

At that time city politics were in flux, and no notable progressive candidate arose to succeed Mayor Taylor. Republican and Democratic Party candidates were nonentities. The Union Labor Party was revived under the leadership of Patrick Henry McCarthy, head of the Building Trades Council, who mounted his campaign for mayor on the platform of bringing the city together by shutting down graft prosecution. With these forces at play, the political future of many supervisors was at risk. They lapsed into a state of indecision in regard to City Hall.

P. H. McCarthy was elected mayor in November, along with a number of new Union Labor Party members of the board of supervisors. Although McCarthy had campaigned for a new city hall on the old site, the new board of supervisors spent most of 1910 discussing with property owners and developers the notion of a private party constructing an office building to serve as a temporary city hall. On October 25, 1910, the board accepted an offer from the Whitcomb Estate Company to construct a seven-story building on their property on the south side of Market Street between Eighth and Ninth Streets. The building would accommodate all city agencies currently occupying rental space, including the courts.[28] The architectural firm was Wright, Rushforth, and Cahill, with which Bernard Cahill was affiliated. Since the new mayor and board were antagonists to Phelan and civic center advocates, Cahill's involvement presented no difficulties. On December 10, 1910, Mayor McCarthy stood in front of the Whitcomb lot, took off his coat, and started breaking ground for the new office building. The construction of this building would be completed in 1912, and it would serve as a temporary City Hall until 1916 when it would be converted into the Whitcomb Hotel (which still stands today) and replaced by a magnificent new City Hall located at the heart of a grand, monumental Civic Center that the city would finally find a way to build.

The Panama-Pacific International Exposition and the Creation of San Francisco's Civic Center

On January 31, 1911, San Franciscans were overjoyed when the House of Representatives selected their city over New Orleans to host the international exposition celebrating the opening of the Panama Canal. The business community had fought hard for this victory, and the city's rewards and the boost to its self-image would be enormous.

Prominent San Franciscans had visited expositions in American cities during the previous twenty years, and many had suggested that one be held in San Francisco. In January 1904, within a week after Allan Pollok published his jeremiad in the *San Francisco Bulletin* about the ills of San Francisco and the need to overcome them,[1] and at the same time as Phelan was organizing the Association for the Improvement and Adornment of San Francisco (AIASF) to develop a new city plan, Reuben B. Hale, an executive with the family-owned Hale Brothers Department Store and civic leader, wrote to the San Francisco Merchants' Association referring to Pollok's article and asking, "Isn't the time ripe to consider a World Exposition in San Francisco in 1915" to celebrate the opening of the Panama Canal? The association delivered Hale's letter to other business groups, who sent representatives to a meeting on April 26, 1904, at the Merchants Exchange Building, where there was unanimous support for the proposal. These men formed a committee to pursue the idea.[2] At this point, Hale's idea was speculative, since the revolution that established the Republic of Panama had just occurred and Congress had just approved a treaty with the new nation. No matter: These men were motivated to improve and promote San Francisco. Many of them, including Hale, would shortly join Phelan's AIASF. On December 1, 1906, Hale invited the members of the committee to a meeting where they established the Pacific Ocean Exposition Company.

Although there had been numerous difficulties in the engineering work on the Panama Canal, by 1909 work was progressing well. On October 5, President William Howard Taft, who was in San Francisco on a West Coast tour, told local leaders that he expected the canal to open by January 1, 1915, if not earlier.[3] San Francisco's exposition committee was aware that other cities were competing to sponsor a world exposition to celebrate the opening of the Panama Canal and felt pressure to seriously organize their work. The first step was to hold an open "mass meeting" at the Merchants Exchange on December 7, 1909. At the meeting, filled to capacity, business leaders spoke about the exposition's value to the city and the need for support. The outgoing mayor, Edward Taylor, backed the idea, but his support was marginal. Significantly, Mayor-elect P. H. McCarthy did not attend. Bolstered by the group's enthusiasm and pledges of financial support, the committee reorganized itself into the Panama-Pacific International Exposition Company, with a board of directors composed of businessmen headed by Charles C. Moore, with Hale and James Rolph Jr.—a well-liked and successful San Francisco-born businessman—among the directors. To provide the capital to back the new company, a large fundraising meeting was held on April 28, 1910, where more than $4 million was collected, which shortly grew to $6 million. The company now had the resources to solicit support for the Exposition throughout California and other Western states and aggressively campaign to convince Congress to designate San Francisco as the host city.

The San Francisco business community was eager to obtain the Exposition to show the world that San Francisco had been restored and was once again the most magnificent city on the West Coast. Many of these individuals also hoped that organizing the Exposition would bring the city together after the years of corruption trials and political disputes and help accomplish the many city projects which had been languishing, particularly a new city hall and a civic center. Hosting the Exposition would be an opportunity to take bold directions in San Francisco's planning and development—because, in their minds, it would be unthinkable to invite the world to visit without having a proper place to greet the many dignitaries and millions of people who would come. These men hoped to see San Francisco's urban architecture reflect a grander vision modeled on City Beautiful ideas.

After an extraordinary campaign to raise money and persuade Congress to choose San Francisco to host the Exposition, President Taft signed authorizing legislation at the White House on February 15, 1911, designating San Francisco as the host of the 1915 Panama-Pacific International Exposition. Hale and several other organizing committee members attended.

Although San Francisco had the green light, the committee had only four years to plan and construct the massive fair and adorn the city to show itself off to millions of visitors. At this point, no agreement had even been reached on exposition locations within the city. Another major concern was the business community's lack of confidence that Mayor P. H. McCarthy and his administration were up to the task of preparing San Francisco for the Exposition. McCarthy had helped end the graft trials, but he had not unified the city. He catered to his Union Labor Party working-class base, appointed cronies to important city posts, allowed vice and crime to rise, and could not start or complete important public works projects, such as the new Geary streetcar line, which had been approved by voters in 1909.

To produce the Exposition and prepare the city, business groups wanted a city government with aggressive leadership staffed by competent experts. To achieve this end, they organized the Municipal Conference in March 1911 to recruit and support suitable candidates for mayor and the board of supervisors.[4] The initial conference members consisted of business and professional men, a number of whom were also directors of the Panama-Pacific International Exposition (PPIE). The primary election in the mayor's race was scheduled for September 26, 1911, leaving the conference six months to recruit a mayoral candidate and organize his campaign. Their overwhelming choice was Rolph, a vice president of the PPIE; however, it took organizers a month to convince him to enter the race.

Rolph was an ideal candidate. Born and raised in the Mission District, he resided there with his family. He had led the Mission District rescue efforts after the earthquake and fire. A self-made, well-to-do shipowner and banker, he was a progressive businessman in the Phelan circle. He supported unions and was particularly popular with those in the powerful maritime trades. He had served as president of the Merchants Exchange for several terms and was popular with businessmen. He also had a gregarious and energetic personality.

Rolph accepted the nomination offered by the Municipal Conference on April 15, 1911.[5] Within weeks, the local Republican and Democratic Parties endorsed him, and neighborhood and ethnic "Rolph Clubs" surfaced throughout the city. On August 11, 1911, Rolph issued his "Declaration of Principles" for his candidacy. He pledged to be "Mayor of All the People," representing no faction and willing to work with labor and business to bring harmony to the city. This would be the slogan of his campaign. One of Rolph's major campaign themes was the construction of a new city hall—and not just one that would merely house city agencies, but one that would inspire people. "We must have a city hall," he wrote. "One convenient for the conduct of public business. More than this, it should be a structure of architectural beauty and dignity, a building that will express the greatness and good taste of San Francisco."[6] Rolph's ideas were emblematic of Phelan's City Beautiful ideals. He called for a new city hall and civic center in most of his campaign speeches. Mayor McCarthy, on the other hand, ran a narrowly focused campaign, appealing

James Rolph (*left*) campaigning by shaking hands with a voter, circa July 1911.
Source: Courtesy of the San Francisco History Center, San Francisco Public Library.

to the working class and labeling Rolph an out-of-touch wealthy businessman and part of an anti-labor faction. Nevertheless, Andrew Furuseth, head of the powerful Sailors' Union of the Pacific, endorsed Rolph and brought along other labor leaders, who often showed up at Rolph rallies. On September 26, 1911, primary election day, Rolph received overwhelming support (47,417 to 27,048 votes) and with more than 50 percent of the vote, under city charter, he automatically became the mayor-elect.

During the next six weeks, Rolph busied himself learning about city government. He remained vice president of the PPIE and involved with Exposition preparations. The general election was held on November 7, 1911, and seventeen of the newly elected supervisors pledged to work with Rolph. Only one of the Union Labor Party supervisors' remained. With this strong mandate, Rolph set to work, focusing on a new city hall and civic center.

On November 15, 1911, the seventeen members-elect of the board of supervisors met with Rolph for the first time at the Merchants Exchange. Rolph stated that they all must work together to prepare the city for the Exposition by January 1, 1915: "There is no room for drones in the city's beehive during the next four years." He went on to speak of general civic improvements. "We must have a city hall . . . which will express our confidence in the city." Rolph then read a letter from the PPIE inviting members of the new board to meet with its directors to discuss an offer to erect an auditorium in conjunction with the building of a new city hall as a component of a new civic center. He also spoke of the need for a public water supply, better transit, and improved streets, but city hall was clearly his priority.[7] The supervisors-elect met again on November 24, 1911, to organize their committees. Paul Bancroft was made chair of the San Francisco Public Buildings Committee, the committee most responsible for city hall and a civic center. Bancroft was a seasoned supervisor, having first been elected in the reform sweep of 1907 and having survived the Union Labor Party election of 1909. He was in the real estate business and the son of Hubert Howe Bancroft, the publisher and great historian of California. He was a business progressive on whom Rolph could rely.

On December 7, 1911, the supervisors-elect met with Rolph, the PPIE directors, and the PPIE architectural commission. By then the PPIE Company had decided to locate the Exposition on the marshlands by the Bay known as Harbor View next to the Presidio (afterward the area would become known as the Marina neighborhood). However, Rolph pressed them about city hall, saying, "In my inaugural address, I want to say that the city hall will be ready for the exposition and I don't want to make any mistakes about it, no matter where it is to be located." PPIE Company President Moore spoke about other buildings, including an auditorium, that should be grouped around the city hall. "All these buildings must be clustered. It is ridiculous to think of permanent buildings located in [Golden Gate] Park or Harbor View. No one would support them. They must be centrally located and in the civic center." The meeting turned to the location of city hall, which everyone felt needed to be decided as soon as possible, as well as the amount of land to be acquired for the civic center. They also agreed that an architectural advisory committee should be created to assist the supervisors' public buildings committee in determining these actions.[8] It would consist of John Galen Howard and five members from the PPIE architectural commission—Willis Polk, the chair of the architectural commission, who was practicing architecture on his own, having left the employ of D. H. Burnham and Co. in 1910; Edward Bennett, the Exposition planner who had been recruited for that post from Chicago, where he had set up his own planning practice after completing the Chicago Plan with Burnham; Clarence Ward, a local architect; Harris Connick, director of works for the Exposition and an engineer; and William B. Faville, an architect trained at the Massachusetts Institute of Technology (MIT) and an alumnus of McKim, Mead, and White. It was readily apparent that Polk and Bennett would continue to advocate Burnham's Market–Van Ness location. However, although the others might have supported that location in 1909, they now were open to alternatives.

Among the architects selected for the supervisors' advisory committee, the most eminent member was Howard, probably the most prominent architect on the West Coast at this time. Well-regarded, he had served as the president of the San Francisco chapter of the American Institute of Architects and was frequently consulted on city matters. He had studied architecture at MIT; worked in the office of McKim, Mead, and White; and, with their support, enrolled in 1891 at the École des Beaux-Arts for two years. He returned to New York City and opened his own architectural office, which was immediately successful. The Pan-American Exposition of 1901 in Buffalo, New York, invited him to be one of eight architects to plan and design the fair's buildings. Howard had also submitted a design to the International Competition for the Phoebe Apperson Hearst's University of California Plan in 1898, but, when the results were announced in 1899, his submission was ranked fourth. The winning architect, Émile Bénard, turned out to be difficult to deal with and unwilling to move to Berkeley to oversee the work. In February 1901, Hearst had chosen Howard to design a building for the School of Mining that she was also donating to the university and therefore was well acquainted with him. As the problems with Bénard continued to fester, on December 21, 1901, the university's board of regents (including Hearst who had been appointed regent in 1897) finally terminated the relationship with him and engaged Howard as the university's consulting architect to oversee the plan and serve as professor of architecture.

On December 8, 1911, members of the public buildings committee, Howard, and the exposition architects commission met for further discussion of the civic center. Polk suggested that the mayor invite the city's architects to submit ideas for a civic center, which the others agreed was a fine suggestion. Rolph supported the plan so long as it was clear to the participants that they could not submit a bill to the city for work done. The honor of competing, he felt, would be sufficient inducement. An invitation was issued with a request that submittals be delivered no later than December 27, 1911.[9]

Rolph, the supervisors-elect, and the PPIE directors met again on December 19. They concluded that all the land needed for a civic center should be acquired before any construction began, but left the location an open issue. The PPIE's president, Moore, reiterated that the exposition company would pay to build an auditorium, but the city would have to furnish the land. He stressed that the PPIE board could contribute nothing further to a civic center. Conservative banker William H. Crocker concluded the meeting, saying that this was the right time to undertake the project, since the new Rolph administration would have the full confidence of the people. Since the city would need to raise money through bonds to finance much of the construction, this was an important affirmation from someone who might have opposed the 1909 city hall bond issue.

John Galen Howard, the most prominent architect in the Bay Area. Mayor Rolph recruited him to design and guide the development of the Civic Center. Source: Courtesy of the Environmental Design Archives, University of California, Berkeley.

Forty-four architects, both prominent and obscure, submitted civic center proposals, which were publicly displayed at the Merchants Exchange. On December 28, 1911, Rolph and the supervisors-elect met at the Exchange to review the plans and hear the architects' comments.[10] Most of the proposals favored the old City Hall site with a civic center extending to the west. Several proposed that a center should extend south along Eighth Street to Mission Street. Some supported the Van Ness Avenue and Market Street location that had featured in Burnham's earlier plan, and a few proposed using property at Dolores and Market Streets owned by the Spring Valley Water Company. Rolph and Bancroft also requested that the advisory committee chaired by Howard prepare its own report on a potential civic center site by January 12.

The public buildings committee met again on January 3, 1912, to allow those architects who had not previously made comments on their plans to do so. At this meeting, former mayor James Phelan took the occasion to offer his thoughts on possible plans, speaking in favor of Polk's revised 1909 Market–Van Ness plan. On January 5, the supervisors-elect and the PPIE board held another joint meeting with Rolph, who emphasized that the time for discussion about the civic center was nearly over. "I intend to go to bat next Monday morning [Inaugural Day] on the proposition for a new city hall."[11]

On inauguration day, after expressing a number of courtesies, and without any pomp, Rolph gave a rather concise inaugural address: "The nation," he said, "has selected our city as the place for the celebration of the opening of the Panama Canal. . . . The world will come and we must be ready." He listed three urgent matters: a new city hall, a public water system, and better streetcar transportation. For the city hall, he said that the first task was to select a site. Acknowledging that the architectural advisory committee had not yet tendered its report, he expressed his personal preference for the old site. "This site commends itself to every practical consideration and only by building there can we be ready within the limited time."[12] That afternoon, the mayor and supervisors had their first regular meeting and passed an urgency declaration of public necessity calling for the construction of a city hall and civic center and setting a bonds election for that purpose. At this point, the measure did not specify the site, but the legislation would start the process to organize a bond election as soon as possible. The popular new mayor had spoken and had finally broken through six years of argument and indecision.

On January 10, 1912, the public buildings committee met to hear the architectural advisory committee report, and most of the members of the board of supervisors attended, as well as former mayors Phelan and Taylor. Howard, Faville, Ward, and Connick recommended the old site, which Howard said was conveniently located near the center of current city activity. It was also more spacious than other locations and offered the easiest and least expensive starting point from which they could acquire additional land along Fulton Street. Howard concluded by saying, "We conceive of civic center as a great metropolitan grouping, along large lines, not only for the city hall and other public buildings . . . but for other semi-public buildings."[13]

In the end, the determining factor for these men in choosing the location and scheme did not appear in their criteria or public remarks—Rolph wanted them to come up with a scheme that could be built in time for the Exposition. Since the old site was already in public hands and the adjoining properties were easily obtainable, this location was the most expeditious choice. Properties at Van Ness Avenue and Market Street might have taken more than a year to assemble. Rolph endorsed Howard's remarks and asked the supervisors to call for a bond election on March 28, 1912, to secure the funds. The public buildings committee then unanimously passed a resolution supporting that view and recommended acquiring six blocks west of the old site.

When the full board of supervisors met on January 15, 1912, and approved the public buildings committee's report and the bond election, Polk was allowed to speak for himself and Bennett, who had submitted the minority report on

Mayor James Rolph Jr. at his inauguration on January 8, 1912, being congratulated by outgoing Mayor P. H. McCarthy. Rolph in his remarks advocated for the old City Hall blocks to be used for the new civic center and city hall. Source: Courtesy of California Historical Society.

the site location. He said that the city was making a mistake and had given the committee too little time to prepare its analysis. Rolph interrupted him, saying, "Didn't you say that the advisory committee of architects was the equal of any in the world?" Bancroft reminded Polk that the committee was his idea and he had suggested the members. These remarks received a large hand from the public audience. At this point, Polk left the room. Rolph called him back and thanked him for all the work he had done. Several supervisors who had previously supported the Van Ness and Market site announced that they were prepared to vote for the old City Hall site, and former mayor Edward Taylor sent a communication expressing the same opinion.[14] Although the actual location of the city hall would still need to be decided, the contentious issue of the general site for the civic center was finally closed.

Bernard Cahill also spoke at the supervisors' meeting. He had responded to the mayor's invitation to prepare a plan for the Civic Center by submitting his 1904 and 1909 plans. True to form, he also lobbied members of the architectural advisory committee, particularly William Faville, about the old site and his plan. Cahill managed to get the *San Francisco Chronicle* to run an article illustrated with his drawings in the Sunday, January 14, 1912, edition, declaring that using the old site was his idea. Part of his motivation was no doubt his animus against Polk and Bennett and their participation on the committee that still lingered from having his earlier plans and ideas dismissed by Burnham. Cahill addressed the supervisors and expressed his pleasure at the expected adoption of the old site for which he had advocated so long. He then said, "[His] plan was submitted to Mr. Burnham in 1904 and he had expressed approval, but he was afterward induced to favor the Van Ness location by those who were interested in the extension of the Panhandle at that point." In this company, it did not serve him well to take such a gratuitous swipe at Phelan and the AIASF members.

Cahill did not let his resentments rest. On April 18, 1912, he wrote to Mayor Rolph, complaining about being unrecognized for his thirteen years of work on his Civic Center plan, which he claimed had finally been adopted. "I have opposed the active missionary work of a very powerful opposition which has attempted to fashion an irrational Civic Center on a community at the wrong time and in the wrong place. . . . This opposition has caused me much suffering and bitterness and brought abuse and ridicule upon my head." He concluded by asking to be engaged to work on the project, saying, "I am subjected to the final humiliation of asking that I not be overlooked."[15] There is no record of this letter having been answered.

It had taken Rolph only two months to resolve the impasse preventing construction of a new city hall and civic center. He devoted virtually all of his time and energy to the project, sharing the belief of the PPIE company members that it would have been unthinkable to host an exposition without a grand building to house the city's government. As an officer of the PPIE, he understood clearly that the exposition would convince the world that San Francisco had fully recovered from the earthquake and was a leading American city. The *San Francisco Chronicle* published an editorial on January 17, 1912, hailing both the city's decision to build and Rolph's businesslike leadership; it also noted, "One element of the Mayor's success is his infinite tact. Resolute and vigorous as he is . . . his plans are only announced after consultation with all who have the official right to be heard." During much of the time he fought for new public buildings, Rolph was not yet officially mayor, so he had to rely on the help of others, particularly directors and officers of the PPIE. In addition to devoting their time and energy to the effort, the PPIE pledged $1 million for a new auditorium, which would be a critical factor in motivating the public to support the project.

Although the groundwork for developing a civic center in the city had been laid over many years, it is safe to say that the Panama-Pacific International Exposition was the catalyst for the San Francisco Civic Center, and the two great projects were inextricably linked. It is worth noting that, during all of the discussions about new development, City Beautiful concepts underlying the ideological and architectural motivations for having a civic center went largely unquestioned. Monumental architecture based on Beaux-Arts principles was the standard for the new civic center, just as it would be for the Exposition. None of the new City Practical thinking had yet seeped into San Francisco.

Breaking Ground
on the Civic Center

Now that the major issue of the general location of city hall and the civic center appeared to be resolved, Mayor Rolph and Supervisor Bancroft had to determine a course for the project to be designed and built. Under the city charter, the board of public works, which included the offices of city architect and city engineer, was responsible for all of the city's building projects. The board comprised three paid members appointed by the mayor. At this time, the board was still controlled by McCarthy appointees and had a reputation for inefficiency and delays. The finance committee of the board of supervisors had recently raised questions of cost overruns and other financial irregularities in the department.[1] But the president of the board, Michael Casey, a longtime labor leader, was determined to serve out his term. Rolph probably did not want to pick a fight with him, but he did not trust the board and the department to move forward rapidly and competently with the civic center project. Therefore, Bancroft and Rolph developed an alternate arrangement—setting up an official committee to oversee the project that would operate independently from the board of public works.

During the board of supervisors meeting on January 29, 1912, members requested that the mayor officially appoint a committee of architects to advise the building committee and board of public works on planning the civic center and running a competition for the design of city hall. The mayor immediately agreed and announced John Galen Howard as chairman and John Reid Jr. and Frederick H. Meyer as members of this new advisory group.[2] Reid had graduated first in his class from the University of California architectural department, where he had studied with Howard, and then had received a stipend from Phoebe Apperson Hearst to enroll at the École des Beaux-Arts, where he had won several gold medals. He was Rolph's brother-in-law; Rolph informed the supervisors about that right away, asking if they had any objections. There were none. Meyer had learned architecture as an apprentice and ran a successful practice designing apartment houses and commercial buildings in San Francisco. Since Howard and Reid were Beaux-Arts–trained architects and many architects in San Francisco were not, Meyer's appointment may have been intended to reach out to the latter. The supervisors appropriated $5,000 to compensate the advisers as well as $2,500 to further examine the old City Hall foundations to ensure their suitability for a new structure.

The city's financial advisers reported that the city could support $8.8 million in bonds for the purchase of land for the civic center and the construction of city hall. The city engineer presented to the committee an estimate of $6 million to purchase the designated six blocks as well as the property along Market Street. It was noted that a new public library would be included on one of the blocks; a possible land exchange with the public library for its Van Ness Avenue block could reduce the total cost of land by approximately $700,000.[3] The advisory committee had to not only prepare a specific plan for the civic center and designate property acquisitions but also keep the cost of land within the available funds.

The PPIE board had formally offered to pay up to $1 million for a new auditorium to house conventions and meetings at the civic center if the city would contribute the land. The assumption was that the auditorium would be built on the block where the old Mechanics' Pavilion had been located. On February 12, 1912, the mayor announced that he had received a communication from the Music Association of San Francisco that it and its members would also contribute $750,000 to construct an opera house at civic center if the city would provide the land.[4] The state legislature in 1909 had appropriated $500,000 for a State Building in San Francisco and the state had bought a parcel at Polk and Fulton Streets for that purpose. Thus, the committee had concrete building projects with which to begin developing the civic center plan.

On February 28, 1912, the mayor held a meeting to discuss the civic center with the board of supervisors' public buildings committee, other supervisors, the architectural advisory committee, and Moore, the president of the PPIE, which would organize and build the auditorium. Everyone agreed to coordinate the auditorium's design with those of other proposed civic center buildings. They also discussed the civic center bond election, which required a two-thirds vote to pass, and agreed that Supervisor J. Emmett Hayden, would organize the campaign, which the PPIE board would vigorously support.[5]

The mayor personally kicked off the bond campaign on Monday, March 4, 1912, at a packed meeting of his home organization, the Mission Promotion

Association. He told the crowd that the civic center bonds showed he was delivering on his commitment to build a new city hall and a civic center and emphasized that the PPIE board's offer to build an auditorium for conventions and meetings would benefit the city's economy and create jobs. He promised that the work would "be done honestly, efficiently, and expeditiously; and I guarantee that it will be done." He underscored his practical arguments by calling the Civic Center the People's Center and saying that it would be a symbol of unity for a great city along the lines of a City Beautiful civic center. The association unsurprisingly endorsed the bonds without dissent and voted to contact thirty other improvement clubs around the city to set up similar meetings. Within a few days, dozens of groups that had supported Rolph's election had scheduled meetings.[6] The association also reached out to labor unions, with the Bricklayers Union Number 7 being the first to endorse the bonds, on March 6, 1912.[7] A labor committee was quickly organized to seek support from other unions and organize worker rallies. For the next three weeks, Rolph, the supervisors, members of the architects advisory committee, and other civic leaders crisscrossed the city every night to speak about the bonds. The architects also produced sketches of possible buildings in the civic center, including interiors of the auditorium, as advertisements for the bonds. The imaginary buildings were all grand neoclassical showpieces.[8]

Campaigners made a special effort to reach women, who had been given the right to vote in California in the October 1911 election. The men in the state had supported suffrage by a slight margin, with San Francisco voters strongly against it. Local suffragettes, operating through the New Era League, wanted to make a show of women interested in civic affairs and so made a concerted effort to register them to vote so that they could be a factor in the bond election. It was estimated that at least 12,000 new female voters were added to the rolls. On March 19, 1912, the New Era League and the California Club, a women's civic improvement organization, held a joint meeting featuring speeches by the mayor, several supervisors, and architect Meyer. After going into great detail about the need for a city hall and civic center, Rolph appealed to the women's desire to be good hosts during the Exposition. "We have no right to invite people from other parts to come here unless we have a proper place to receive them, no more than we have a good justification to ask people to visit our homes if we have no homes."[9]

The four city newspapers all strongly endorsed the bonds. The *San Francisco Chronicle*, which only three years before had opposed bonds for the Market–Van Ness Civic Center as an extravagance, ran several editorials extolling the project's virtues and urging support for the bonds. The campaign culminated in the Mission District, where Mayor Rolph whipped up his supporters in a packed house at the Lyceum Theatre on March 25, 1912.[10] By this point, virtually no opposition to the plan had been expressed.

The election results of Thursday, March 28, 1912, exceeded the most optimistic expectations. Voters approved the bonds with 92 percent (45,133 to 4,035) of the vote, and support came from every district and group in the city. It was estimated that 8,000 women voted, with greater participation in middle-class and wealthy neighborhoods. Election results were a stunning endorsement of Rolph's leadership, Exposition plans, and City Beautiful ideas. After more than a decade of feuding, violence, corruption, and factionalism, Rolph had unified the city in less than six months.

The Design Process Gets Underway

On Friday morning, the day after the election, Rolph and the board of public works announced their reorganization of the city's bureau of architecture, converting the advisory architects into consulting architects and placing them in charge of the bureau whose primary task was to plan, design, and construct City Hall and the Civic Center.[11] For this work, each would receive a $2,500 retainer and $25 per day for city work. They could also continue to work on private projects. Alfred I. Coffey, Mayor McCarthy's appointed city architect, promptly resigned.

The new consulting architects announced a city hall design competition. It would be open to all architects who had been legally practicing in San Francisco on January 1, 1912. These architects were invited to submit applications and credentials to the board of public works by April 5, 1912.[12] The consulting architects said that they would publish a list of architects accepted to participate in the competition on the day after receiving submissions.

Later on in the same day, Rolph made an unannounced visit to the offices of the PPIE, where he declared to its officers that the city would give them land for an auditorium. They were a bit taken aback by the mayor's visit, but they promised to respond to him on the following Tuesday, April 2. Rolph then announced that in November he would ask the voters to authorize the public library to exchange its Van Ness Avenue block for one in the new Civic Center area and permit the city to sell the former library block.

On Monday, April 1, 1912, the board of supervisors approved the previous week's election results, which gave the board the power to bring condemnation suits against 108 parcels of property in the area bounded by Market Street, Hayes Street, Van Ness Avenue, and Golden Gate Avenue. City Attorney Percy Long told the supervisors that he hoped that the suits would be a formality, since he expected many people to sell their property willingly at a fair price. Once the vote was taken, he rushed to the county clerk's office to file the suits.[13]

Although the old City Hall site had previously been settled as the site for the civic center more generally, the consulting architects still needed to prepare a plan for the acquisition of the blocks to the west and move forward with a final decision about where to place the new City Hall. Supervisor Bancroft showed the board the consulting architects' tentative land use plans for the Civic Center, which he presented as two alternatives: both schemes proposed a street grid at the old City Hall site with an extension of Hyde, Grove, and Leavenworth Streets to Market Street. One plan, however, located the new City Hall on the old site and placed the public library and opera house on Van Ness Avenue, with a large plaza between those two buildings and City Hall. The other plan placed City Hall on Van Ness Avenue between Grove and McAllister Streets and the public library and opera house facing the plaza on the old City Hall site. There were numerous reasons for each plan's strategies, but one of the rationales for considering the Van Ness site was almost certainly the recent knowledge that the soil underneath the old City Hall was unstable because of an underlying slough.

For both plans, the architects proposed acquiring and clearing properties from City Hall Avenue along Market Street to McAllister Street, thus opening up the vista for either the City Hall or Opera House. They placed the auditorium, as expected, on the old Mechanics' Pavilion block and proposed that an art museum face it from across the plaza.[14] In both plans, the State Building was located on the reconfigured block bounded by McAllister, Leavenworth, Fulton, and Hyde Streets, where the old Hall of Records still stood. Commerce High School, completed in 1910 with funds from the 1908 bond issue, stood on the Grove Street side of the plaza. The architects proposed moving it rather than demolishing it.

Bancroft's discussion of the Civic Center proposals and drawings was the first public exposure of the official Civic Center strategy. Although the plans reflected previous local efforts, they showed City Beautiful ideas that had developed during the previous twenty years. Howard's Beaux-Arts training, experience planning the University of California campus, and participation in planning two international expositions influenced his work. He was the dominant influence among the group comprising Mayor Rolph, Supervisor Bancroft, and the consulting architects.

On April 3, 1912, the *San Francisco Chronicle* editorialized about the unprecedented speed of events over the previous days: "We believe that breaks all municipal records."

On April 6, 1912, the consulting architects announced that 110 architects were certified to participate in the City Hall design competition and receive rules and the building guidelines. That document was prepared in the rigorous and concise fashion typical of the École des Beaux-Arts. Architects who had studied in Paris had no problem understanding it. Some of the others, particularly those who had learned architecture as apprentices, had some difficulty deciphering it. The programmatic sections consisted of mostly utilitarian requirements, except for this statement: "The main portions of the building are not to exceed four stories in height above the ground, but a dominating monumental feature may be introduced at the intersection of the street axes indicated on the plan of the site."

The architect who created the submittal judged best would be awarded the first prize of $25,000 and be engaged by the board of public works to design the building, with compensation following the schedule published by the American Institute of Architects for such projects. Architects who designed the next twenty best submittals would each receive $1,000 for their work. All submittals were due at noon on June 15, 1912, when they would be publicly displayed. The final decision would be made by a jury consisting of Mayor Rolph, a member of the public buildings committee, a member of the board of public works, the consulting architects, and one architect voted on by the participants from a list of three chosen by the consulting architects. This final architect turned out to be the New Yorker Walter Cook, the president of the American Institute of Architects and a close friend of Howard. On May 28, 1912, the consulting architects submitted their extensive Civic Center report to the mayor and supervisors. In the end, they recommended placing City Hall not on the old City Hall site, but instead placing it on the Van Ness site. In addition to the soil issues at the old site, that location had other advantages, such as being away from Market Street traffic; presenting the front, rather than the back, of City Hall to the plaza; providing the plaza shelter from the west wind; saving the cost of rent to the city, since the old Hall of Records could remain standing during the center's construction; and probably saving construction costs.[15] They recommended that issues raised in the report be subject to public discussion before recommendations were adopted.

One complication for the project was the condemnation of parcels, both from a budget standpoint, but also from a legal one. Determining that the government's original number of condemnation suits had gone over budget, in April, the consulting architects recommended that the board of supervisors rescind condemnation suits against parcels along Golden Gate Avenue between Hyde and Larkin Streets to conform the land acquisition costs closer to the budget. Legal issues were also raised against the project, with two property owners of key parcels challenging their property condemnations by arguing

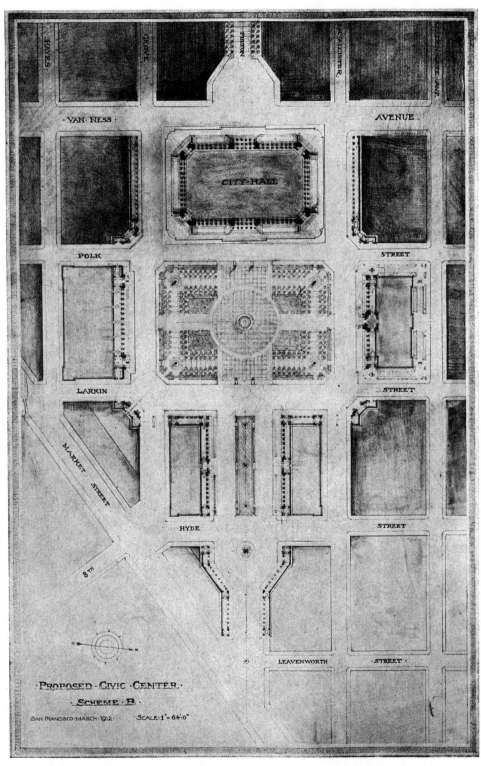

Howard's final design for the Civic Center with City Hall at Van Ness Avenue.

Source: Courtesy of the San Francisco History Center, San Francisco Public Library.

that, in authorizing the city in 1870 to build a city hall on the old Yerba Buena Cemetery land, the state legislature had limited the city to that site and thus the city could not take other property for a city hall or civic center. Judge James Seawell dismissed those arguments in a decision rendered on June 27, 1912, saying he did not see how the legislature in 1870 could anticipate the needs of the city in 1912. Reflecting the spirit of the time, he admonished the plaintiffs by saying, "The court had supposed that the citizens of San Francisco would be so patriotic that they would come forward and say, 'Here is my property; give me what it is worth,' but it seems that they [the plaintiffs] have met the call in quite another spirit."[16]

In June the consulting architects and other city officials completed their discussion of Civic Center alternatives with a number of civic groups and received unanimous support among those groups for a Van Ness Avenue location for City Hall. However, some supervisors argued at their meeting on July 1, 1912, that Mayor Rolph, in his inaugural address, had told the public that City Hall would be located on the old site and voters had approved bonds for a new city hall they thought would be built at that location. The dissenting supervisors thus felt they had a moral obligation to proceed accordingly. City Attorney Long opined that the board could legally choose either location. The vote on the matter ended with fourteen supervisors in favor of the Van Ness site and four opposed.[17]

From his editorial pedestal at *Architect and Engineer of California*, Bernard Cahill commented on the Civic Center plan and City Hall competition in the issue published in July 1912. He denigrated the process for allowing the competition to proceed without first confirming the building's location. This, he said, rose from not allowing for sufficient deliberation on the issues because of the "usual wasteful haste so typical of some wise men of the West." He charged that relocating City Hall from the old site was "immoral and injudicious" and added nothing architecturally. He decried—in an attack on Beaux-Arts land planning—"[T]he mania for uniformity and formality—for straight streets and square buildings—[which] seems to over ride every other consideration. One would welcome a curve, a bend, an angle or a little irregularity." He also claimed that the City Hall on Van Ness Avenue did not require a dominating monumental feature, particularly a dome, which he considered more appropriate for state capitols. He felt that an office tower with space for city departments would be more suitable. In his opinion, "It would not be surprising if the whole Civic Center project were to come to naught and even the construction of City Hall indefinitely delayed."[18] Cahill's views were certainly contrary to those of Rolph and the men behind the PPIE. Cahill could still have been suffering from Rolph's snub, when the mayor did not respond to Cahill's pleading letter.

Meanwhile, the City Hall competition had produced an astonishing response from architects for the board of public works and had received seventy-three submissions on June 15, 1912. All of the entries were numbered so that the jury could not identify the designers. The members of the jury, led by Cook and Howard, immediately set to work, first eliminating fifty-two entries that would not qualify for first or second place. Among those entries were several submitted by well-known architects, such as Bernard Maybeck, Albert Pissis, and William Faville. The next twenty-one entries each qualified for the $1,000 second-level award. Of these twenty-one, twelve architects had attended either the École des Beaux-Arts or noted American schools of architecture and had worked in prominent Eastern offices, such as McKim, Mead, and White. Of the remaining, six had learned architecture working as draftsmen in architecture offices. The drawings from the twenty-one finalists were shown at the Merchants Exchange for several days for public viewing.

On the afternoon of June 20, 1912, the jury announced that the City Hall plan by the firm of Bakewell & Brown (John Bakewell Jr. and Arthur Brown Jr.) was the first-prize winner and confirmed the firm's appointment as City Hall architect. The submittal described a four-story rectangular structure in neoclassical or French baroque revival style covering two square blocks. The building was

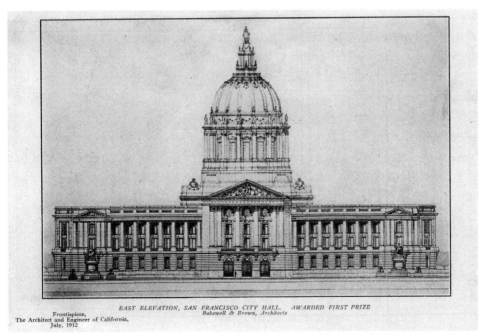

EAST ELEVATION, SAN FRANCISCO CITY HALL.   AWARDED FIRST PRIZE
Bakewell & Brown, Architects
Frontispiece,
The Architect and Engineer of California,
July, 1912

Bakewell & Brown's east front drawing for the new City Hall won them the first prize and the commission to design the building. From Architect and Engineer. Vol 29, July 1, 1912.

Source: Courtesy of the San Francisco History Center, San Francisco Public Library.

divided by two internal light courts, and rising from the top of the structure was a massive dome, 243 feet high from the street and topped with a lantern. It was modeled after the dome on the L'Église Saint-Louis des Invalides in Paris, with which Arthur Brown Jr. was very familiar from his days at the École des Beaux-Arts.

Brown's selection as one of the architects for City Hall was a fitting recognition for someone with a background so steeped in architecture and the arts. Brown's father had been chief engineer of the Central Pacific Railroad and was often called upon to design structures, the most notable of which was the Hotel Del Monte in Monterey, California. The family was well connected to business and artistic circles. For example, young Arthur accompanied his parents frequently when they visited the painter William Keith at his house in Berkeley. In the early 1890s, Brown enrolled at the University of California, Berkeley, studying in the engineering department (Berkeley did not yet have an architecture department). Brown eventually joined Maybeck's Saturday drawing class, where he became friends with other students who would also become well-known architects. After Brown's graduation, Maybeck arranged for him to receive a stipend from Hearst to study at the École des Beaux-Arts, which he entered in 1896. Brown was considered one of the most outstanding Americans to study there, was encouraged to seek a *diplôme* (which few Americans achieved), and was awarded several important prizes. He left Paris in 1903 and, after two years of testing his options, he decided to partner with his fraternity brother from Berkeley and fellow École student, John Bakewell, in their own practice.

The young architects struggled at first, with few of the post-earthquake-and-fire projects coming their way. However, their reputation grew with the Berkeley City Hall commission in 1907 and, in 1908, the rehabilitation of the damaged City of Paris department store building on Union Square in San Francisco. Brown had also been named in 1911 a sub-architect for the PPIE. Nevertheless, in the early months of 1912, their office did not have much work. Brown's biographer, Jeffrey Tilman, speculates that the reason the Bakewell & Brown submission was so well conceived and its drawings and presentation so finely prepared was that the two men had little else to do.[19]

The initial public reaction to the Bakewell & Brown City Hall was uniformly positive. The *San Francisco Chronicle* stated that "the plans for the structure give promise of a building that will at once be well adapted to the transaction of business and be dignified and imposing in appearance. . . . There is every reason to believe that San Francisco in 1915 will have one of the finest municipal homes in the country."[20] Even Cahill, despite his grouchy analysis of the Civic Center plan, praised the City Hall selection. He called the plan bold and the dome and

(From left to right) City Hall designers— John Bakewell, Arthur Brown Jr., Jean-Louis Bourgeois, and John Baur. Source: Copyright © 2009 The Regents of The University of California.

square gallery around it "splendidly conceived." He wrote, "The plans of Bakewell & Brown give all evidence of complete and exhaustive study. . . . The actual rendering had the lightness and daintiness of the etcher's needle."[21] With nothing but praise elicited by the selection, the board of public works made arrangements to pay Bakewell & Brown their prize and engage them to prepare the working drawing, even though some of the property for the building had yet to be acquired.

Exposition Auditorium

The board of the Panama-Pacific International Exposition was eager to move forward with the auditorium building for which they had agreed to pay. It was integral to their plans for holding conventions and meetings during the Exposition—the American Medical Association was already interested in using the building. The PPIE had developed specifications for halls and meeting spaces to accommodate up to 10,000 people and had been discussing them with the mayor and supervisors with the aim of harmoniously coordinating the auditorium design and that of the Civic Center. To meet the auditorium's planned opening date in January 1915, the PPIE board decided on June 26, 1912, to request that the city allow the consulting architects to design the façade of the building at the exhibition's expense, dispensing with a time-consuming architectural competition. At this time the city was still in negotiations with the Mechanics' Institute and would not acquire the block until October.

The rush to have the auditorium under construction as soon as possible produced a variety of reactions. Several architects came to the supervisors' public buildings committee on July 2, 1912, to complain that the city was not following its own policy to hold architectural competitions for Civic Center buildings. They were particularly upset that the auditorium design project had been given to the consulting architects. As one architect told the committee, "If the consulting architects consider themselves better able than other architects in San Francisco . . . they should vacate their official positions and enter the competitions."[22] The board of supervisors finally sorted out the issue at a meeting on August 19, voting to require that all the publicly supported buildings proposed for the Civic Center be subject to architectural competition. However, they approved the arrangements with the PPIE for the auditorium design because that building was being financed and constructed as part of the exposition, which did not require competitions, clearing the way for the speedy commencement of work.

However, procedural clarifications and arrangements about the auditorium did not satisfy the dissident architects. Their leader was William Mooser, a San Franciscan who had apprenticed in his father's architecture office and served as city architect under Mayor Phelan. Others included William Toepke, who had apprenticed in Mooser's office, and Edgar Mathews, who also had been born in San Francisco and had apprenticed in his father's office. Mathews was the brother of Arthur Mathews, the well-known painter and a leader in the American Arts and Crafts movement. Although these men had prosperous practices, they appeared to resent the growing number of Beaux-Arts–trained architects working in San Francisco and the prestige they were granted. The dissenting architects were particularly hostile toward Howard, who had arrived at the University of California from the East only ten years before and now controlled work on the campus.[23] During his term as president of the San Francisco chapter of the AIA, Howard gave the speech "The Future of Architecture on the Pacific Coast," in which he described the professional standards in the area as poor and stated that practitioners were "snatching" work from each other and disparaging each other behind one another's back. He said "draftsmen are not architects," and he called for more education and stiffer certification requirements.[24] Needless to say, these remarks did not sit well with Mooser and his colleagues.

The disgruntled architects managed to take over the San Francisco chapter of the AIA in 1912 by getting their candidates elected to the board of directors. Their number included George McDougall, an apprentice-trained architect, who was elected president and would soon be appointed as state architect. At the chapter meeting on February 2, 1913, Mooser, Mathews, Toepke, and Faville submitted a report charging the consulting architects with taking the auditorium design commission for themselves instead of organizing a competition as the chapter had desired. (Faville was the odd man in the group; he had trained at MIT and worked at McKim, Mead, and White, as Howard had.) The report also accused the consulting architects with arranging for the winning City Hall architects to receive a lower fee for their efforts and be excluded from supervising work on the structure. They asked that the chapter suspend the three consulting architects from its membership.[25] When Mayor Rolph learned of this action, he was furious and, on March 27, 1913, denounced the chapter for dictating to and harassing the city since the beginning of work on the Civic Center. He said, "This entity of architects is the worst kind of a [business] trust," and he demanded that the accusing architects meet with him immediately.[26] They refused. The next day the *San Francisco Chronicle* editorialized, "It certainly does not comport with the dignity of the city that the designing and construction of buildings for our Civic Center should become the subject of a local squabble among local architects."

The chapter held an extraordinary trial of the consulting architects on April 25, 1913, where, by a vote of 37 to 24, charges of "evasion, duplicity, and discourtesy" against them were upheld. The vote had little practical consequence for the consulting architects or their work at Civic Center, and Howard and his fellow consulting architects did indeed design the façade for the Exposition Auditorium. In May, eighteen prominent architects joined them to establish an alternative professional organization, the Society of San Francisco Architects.[27] The breach among the city's architects would continue for many years.

City Hall

In spite of intramural feuding among local architects, work on the Civic Center progressed rapidly: the city sold bonds, acquired land, began excavations, and ordered steel for the City Hall.

In December 1912 the consulting architects and Bakewell & Brown deliberated on the appropriate stone for City Hall—granite or limestone. To determine the appropriate color, they consulted with Jules Guérin, who had been engaged as the PPIE colorist.[28] A well-known illustrator, he had done the drawing for Burnham's Chicago plan. They agreed on Sierra White granite to present the right image. The consulting architects had also begun to draw an elaborate ground plan for the Civic Center with an overhead perspective, which they asked Guérin to color. The drawings included all of the proposed buildings and representations of the corner lots. Guérin's color renderings would generate great interest when revealed to the public on June 11, 1913.[29]

A ceremonial groundbreaking for City Hall was held on April 5, 1913, before a great throng of citizens and city officials. The program began with a chorus

John Galen Howard's rendering of the complete Civic Center plan included real designs for City Hall on Van Ness Avenue, the Opera House, and the Exposition Auditorium, as well as imagined plans for other buildings, published June 1913. Source: Courtesy of the San Francisco History Center, San Francisco Public Library.

of 500 schoolchildren singing "Columbia, the Gem of the Ocean." Howard gave a speech describing the undertaking and then led the assembled celebrants in three cheers for Mayor Rolph, the supervisors, and other officials. Rolph followed, saying, "The beginning of operations today is evidence of progress made possible only by unity of purpose. . . . We all feel the same city spirit that makes us linked together for the common good and for all things that help make San Francisco the greatest city on earth." Rolph took up a silver shovel made for the occasion and, joined by the supervisors with "common garden variety" shovels, started turning the earth on the site of the new City Hall.

James Rolph holds a silver shovel at the groundbreaking for the new City Hall.
Source: Courtesy of San Francisco History Center, San Francisco Public Library.

Among the many speakers was Bakewell, who stated that the "complete ed-
ifice will be 14 feet higher than the US Capitol." What he meant was that, as
measured from the base of both buildings to the top of their lanterns, the San
Francisco City Hall would be higher. Most likely based on this comment, Rolph
said numerous times that the San Francisco City Hall dome was thirty-seven
feet higher than the US Capitol dome. The *San Francisco Chronicle* later published an article, on March 31, 1928, accusing Rolph of "deceiving the people."
Comparing the two domes, the newspaper staff had calculated that the city's
dome was forty-two feet lower than that of the US Capitol. They then did a lan-
tern-to-lantern comparison and found that San Francisco City Hall was nine
feet higher. The writers, with obvious delight, concluded, "The thirty-seven feet
advantage of his City Hall is an exploded fallacy."[30] However, the actual dome-
to-dome comparison puts the City Hall dome at nineteen feet taller than the US
Capitol's, but on a much smaller drum base.

Opera House

The Music Association of San Francisco for its part pledged construction funds
to build an opera house in the new civic center and offered to operate the theater.
The prospect of an opera house was greeted enthusiastically. Supervisor Henry
Payot led the relevant efforts on behalf of the city, which had promised to provide the land. The Music Association had been founded in 1909 by a number of

prominent men to "foster Musical Arts in all forms, and to particularly establish a Symphony Orchestra and to build a great opera house." The PPIE's building and operating the Exposition Auditorium and then giving it to the city was the model—however, unlike the PPIE and the Auditorium, the Music Association expected to control its building in perpetuity.

After much discussion about the site, the south block on the old City Hall site (known later as Marshall Square) was designated the best location, since it had good access to Market Street for patrons. By the end of 1912, the association had engaged Willis Polk as the architect. His design, with its grand staircase, resembled the Palais Garnier, home of the Paris Opera. William Crocker of Crocker National Bank, Isaias W. Hellman of Wells Fargo Bank, and William Bourn of the Spring Valley Water Company agreed to lead fundraising efforts, which eventually became a $1 million commitment. Potential Opera House donors were told that in return for a substantial contribution, they would receive first rights to a box or seat. However, they would still have to pay the regular ticket price to attend performances.

The Music Association and its donors wanted not only to operate the building but also to control it through a board of directors. However, this made city lawyers and officials concerned. They argued that if the Opera House was located on city land, the city should have at least an equal say in its operation. Newspaper editors made derisive comments about the city running the Opera House, suggesting that municipal managers would end up producing ragtime rather than grand opera. It took the rest of 1912 for the association to secure the individual $15,000 pledges for the thirty opera boxes and smaller sums for individual seats to secure the $1 million pledge, and to negotiate an acceptable agreement with the city. On February 3, 1913, the board of supervisors passed the agreement without debate and the mayor signed it immediately.[31] The agreement called for a fifteen-member board of directors, nine of whom would be selected by the association and six by the city or other entities, such as the presidents of the University of California and Stanford University.

With the successful enactment of this Opera House legislation, everyone was eager to begin construction in the fall. However, lawyers for the city and the Music Association decided to bring a friendly lawsuit to settle potential charter issues. The suit reached the California Supreme Court, which found, on June 11, 1913, that the agreement between the association and the city violated the city charter. This came as a shock to everyone. The court expressed regret and suggested ways to get around the problem, but it said that San Francisco had no right to turn over city property to a private party in perpetuity without retaining control of it.[32] All parties viewed the decision as a setback, but not a fatal one.

WILLIS POLK AND CO. ARCHITECTS

Willis Polk's drawing of the façade for the proposed Opera House to be built on Larkin Street across the plaza from City Hall, circa 1913. Source: Courtesy of professor Jeffrey Tillman.

Supervisor Payot and the Music Association and its lawyers set about developing a new version of the agreement that could pass the courts. The new iteration, calling for a self-perpetuating board of directors consisting of five city officials and ten members appointed by the mayor, finally reached the board of supervisors on November 10, 1913. The assumption was that the mayor would appoint ten members of the Music Association. A. J. Gallagher, the lone supervisor affiliated with the Union Labor Party, spoke against the agreement, arguing that the city should have exclusive control of the Opera House. The measure passed 13 to 5, in spite of Gallagher having convinced four supervisors to join him.[33] The municipal election affecting half the members of the board was scheduled for the following day.

Within the week, word was circulating that Mayor Rolph was considering vetoing the measure since he did not like the provision that subscribers with rights to boxes and seats could pass those rights to their heirs. The mayor's change of attitude came as a great surprise, because the same language had appeared in the earlier version of the agreement, which he had approved in February. The business and society elite of the Music Association, their lawyers, and the city attorney visited the mayor to ask him to reconsider. He told one group that he felt that the city should control the Opera House board of directors, lest the organization fall under objectionable management that would permit the "tango dance and the Black Crook" to perform there.[34] He asked the gathering whether the Music Association would simply donate the Opera House to the city, free of conditions.

The mayor's veto message was released on November 20, 1913, with assertions that the agreement would violate the city charter, that granting hereditary rights to boxes and seats would create a local aristocracy, and that donors—not the public—would control the board of directors. All the parties that had worked on the project for almost two years were flabbergasted. Supervisor Payot said, "It just makes me sick." Crocker said that he and his associates were "only trying to do something big and fine for San Francisco." He pointed out that the people who would lose in the immediate future were laborers who would have constructed the building (there was considerable unemployment at the time) and musicians and other artists who would have performed within it. City Attorney Long announced that his office had nothing to do with the mayor's veto. Both the *San Francisco Chronicle* and *San Francisco Examiner* ran editorials condemning the veto.

Rolph's actions seemed completely out of character. Although leaders of the Music Association might have been older and more conservative than Rolph, they were people with whom he worked and socialized. He had a close working relationship with them from his position as vice president of the PPIE, and they all held him in high esteem. On November 22, 1913, the *San Francisco Chronicle* asked, "Why did he do it?" and reported what the newspaper viewed as a craven political deal. At a gathering in Fresno, California, the paper reported, Governor Hiram Johnson (who had recently been Theodore Roosevelt's vice presidential running mate on the Progressive "Bull Moose" ticket), met with political advisors Mayor Rolph, Matt I. Sullivan, and Eustace Cullinan and plotted a scheme whereby Johnson would run as the Progressive Party candidate for US Senate in 1914 and Rolph would run as the party's candidate for governor. To enhance his progressive appeal, Rolph would have to veto the Opera House agreement to show that he was a crusader against privilege and wealth, the opinion being that this could hurt him in San Francisco, but not statewide.[35]

On November 21, 1913, the *San Francisco Bulletin* jumped to Rolph's defense, characterizing his veto as a "courageous and democratic act. . . . All good citizens who are opposed to special privilege, discrimination or use of public property should praise the Mayor." Sullivan, a prominent lawyer and friend and adviser to the mayor, was given a column to argue the merits of the veto and counter criticism from the "morning press."[36] The following day, Cullinan submitted a letter claiming that the *San Francisco Chronicle* story about a back-room deal was preposterous.[37] He admitted to a Fresno automobile ride, but he claimed that they had not discussed politics.

Whether or not a deal in Fresno between Rolph and the others took place as part of some broader political calculation, Rolph's veto would block the construction of the Opera House at this time and leave a vacant block in the Civic Center that would remain empty for the next eighty years. Many of the people who had recruited Rolph to run for mayor and had supported him enthusiastically in his first years in office were bitter; some never forgave him.

The Opera House debacle undermined support for Rolph and the Civic Center, diminishing their luster. Rolph had promised during the bond campaign that the Civic Center would be complete by the opening of the Panama-Pacific International Exposition. Now people wondered what was going on and asked why the area was such a construction mess. On February 19, 1914, the *San Francisco Chronicle* reported, "The officials responsible will have to get busy if they are to escape the censure inevitable in the event that the Civic Center exhibit consists more of contractors' junk than of finished edifices."[38]

Public Library

Planning for the main library continued as well, but several obstacles had to be overcome. The building's financing was the most immediate issue. Three-quarters of the $1 million cost of the building was to come from a $750,000 contribution to the city's libraries from Andrew Carnegie. The San Francisco Labor Council urged that the gift be rejected since Carnegie's steelworks were notoriously anti-union; the council collected 10,000 signatures to put the matter on the ballot for the November 5, 1912, election. But voters overwhelmingly favored accepting the gift.[39] On December 10, 1912, voters approved the transfer of land and the sale of the 1903 bonds. Once the financial and land-transfer hurdles were cleared, the consulting architects were able to prepare a competition for the design of the library building.

The independent public library trustees spent the year of 1913 arranging financing for the new library with Carnegie and city donors. They had also negotiated with the consulting architects to ensure that the new building's design would conform to that of other buildings in the area. Finally, in late April 1914, the consulting architects announced a closed competition for the library and invited a preselected group of six architects to submit proposals by May 4, 1914.[40] Three of the architects were Beaux-Arts–oriented: George Kelham, Pissis, and G. Albert Lansburgh. The three remaining selections were apprentice-trained: the Reid brothers (James, Merritt, and Watson), who had completed the 1910 design for the library trustees; Ward and Blohme; and Edgar Mathews. In terms of architectural politics, Kelham had been the consulting architects' defender at the AIA trial, and Mathews had been the complainant.

Unlike the procedure in the City Hall competition, the consulting architects did not judge the library proposals. Instead, they set up an independent jury composed of the former mayor and library trustee James Phelan and two of the country's most distinguished architects, Cass Gilbert and Paul P. Cret. Gilbert was from New York and a former president of the AIA. He designed the Minnesota Capitol in St. Paul, the Woolworth Building in New York, and the St. Louis Public Library. Cret was a French École des Beaux-Arts–educated architect who had joined the University of Pennsylvania faculty in 1903. His best-known building at the time was the headquarters of the Pan-American Union in Washington, DC. Phelan reportedly said that he would support the project these two architects selected.

Six plans were duly submitted, and the jury gathered to review them the following day. One of the architects' tasks was to design a building in harmony with the rest of the proposed Civic Center. However, the library budget did not allow for the building to cover a whole block. Mathews and Pissis resolved the problem by planning a rectangular building with façades on all sides that covered only half the block. Thus, people coming up the Fulton Street axis would find a large lot behind the library. The other four submittals solved the problem by designing façades along both Larkin and Fulton Streets, but leaving a large corner off the building at Hyde and McAllister Streets, the so-called "d" design. On May 8, 1914, the jury announced that the award would go to Kelham, creator of one of the four "d" designs.

Kelham's proposed building had rows of arched windows above a baseline along the Fulton Street side. His design was similar to Charles F. McKim's 1895 plan for the Boston Public Library, which was derivative of Henri Labrouste's 1851 design of the Bibliothèque Sainte-Geneviève in Paris. Kelham located the main entrance on the Larkin Street façade, on which he placed a series of massive columns to better reflect the Civic Center's neoclassical nature. Such a feature did not appear on either Labrouste's or McKim's library buildings. The building's internal layout and function were considered superior to those in the other submittals. In the May 1914 issue of *Architect and Engineer*, B.J.S. Cahill praised the competition and the jurors, whom he described as ideal. He praised Kelham for creating a "clean-cut plan, perfectly balanced and admirably arranged. . . . The fronts are marvels of fine draftsmanship, both in felicity of design and elegance in rendering."[41]

The invitation to participate did not lessen Edgar Mathews's antipathy toward Beaux-Arts architects. In the library trustees meeting to confirm the award to Kelham, held in late May, Mathews complained that the competition had been unfair and manipulated to his disadvantage. The previous year, in 1913, the Detroit Public Library had held a competition for a new library building with a jury that included Paul Cret. The jury awarded the project to Cass Gilbert, whose design was modeled on the Boston and Paris Sainte-Geneviève libraries. Since Kelham's plan resembled the Detroit design, Mathews charged that Kelham had copied Gilbert's work. He even charged that Kelham had hired one of the draftsmen who had worked on the Detroit project to help prepare the drawings. He suggested that Gilbert and Cret, seeing a familiar plan, were flattered and thus were biased against the other plans. But the library trustees rejected Mathews's charges and engaged Kelham.[42] However, the discord among the architects did not escape notice, and the *San Francisco Call* described the sad state of the local architectural profession, whose architects frequently tried to demean the work of their colleagues. They wrote, "The art of architecture is the art of plagiarism," pointing out that copying had been going on for two thousand years and reporting that local professionals considered Mathews's charges ridiculous.[43] However, Mathews continued to nurse his grievances, and two years later on May 12, 1916, he would file a lawsuit against the library trustees for $11,190 in damages, asserting the same charges he had made two years earlier.[44] The suit was eventually dismissed, but it showed the raw division still in place

The Main Public Library designed by George Kelham, shortly after its completion in February 1917.
Source: Courtesy of the San Francisco History Center, San Francisco Public Library.

among San Francisco architects. After the various bureaucratic and fundraising problems, construction on the library finally began on April 15, 1915, well into the Panama-Pacific International Exposition, and the library would be dedicated nearly two years later, on February 15, 1917.

State Building

The only remaining undesignated half block facing the Civic Center Plaza was on McAllister Street. Although this site had originally been reserved for an art museum, the state's needs were more immediate, since it lacked a large building to accommodate courts and other agencies. A deal was struck whereby the state would exchange a state-owned lot that was destined to become part of the plaza for the city's parcel on McAllister, where it would build a large compatible office building at the cost of $1 million. However, the state did not have the funds on hand, so a bond measure was proposed for the November 3, 1914, state ballot which voters approved. The state did not sell the bonds until February 1916 delaying the time that work on the building could begin. The design competition for the State Building was the responsibility of George McDougall, the state architect. McDougall's father, Barnett, had come to San Francisco in 1856 and had become a successful builder and architect. George and his two brothers trained in their father's office. In the 1890s they set up McDougall Brothers and completed projects throughout the state, particularly in the Central Valley. In 1913 George McDougall served as president of the San Francisco AIA chapter during the consulting architects' trial and thus was intimately familiar with architectural politics in San Francisco. In the fall of that year he was appointed state architect.

In September 1916 McDougall announced a two-tiered competition. All architects in the state were invited to submit designs. A jury comprising the governor, four state officials, and three architects chosen from a list of five submitted by the San Francisco AIA chapter (still under the control of the dissenters) would make a first-round review and select eight finalists. These eight finalists would then be asked to prepare detailed plans, from which the award winner would be selected. On November 16, 1916, McDougall announced the three architects on the jury: Edgar Mathews; James W. Reid, of Reid Brothers; and Robert D. Farquhar, from Los Angeles.[45] Mathews was a provocative choice because of his two prominent feuds over Civic Center buildings. His selection also turned the tables on the domination by Beaux-Arts–trained architects, since only Farquhar had that background. On November 24, 1916, the jury announced that it had reviewed fifty-two proposals, from which eight were selected for further development, including proposals from Bliss and Faville, Lewis P. Hobart, Charles

State office building completed in 1926 showing the high base and arches and lack of decorated columns, which upset Mayor Rolph and the Civic Center designers. Source: Courtesy of the San Francisco History Center, San Francisco Public Library.

Peter Weeks, Bakewell & Brown, and Loring Rixford. On February 24, 1917, the award went to Bliss and Faville.[46]

The Bliss and Faville building was severely Italian renaissance. An undecorated three-story base with small windows supported two-story arched windows fronted by a balcony balustrade held up by flat Ionic pilasters. These five stories were capped by a strong cornice line and another floor with small windows. The building was to be clad in Civic Center granite and would conform to area height limits.

Within days of its public presentation, the State Building design was subject to criticism from the architects of the Society of San Francisco Architects. Its president, Charles Peter Weeks, said, "We were unanimous that the design by Mr. Faville ... does not harmonize with the buildings now in the San Francisco Civic Center." Mathews, who by now had succeeded William Faville as the president of the San Francisco AIA chapter, responded by calling the Society of San Francisco Architects a "corpse."[47] The architects' feud raged on. Polk wrote, "The winning design disregards the cornice and does not . . . reflect the scale of the buildings already built. . . . It would, if built, be a disturbing note in the uniformity and harmony necessary for the successful completion of the Civic Center."[48] The society communicated with Farquhar, who responded in writing that he had favored the Bakewell & Brown, and not the Bliss and Faville design.[49] However, Mathews, Reid, and McDougall were advocates for Bliss and Faville, and the lay members of the jury went along with their judgment. The dispute was another case of architects with Beaux-Arts values bitterly disagreeing with architects who had been apprenticed.

Mathews convinced the AIA chapter to pass a resolution stating that the Bliss and Faville design was the right selection and the competition had been conducted properly. Mayor Rolph and Supervisor Ralph McLaren, now the chairman of the public buildings committee, stepped into the fray on March 7, 1917, suggesting that the consulting architects be recalled to try to work things out. However, Faville, who detested Howard, refused to meet with them.[50] The mayor appealed to Governor Hiram Johnson, who refused to get involved. By June, state officials said that the matter was closed and they would not discuss the project with the city any further. They had signed contracts with Bliss and Faville to prepare drawings for the building exactly as it had been presented.

The *San Francisco Chronicle* chimed in on June 5, 1917: "The State Building, as planned, is not hideous in itself, but it will be unsightly as a violently discordant note in an otherwise harmonious architectural scheme. If it were intended to be used as a jail and if it were erected at the back of Twin Peaks or on the mud flats near Islais Creek, it might not be so objectionable, but as part of the Civic Center it will be barbarous."[51]

Even though San Francisco had lost control of the strict Beaux-Arts plan for the Civic Center after the Panama-Pacific International Exposition closed at the end of 1915, and the area had become subject to more common and open pressures, clearly, the city government and the public remained attached to the original aesthetic impulse.

After the US entered World War I on April 6, 1917, steel was unavailable and the construction of the State Building was postponed. The structure was finally completed in 1926 at twice the original cost.

The Exposition

In the summer of 1914, six months before the opening day of the Panama-Pacific International Exposition, the Civic Center was still a huge construction site. City Hall, which Mayor Rolph had hoped would be finished before the Exposition opened on February 20, 1915, had a granite façade that covered only the first two floors; it was expected to be completed by June 1915. The plaza was a two-block demolition site occupied by several structures earmarked for removal, including the Central Fire Alarm Station. On the old City Hall site, the contractor was still removing the foundation and crushing bricks and stone, while city employees worked nearby in the old building's McAllister-corner offices and the Hall of Records. Hyde, Grove, and Fulton Streets had been constructed only partway to Market Street, and a corner of an old building still sat in the Grove Street right-of-way. Fortunately, the Exposition Auditorium was well on its way toward completion by December. Nevertheless, the media began running articles accusing the board of public works of indolence.[52]

On May 11, 1914, the board of supervisors approved the plans of the consulting architects for the plaza, which had appeared in the 1913 Jules Guérin rendering and were now complete. Besides landscaped quadrants and two round pools, the architects created generous paved spaces, including one from the steps of City Hall to Larkin Street for public gatherings of up to 20,000 people. They proposed to install during 1915 a plaster faux-travertine balustrade with entrances decorated by statues of bears and other creatures surrounding the plaza's perimeter. In addition, a plaster statue serving as a fountain would grace each of the two ponds. The temporary plaster works would test whether or not

City Hall under construction with granite in place up to the second floor, 1914.
Source: Courtesy OpenSFHistory / wnp36.00486.

these adornments would be suitable for the site and appreciated by the public.[53] (The following year they were determined not to be suitable and were removed.)

Among the notable construction issues that had been resolved in preparation for the plaza's construction was the moving of the Commerce High School building from its original location on Grove Street—an area now intended for the plaza—to a new location on the block that had previously been owned by library trustees but that had been transferred to the city. The task of moving the 8,000-ton, three-story brick building was a considerable engineering feat for the time and included removing the foundations and placing the structure on rollers and rails. It was then towed slowly for several blocks on streets with sharp angular turns. The move began on May 8, 1913, and the large structure reached its new Fell Street location at the end of November.[54]

Plaza construction began in early 1915, and by March, John McLaren, the park superintendent, had planted two rows of sycamores around its perimeter and Irish yews and pyramidal boxwood trees within.[55] It was not until July that the work was complete and the fountains ran with water. By that time, all of the area's streets had been finished and paved. Unfortunately, convention visitors approaching the auditorium during the first four months of the Exposition saw only an active construction site.

In spite of the area's disheveled appearance, the year 1915 opened with the PPIE holding a grand masked ball to inaugurate the Exposition Auditorium. The occasion was a precursor of things to come at the Exposition. The auditorium's interior was decorated with gems from the Tower of Jewels, plants and flowers from the Exposition hothouses, and flags from the participating states and nations. The Exposition Electricity Bureau lit up the exterior with electric lights. The program included ethnic dance performances by artists from many of the domestic and foreign pavilions. All ranks of people—from members of the PPIE board of directors to the most ordinary citizens—purchased tickets, and more than 20,000 people attended, wearing either their own costumes or masks that could be purchased on entering. The auditorium dance floor accommodated 2,500 dancers at any one time, and side rooms held banquets and other entertainment.[56] The ball, considered a huge success by all, began the Exposition year in San Francisco.

On opening day of the Panama-Pacific International Exposition, the public was invited to walk to the end of Van Ness Avenue into the fairgrounds by the Bay with Mayor Rolph, accompanied by the Catholic bishop, a leading rabbi, and the Episcopalian bishop. Governor Johnson, Mayor Rolph, and other luminaries made short speeches and the religious leaders offered prayers. After President Woodrow Wilson used the telegraph to activate the Exposition grounds' machinery, the Exposition was officially opened. Visitors on opening day numbered 255,149,

The Exposition Auditorium after its completion in January 1915. It was the only Civic Center
building available for use during the Panama-Pacific International Exposition.
Source: Courtesy of the San Francisco History Center, San Francisco Public Library.

and most were overawed. While millions of visitors enjoyed the Exposition located along the north shore of San Francisco Bay, work continued in the Civic
Center well past its closing date of December 4, 1915.

In addition to the large monumental buildings in the Civic Center plan, the
consulting architects' plan also called for small buildings with rounded chamfered, or notched, corners at the plaza's four corners. But with the funds available the city could only purchase three of the four corner lots for that purpose.
The Polk-Grove corner was designated for the health department headquarters,
and a small central emergency hospital stood there while plans for the department's building were developed. The Polk-McAllister corner was intended for
police and fire department headquarters, but the property was left empty.

Work on the City Hall façade came to a halt on June 1, 1915, the victim of a
statewide strike of the granite cutters' union, which was supported by the stone
setters' union. The McGilvray-Raymond Granite Company, which had the contract to provide and install stone in City Hall, had completed its installation
work, with the exception of the dome. Although all of the granite had been cut,
the company could not transport it to San Francisco or install it because of the
strike.[57] Mayor Rolph could not move into the building until the stonework was
done. The strike would not be settled until November 11, 1915, pushing the building's completion back to March 1916.

At the end of June 1915, the contract with the consulting architects expired,
and they terminated their duties. John Reid Jr. was retained as a consultant to
look after any remaining problems;[58] in 1918, Mayor Rolph would appoint him
to the post of city architect, a position he would occupy until 1930.

The completed City Hall, circa 1917. Source: Courtesy OpenSFHistory / wnp36.01705.

Although it did not happen in time for the Exposition, Rolph insisted that he would keep his promise that City Hall would open in 1915, so he scheduled a dedication ceremony for December 28, 1915. It took place in a light rain, on Polk Street, below the new dome decorated with $5,000 worth of gold leaf.[59] The ceremony was officiated by Supervisor Ralph McLaren, the chair of the building committee. McLaren exulted about designing and building the mammoth building in little more than three years, which he compared to the twenty-seven years it had taken to complete the old City Hall. Howard and Arthur Brown Jr. attributed the project's success to the leadership of Mayor Rolph. Rolph then declared, "I love that building. It is marvelous how it has risen. It has been built without a breath of scandal and on time. . . . It is the finest public building in the world." Rolph unlocked the main door with a golden key and invited the public inside.[60]

Two days later—and four weeks after the closing of the Exposition—the PPIE board turned the Exposition Auditorium over to the city during an evening ceremony attended by about 5,000 people. They heard a concert by the San Francisco Municipal Band and Chorus and Governor Hiram Johnson's remarks delivered by telephone, and they witnessed the symbolic transfer of ownership when President Charles C. Moore of the PPIE gave a key to Mayor Rolph.[61] A few weeks earlier, the PPIE directors had announced that the PPIE would give the city the 11,000-pipe Exposition Organ, which would be installed in the auditorium and played during public concerts. The organ had been located in the Exposition's 3,000-seat Festival Hall, where performers had used it frequently. This gift produced great interest and began speculation about whom the city would engage in the new, prestigious post of municipal organist. The amazing year 1915 ended with the Ball of All Nations, held on New Year's Eve at the Exposition Auditorium, which was jammed to capacity.[62]

Completion

After contractors finished the final construction work on City Hall in March, the more mundane task of moving city departments and staff into the new building and finishing up the detail work continued until the end of the year. The board of supervisors held its first meeting in the new oak-paneled chambers on October 9, 1916.

Since city offices would be vacating the functioning remnant of old City Hall on McAllister Street, the board of supervisors quickly signed a contract to demolish the structure. However, making a decision about the fate of the Hall of Records was more difficult. Some felt that it should be retained and possibly used as offices for the board of health, because it was in relatively good condition. Others pointed out that it was in the way of extending Hyde and Fulton Streets to Market Street. Finally, in August 1916, the board of supervisors voted to demolish it. The *San Francisco Chronicle* wrote, "It has no place in the architectural scheme of Civic Center. On the contrary, if retained, it would strike a discordant and anomalous note. Better forget it."[63] On August 2, 1918, while clearing the old City Hall site of debris, the hall's cornerstone was discovered near the corner of McAllister and Leavenworth Streets. The granite stone, weighing several tons, was a relic from 1872, when it had been laid during a grand Masonic ceremony.[64]

After several more months, street extensions and landscaping were complete. With that, San Francisco had finished the first phase of creating a grand Civic Center. The Civic Center was the second dimension of the Panama-Pacific International Exposition—the one that has become a permanent and developing part of San Francisco's identity. James Rolph Jr., on behalf of the Panama-Pacific International Exposition, made it happen, and John Galen Howard laid out the center's monumental design and saw that it was properly built. They should be remembered as the Civic Center founders.

1920s and 30s:
Mayor Rolph Forges Ahead

Even as the City Beautiful movement declined nationally, replaced by an approach to city planning that valued pragmatic matters over aesthetics, San Francisco's leaders continued their work on the Civic Center in the spirit of the original scheme. By 1920, much of the original plan was complete. Three of the four proposed buildings had been constructed, the State Building was ready to start, the plaza had been attractively landscaped, and Grove and Hyde Streets had been extended and connected to Market Street, albeit leaving the Pioneer Monument awkwardly located on the corner's edge.

The eastern area of the plan, however, remained undeveloped and problematic. City Hall bond monies had been insufficient to purchase all of the properties that had been desired, so the corner of Grove and Larkin Streets remained in private hands. A more serious matter was that the remainder of the old City Hall triangle-shaped block, east of the new section of Hyde Street, still fronted on the remains of City Hall Avenue, and private parcels between it and Market Street blocked access to the Civic Center from downtown. The area was ungraded and open, except for a few one-story buildings on Market Street. Neither Fulton nor Leavenworth Street had been extended and built out to connect with Market Street.

Mayor Rolph remained the chief advocate for completing the center. Anticipating a huge Shriner's convention in June 1922, he wrote a paean to the Civic Center that was published in the *Chronicle* where he extolled each existing building and called for a new health department building on the southwest corner of the plaza and a fire department headquarters on the northwest corner. He concluded by calling the buildings "monuments for our descendants so that they will say 'This was a generation with vision.'"[1] In April 1922 he publicly called for the city to purchase all private property in the triangle between Hyde, Fulton, and Market Streets, saying, "I believe that this property is needed to round out our Civic Center."[2] Now that ten years had passed, several sizable private building projects were underway in the mid-Market area, and real estate interests protested such an acquisition as interrupting the continuity of Market Street buildings. The board of supervisors was not amenable to spending the large amount of money required to purchase the land, but after a great deal of arguing, it appropriated $100,000 to start acquiring parcels to extend Fulton Street to Market Street.[3]

At the same time, other construction projects were underway that would enhance the Civic Center area. Back in 1913, after the library trustees had transferred to the city the block they had owned on Van Ness Avenue, Commerce High School, previously located on Grove Street on land intended for the plaza, moved its building to a new location at 150 Fell Street.[4] But by the start of the next decade, Commerce High School had outgrown the old building. New high school buildings were proposed to fill in and improve the rest of the block facing into the Van Ness Avenue side of Civic Center. On November 21, 1922, voters had approved a $12 million bond measure for school construction, which included buildings for Commerce High School. John Reid Jr., now the city architect, took responsibility for designing and building a three-story structure with thirty-five classrooms and an adjacent 1,840-seat auditorium. He chose an early French renaissance style influenced by the Château de Blois. The artistic façade's terra-cotta decoration, the art enhancement of its day, was made by the well-known firm Gladding, McBean, and Co.[5] Costing more than $1 million, the new structure would be dedicated on September 25, 1926.[6] Students had access to athletic fields across Hayes Street on the block recently acquired from the War Memorial board of trustees.

Competition between private and public interests for the land around the Civic Center, however, would be a persistent issue. In January 1923 the city discovered that real estate interests intended to purchase private parcels on Market Street, off of Hyde Street, to construct a sixteen-story Auditorium Hotel. Rolph was outraged, exclaiming, "We don't want such a building towering over Civic Center," and he asked the supervisors to condemn the property.[7]

In response to the business community's opposition to the mayor's sweeping approach, city architect Reid proposed a compromise that would allow the hotel project to move forward if the city could acquire a strip of the property that would permit the city to extend Fulton Street in a grand manner to Leavenworth and Market.[8] Although the hotel developers suggested this would put their project in jeopardy, on January 30, 1923, the supervisors voted in favor of this acquisition, ultimately leading the developers to cancel their project, and handing Rolph a victory in his efforts to prioritize the Civic Center over private interests in the area.

On January 7, 1924, in the inaugural address for his fourth term as mayor, Rolph laid out a long list of projects he said were necessary as part of the original Civic Center plan, including buying the Market-Hyde-Fulton triangular properties, constructing a health department building at the corner of Polk and Grove Streets, and building a combined headquarters for the fire and police departments at the corner of Polk and McAllister Streets.[9] In July 1924 the city finally acquired four parcels for $225,000 that allowed it to extend Leavenworth Street to Market Street.

Despite Rolph's opposition, real estate developers remained interested in properties in the Market Street triangle. Frank Leis acquired the parcel next to the city's lots on Leavenworth Street, and William Wagnon acquired the remaining parcels adjacent to Hyde Street. In January 1925 Wagnon announced plans to construct an $8 million four-story multiuse building with a 2,400-seat theater facing Market Street which he would lease to Alexander Pantages, a major West Coast vaudeville operator.[10] Pantages had built a smaller theater in San Francisco in 1911, but he was willing to give it up for the new, larger facility. Wagnon agreed to use Pantages's longtime architect, Benjamin Marcus Priteca. Priteca was a Scotsman who had studied architecture at the University of Edinburgh and then came to Seattle, where he met Pantages, who gave him the commission to design his San Francisco theater and, eventually, twenty-one others. They chose to design the building and the theater's interior in the Spanish Gothic style. Wagnon agreed to grant the city a 22-by-36-foot portion of his property in the back to become part of Fulton Street and to leave a portion of the Hyde Street façade and the back wall of the building blank so that it could be built out in a design suitable to the city's plans. Although many people thought this was a splendid plan, Rolph still harbored the view that the city should condemn the property. The original Civic Center consulting architects of Howard, Meyer, and Reid were called in for consultation as to the proper design of the Fulton Street entrance to the Civic Center. They recommended to the board of supervisors that it was not necessary to condemn the property and that the theater could be built, but that a uniform and dignified façade be built on the south side of Fulton Street, possibly with an arcade or loggia. They also recommended that the triangular Leis corner be purchased to ensure the architectural character of the center's entrance.[11]

Nevertheless, when the new Pantages Theater was finished, Rolph could see the blank concrete wall on Hyde Street from his City Hall office and was furious. On November 30, 1925, he publicly blamed Ralph McLaren, the outgoing

From Larkin Street looking down Fulton Street at the blank back wall of the Pantages (Orpheum) Theater building which so irritated Mayor Rolph, circa 1925.

Source: Courtesy of San Francisco History Center, San Francisco Public Library.

supervisor and his longtime ally, for the blight, since McLaren, in his private capacity as a contractor, constructed the theater building.[12] The next day, in front of the press, Rolph asked Rear Admiral Thomas Washington, the new commandant of the Twelfth Naval District who was making an introductory call on the mayor, if the fleet would use the wall for target practice.[13]

Wagnon wrote a letter to the mayor complaining that he was being unfair. Wagnon wanted the wall to be finished and was tired of waiting for the city to make up its mind about the design, and therefore he might just finish the wall himself.[14] The new board of supervisors, which took office in January 1926, was more concerned with cutting taxes than with Mayor Rolph's desire to enhance the Civic Center, so it never acted on the consulting architects' recommendations for Fulton Street. Since Wagnon did not receive any building designs from the city, he decided to do nothing. It would not be until after World War II when then mayor Elmer Robinson asked the city's arts commission what might be done with the blank wall that any ideas were officially proposed—it reported that in lieu of substantial funds for the area's improvement, the city should plant vines along the wall, which would eventually cover it if the greenery was well tended.[15] (This idea is under consideration again today by a consultant helping the city rethink the public areas of the Civic Center.)

Around this same time as Mayor Rolph was expressing frustration about the theater construction, he was planning a major civic event that would lead to the beginning of a notable tradition—the decorative lighting of the exterior of City Hall's dome. In the midst of the arguments over the Market Street triangle, Rolph and other city leaders had been eager for San Francisco to host California's Diamond Jubilee, celebrating the seventy-fifth anniversary of statehood, September 5–12, 1925. The planning committee decided to decorate the Civic Center with lighting "more gorgeous than the glittering diadem displayed at the Panama-Pacific International Exposition." They recruited Walter D'Arcy Ryan to design and execute the jubilee's display.[16] He was the chief illumination engineer for General Electric Company and had designed lighting for the PPIE. Besides creating temporary lighting around the Civic Center and other city locations, Ryan proposed installing permanent floodlights on the roof of City Hall to shine on the dome: the outside of City Hall had never been illuminated. Rolph was particularly enthusiastic, and he arranged for $20,000 to cover the cost.[17] California's Diamond Jubilee was a great success. The Arco de Brilliantes, arches glittering with jewels and lights, graced the Fulton Street entrance to the Civic Center, and plaza buildings were also outlined in lights. Two plaza fountains were adapted to spout water forty feet into the air and were lit with a "radio panchromatophone," which synchronized light, water and musical radio broadcasts.[18] Speeches, of course, played a part in the celebrations, as well as a grand ball with attendant movie stars, a concert featuring the contralto Ernestine Schumann-Heink, and fireworks—all of the hoopla Rolph and San Franciscans loved. The lighting of City Hall's dome was also a success, and the city has continued to do so, recently converting the flood lights to computer-driven LED lighting which can change colors on command.

During these years, Rolph's popularity in San Francisco remained strong. In November of 1927 he was elected to an unprecedented fifth term as mayor, carrying along a number of supervisors ready to work with him on further improvements to the Civic Center. In his inaugural remarks on January 3, 1928, Rolph called for a renewed spirit of harmony and cooperation and presented a long list of projects to accomplish, including his usual requests to finish the eastern portion of the Civic Center and to construct a building on the corner of Polk and Grove Streets for the Department of Health. He added to the list a new courthouse on Marshall Square and an extension of the Golden Gate Park panhandle to Market Street.[19]

While the courthouse on Marshall Square and the panhandle extension were never implemented, the Department of Health building proceeded easily, since the department had already prepared several construction projects, including that of its headquarters. The board of supervisors placed a $3.5 million bond

The lighting of the Civic Center Plaza and City Hall for the first time for Diamond Jubilee of the state of California, September 9, 1925. Source: Courtesy OpenSFHistory / wnp27.4239.jpg.

measure on the November 6, 1928, ballot to cover the costs, and 73 percent of the voters supported the measure. In early 1929, with a budget of $800,000, the San Francisco Board of Health engaged the local architect Samuel C. Heiman who prepared plans for a four-story renaissance palazzo structure faced with granite that also incorporated the one-story Central Emergency Clinic that was already existing on the site.[20]

The building would open its doors to the public in 1932, the same year as the long-awaited War Memorial Opera House and Veterans Building, two major buildings in the Civic Center complex which are discussed in the next chapter.

Federal Capitol of the West

Although it had not been on his 1924 inaugural to-do list, Rolph supported constructing a new federal office building at the Civic Center. Adding a federal building to the Civic Center had been discussed repeatedly since 1916, when the *San Francisco Chronicle* ran an opinion article suggesting such a use for the vacant Marshall Square block since the federal government already leased space in the city and needed more.[21] It was not until the mid-twenties, however, that the US Treasury, the federal department in charge of public buildings, gave serious attention to building offices in San Francisco. Although more than a decade since the

Chronicle's suggestion, the board of supervisors in the summer of 1927, passed a resolution offering the Hyde-Fulton-and-McAllister property to the federal government (they did not also follow the *Chronicle's* suggestion to offer the Marshall Square block). To give the resolution weight, the board placed it on the November 8, 1927, ballot as a policy statement, and 78 percent of the voters endorsed it.

On February 24, 1928, President Calvin Coolidge signed a Public Buildings Act authorizing the funding and construction of new federal office buildings, including one in San Francisco. The US Treasury was willing to build on the Hyde-Fulton-and-McAllister property the city offered in the Civic Center.[22] Although pleased with this development, Rolph learned from the city attorney that it would not be easy to transfer property to the federal government. Because of the way the land had been designated for the old City Hall by the state legislature back in 1870, voters would first have to pass a charter amendment to authorize the transfer, and then the state legislature would have to approve the transaction. The charter amendment was duly approved by the voters on November 6, 1928, by a two-thirds margin, and the legislature approved it in early 1929.

Before construction could begin, design guidelines had to be established, so the layout of Fulton Street and the blank wall behind the Pantages Theater had to be readdressed. William A. Newman, the Treasury's public building engineer for the Western United States, assured San Francisco officials that the new federal building would be designed in an architectural style conforming to the other Civic Center buildings.[23] The city again reassembled the consulting architects, Howard, Meyers, and Reid, who proposed uniform façades for both sides of Fulton Street, perhaps as an arcade or loggia. The city still did not own all of the Fulton Street right-of-way including a corner of the block they intended to convey to the federal government. Therefore, Rolph convinced the board of supervisors to also place before the voters at the November 6, 1928, election a $1 million bond measure for improvements to the Civic Center that would include the façade on the south side of Fulton Street. However, the voters did not provide the necessary two-thirds vote for the measure to pass, leaving the blank-wall issue unresolved. Pantages ran into financial difficulties at this time and sold some of his theaters, including the San Francisco venue, to RKO, the future major film production company, which later reopened it as the Orpheum on September 6, 1929.[24]

The Treasury announced on February 23, 1929, that it had selected Arthur Brown Jr. as architect for the federal building. As the designer of San Francisco's City Hall and War Memorial buildings, he was the obvious Bay Area architect for the task. In addition, the Treasury was already familiar with Brown's abilities from his work as a consulting architect for them. In 1927 the secretary of the treasury, Andrew Mellon, had chosen the noted planner Edward Bennett to be

The new Federal Building designed by Arthur Brown Jr. just before completion, April 22, 1936.

Source: Courtesy of San Francisco History Center, San Francisco Public Library

chairman of a committee to design the Federal Triangle complexs of office buildings on Pennsylvania Avenue.[25] Bennett, in turn, had recruited old friends from
his days at the École des Beaux-Arts, including Brown and John Russell Pope, to
join the board of architectural consultants. Brown would eventually design the
Department of Labor and the Interstate Commerce Commission buildings, and
Pope would design the National Archives.

On September 19, 1930, the US government formally accepted from San
Francisco the deed for the property on which to build the federal building, for
which Congress had appropriated $3 million.[26] By then Brown had developed
plans for a rectangular six-story neoclassical building with an inner courtyard, a
rusticated base, and upper stories fronted by Doric columns clad in Sierra White
granite, similar to City Hall, the War Memorial buildings, and the Federal Triangle
buildings. The Hoover administration called for construction bids in October 1932,
before the presidential election. However, Franklin Roosevelt's incoming administration decided to review all public building projects in the pipeline, so it was not
until February 1934 that work actually began and the Treasury sent a supervising
engineer to oversee the work.[27] The building was finally dedicated on May 16, 1936,
nearly seven years after voters had approved donating the land to the US government. The building was called the Federal Capitol of the West and eventually
contained thirty-three agencies. It would be the last significant architecture added
to the Civic Center complex for nearly fifty years.

The Veterans
and the Temple of Music

The San Francisco War Memorial & Performing Arts Center, as the complex of buildings located across Van Ness Avenue from City Hall is known today, is one of San Francisco's most active cultural landmarks. Today the center offers concerts, opera and ballet performances, exhibitions, and numerous other high-profile public and cultural events every year. The original two buildings of the center are the War Memorial Opera House and the Veterans Building. The complex was expanded in 1980 when the Louise M. Davies Symphony Hall opened across Grove Street from the Opera House. All together, San Francisco War Memorial & Performing Arts Center contributes to the Civic Center functioning in the original spirit of the City Beautiful ideas—a concentrated urban site to generate pride and encourage civic and cultural engagement among the city's residents.

The early history of the Opera House and Veterans Building share many similarities to the planning and construction history of the other major buildings in San Francisco's Civic Center, and like many of those other buildings, the complexity of San Francisco's city politics and the necessity for money and fundraising defined every step of their development. But despite the extensive struggles over the years to be able to be able to move forward on their planning and construction, like the rest of the Civic Center, their eventual completion ultimately also represents a story of civic-minded people with money and influence motivated to come together to encourage not only civic participation, but to also ensure San Francisco's position as the most important metropolis on the West Coast.

In 1913, when Mayor James Rolph vetoed the agreement to construct an opera house at the Civic Center two years before the Pacific-Panama International Exposition was to open and no new compromise was reached, board members of the Music Association of San Francisco moved on to devote themselves to developing the local symphony orchestra. At that time, the city did not have a municipal auditorium in which the musicians could perform, so the association held concerts in privately owned theaters, where scheduling problems were common. Many Music Association members were also on the board of directors of the 1915 Panama-Pacific International Exposition, and their interest in an opera house was put aside as they became preoccupied with overseeing preparations for the fair.

Although Rolph had opposed the terms offered in the earlier agreement, he had always been in favor of an opera house at civic center. Three years later with the PPIE now closed, during the ceremony on April 15, 1916, in which the cornerstone for the Civic Center's public library was laid, Mayor Rolph addressed the crowd and gestured to the adjacent block, stating that he hoped shortly to see an opera house owned by the people of San Francisco erected there.[1] Two days later, it was revealed that the former Music Association opera house donors, led by William Crocker, had been discussing a revised plan for a Civic Center opera house with Gavin McNab, an influential lawyer and local Democratic Party leader who was also the mayor's close friend and adviser. McNab told the press that the new proposed building would serve as a concert hall and opera house and would contain a conservatory of music to be operated under the aegis of the University of California. Similar to the previous opera house proposal, the plan called for the city to make available the Marshall Square block, and donors would contribute $1 million. The Music Association would build the structure and then operate it for a defined term, at the end of which the building would revert to the city. To clear up possible legal questions, a charter amendment to confirm this arrangement would be placed before the voters.

By mid-1916, the new Civic Center had become a functioning place with City Hall open for business, the Civic Auditorium holding meetings and conventions, and the plaza available for walking and sitting. Although the large block of Marshall Square and the plaza remained a void, other buildings were in the works—the State Building and the public library were both in planning or under construction. It was an active and exciting moment in the Civic Center's development, and the addition of a new opera house would continue to expand the Civic Center's growing presence in the city.

Although Willis Polk, who had designed the first plans for the opera house in 1913, went ahead and updated his plans so that construction could start as soon as an agreement for funding was approved, there was no immediate action from the city government and when the United States entered World War I in 1917, all attention on the opera house ceased as San Francisco prepared for war.

Nevertheless, the war didn't stop advocates for an opera house from discussing new plans. In the spring of 1918 when the American participation in the war was at its most intense stage, William Crocker organized a new group of wealthy men who began yet another campaign to build an opera house, but this time independent of the Music Association and beyond city government control. The actual chairman of this informal committee was John S. Drum, a well-connected banker who would spend the next ten years in that role. The planning group expanded the project's scope by adding an art museum, so it was often called the academy of art project or the opera house and art center project. Inevitably, a key obstacle was money, but through pledges from previous opera house subscribers, by 1919 the committee had reached $1,635,000 toward an estimated cost of $2,500,000. Just before September 1919, they went public with the detailed plan and submitted it to the regents of the University of California, hoping that the regents would take fiscal responsibility for the project and appoint a board of trustees to oversee it. They also pushed forward quickly on acquiring property for the project and on September 1 the committee signed an option to purchase an empty block at Van Ness Avenue between Hayes and Grove Streets, where St. Ignatius College had been located before the 1906 earthquake. Willis Polk was once more asked to make plans for a new opera house that would be suited to the new location.

When Crocker went to present the project in person to the regents of California and to appeal for their administrative oversight, the speech he gave drew heavily upon many of the same City Beautiful ideas that had been so instrumental in making San Francisco's Civic Center a reality during the prior decade. "Harmony," he said. "Is the watchword of the plans. We propose to have everyone in the City interested in the creation of the arts center. . . . There will be no special privileges for donors. . . . It will be a center of art and music, free from politics and built by popular universal subscription." Although, he also appealed to the purse strings: "Control and ownership by the University of California is proper," he said. "It will be self-supporting."

The funds, Crocker explained, to purchase the land would come from the San Francisco Institute of Art's sale of the Mark Hopkins mansion property on Nob Hill, which had housed its school before the earthquake and fire. Tying the project to the nation's war time struggles, he concluded with the promise that the new building would be dedicated to the memory of soldiers and sailors who had died in World War I. Crocker's proposal and presentation were evidently persuasive and afterward the regents agreed to take responsibility for the project.[2]

In general, the project for an opera house had wide support among the city's opinion makers. M. H. de Young, the conservative publisher of the *San Francisco*

Chronicle, spoke in support of the project, as did Matt I. Sullivan, a prominent lawyer and lifelong friend of Rolph's, who represented the more progressive segment of the community. At a meeting of fifty prominent men in his bank offices to further these efforts, Drum described the project in grand terms, telling them that no city in America had created a publicly supported opera house and art center; therefore, their task was unprecedented and ambitious but would be successful if the whole city supported the venture. But even with the support of some of the city's wealthiest citizens, funding was a major issue which the public would have to help provide.

The idea that the building would be serving as a war memorial of some kind had been an obvious element of the opera house project from the beginning. As McNab said to Rolph when the mayor had approached him about heading a committee to provide for a war memorial—no memorial could be more fitting than an opera house, since music will "give pleasure and joy to the multitudes and do something worthwhile for the memory of the men who gave their lives for the world."[3]

However, the initial idea had just been to build a memorial court outside of the opera house building. But that would change when Drum met with Charles Kendrick, a successful real estate broker and investor who had volunteered as an Army major in Europe. Kendrick was involved with the American Legion, a newly established veterans organization, and he was the California representative on the national executive committee. He was affiliated with San Francisco American Legion Post 1, one of the largest in the state, whose membership had a large number of former military officers, many of whom were prominent business and professional men.

Kendrick suggested to Drum that rather than just setting aside a portion of landscaping on which to build a memorial court, they should consider making the project itself into the memorial. He told Drum, "I think if you turn the whole project into a War Memorial, I can get the veterans' support." Drum and the opera house committee liked Kendrick's idea and gave their approval to negotiate an alliance. Kendrick went on to meet with at least fifty veterans' groups who offered their support for a War Memorial Opera House and art museum that would also contain meeting rooms for veterans.[4]

With this boost, the committee purchased the St. Ignatius College block on February 28, 1920, for $300,000, which was provided by the San Francisco Institute of Art. Polk adjusted the architectural plans to include a 3,000-seat opera-house auditorium on the western, Franklin Street side of the block, with two wings extending to the Van Ness Avenue side, approximating a U shape. One side would accommodate the art museum and the other side, the veterans, with

40,000 square feet of dedicated space, a memorial court would appear between the two wings.

With this alliance in place, Kendrick organized an extraordinary campaign to secure public donations toward building the War Memorial complex. Virtually every municipal and civic organization enrolled to support the project. The committee recruited school teachers to impress on their students the patriotic significance of the memorial and ministers to discuss its importance with their congregations. The idea was to reach the fundraising goal by Memorial Day. The week of May 17, 1920, was devoted to patriotic activities, religious services, military maneuvers, and band concerts on the empty block purchased for the project. The highlight of the week was a huge rally at the Civic Auditorium (formerly the Exposition Auditorium) at the Civic Center on May 19, with bands and other entertainment presided over by David Barrows, president of the University of California and state commander of the American Legion. Pledges were called out during the evening, including $100,000 from the city government to pay for the memorial court.[5] Later that week, an all-night dance party was held at Dreamland Auditorium, and the proceeds went into the project fund. The appeal was taken to the streets, where volunteers with cans were stationed in pup tents to receive small contributions.[6] By the end of the campaign, some $2.15 million toward the $2.5 million goal had been contributed or pledged by 65,000 people.

Although the lawyers for University of California regents would deem thousands of initial pledge forms inadequate and require new forms (a task that would take another two years accomplish), by the fall of 1922, the trustees felt confident enough to announce the appointment of an advisory board of architects to review the plans that Polk had designed and make recommendations for moving forward with the project. The board consisted of eight Beaux-Arts architects, many of whom had been the major architects of the Civic Center since the very start: Bernard Maybeck, the chairman; John Galen Howard, Frederick Meyer, and John Reid Jr., the three former Civic Center consulting architects; Polk; Arthur Brown Jr.; G. Albert Lansburgh; and Ernest Coxhead.[7] By selecting these architects, the trustees showed their intent to extend the neoclassical and French baroque styles of the Civic Center to the new building. Within a month, the architects reported to the trustees that neither Polk's newly updated design nor the St. Ignatius block could accommodate all the functions proposed for the War Memorial and recommended moving the project to the adjacent two blocks in front of City Hall.

But this newly proposed location presented some problems. Earlier in the year, in May, the Oakland-based Lyon Storage and Moving Company had announced that it had acquired half of the block at McAllister Street and Van Ness Avenue and intended to build an eight-story building with a clock tower, compatible with the Civic Center's design, to house its San Francisco operation.[8] Mayor Rolph and the supervisors were disturbed by the prospect of a commercial development across from City Hall. When the trustees voted on November 3, 1922, to ask the board of supervisors to acquire the two blocks for the new War Memorial buildings, by condemnation if necessary, their proposal was well received. In January 1923 the supervisors authorized condemnation of the rest of the two blocks, and the trustees advanced the funds for the purchases.

During this same month, on January 23, 1923, the trustees presented the design scheme for the two War Memorial blocks: an opera house on the south block and a combined American Legion building and art museum on the north block (the previous idea of one grand building accommodating all functions had been abandoned, partly as a result of the veterans' desire for a separate facility). The board of supervisors approved the plan unanimously.

Throughout the rest of the year, the advisory architects, primarily Polk and Brown, worked on plans and sketches that would harmonize the area with City Hall and the rest of Civic Center. Later that year, they presented preliminary drawings to the trustees, showing two identical neoclassical buildings on

PRELIMINARY STUDY OF WAR MEMORIAL COURT · FACADE OF OPERA HOUSE SHOWN ON RIGHT · AMERICAN LEGION AND MUSEUM BUILDING ON LEFT

The 1927 plan by Arthur Brown Jr. for the War Memorial complex court with colonnade façades and a victory column in the center.

Source: Courtesy of San Francisco History Center, San Francisco Public Library.

A performance of *Lucia Di Lammermoor* with soprano Lily Pons on October 23, 1932 in the Civic Auditorium for a radio broadcast. Note the painted ceiling and the decorative lighting features.
Source: Courtesy of San Francisco History Center, San Francisco Public Library.

either side of a memorial court. This was an exciting concept for San Francisco, drawn from the Place de la Concorde in Paris designed in 1755 by Ange-Jacques Gabriel, the court architect to Louis XV, reinforcing the French cultural aspect of civic center. In 1923 the only American structures with a similar plan were in the Cleveland Civic Center, part of the Group Plan of 1903 prepared by Daniel Burnham. Polk was responsible for the building elevations, which showed a high rusticated base penetrated by large arched entrances, on top of which sat two-story Doric columns on all sides of the buildings. On top of the columns was a high attic with room for lengthy inscriptions on the Van Ness Avenue side. They placed a large victory column modeled after the one in the Place Vendôme in Paris in the memorial court.[9]

The effort to create an opera house was initially driven by people interested in housing the symphony, but there was increasing interest in supporting opera. Up to this time San Francisco had not had a resident opera company, so opera lovers depended on touring companies of varied competence that performed in private theaters. One company even braved performances in the barn-like Civic Auditorium. Gaetano Merola, the conductor of many itinerant troupes, fell in love with San Francisco and settled there in 1921. He convinced Stanford University to sponsor outdoor opera performances in its stadium in the summer of 1922. The performances were an artistic success and attracted huge crowds, but they were a financial failure. Nevertheless, the performances inspired a number of well-to-do opera lovers to try to establish a resident company. The San Francisco Opera Association was formed on April 23, 1923, with Merola in charge, and it presented nine operatic performances that fall in the Civic Auditorium. The season ended with a tiny profit and gave the sponsors the confidence to continue.[10] Now that San Francisco had its own opera company, the push for the War Memorial Opera House gained more momentum.

The trustees were pleased by initial plans for two identical buildings and approved a detailed development. As supervising architects for the work on the Opera House, the trustees engaged Polk and G. Albert Lansburgh. Bakewell & Brown was engaged to work on the Veterans Building. Lansburgh had expertise and experience in building auditoriums, so he would be responsible for the theater portion of the Opera House. However, on September 10, 1924, Willis Polk passed away, so Brown and Lansburgh began working together on both buildings.

Unfortunately, while preparing the studies, designs, and cost estimates over the course of the next year, the architects discovered that the amount of funds proposed for the project could not support the desired buildings, or, as the architects put it, their uses with "the dignity and grandeur the people of San Francisco have a right to expect."[11] Nevertheless, despite the realization that the current funding proposals would not suffice, and despite potential disagreements between the veterans and arts proponents that had become increasingly evident over the recent years—particularly relating to uses for veterans in their building such as a game room, bar and other amenities of a traditional veterans hall, a groundbreaking ceremony was held on Armistice Day, November 11, 1926. The event included a parade from the Ferry Building to the War Memorial site and performances by the San Francisco Symphony, the San Francisco Opera chorus, and the San Francisco Municipal Band joined by Louise Homer singing the "Battle Hymn of the Republic."[12]

The cost issues that the architects had discovered were substantial, and at the end of 1926, after the architects refined plans and developed cost savings, they reluctantly reported to the trustees that the project needed $4 million more. The trustees decided that the only source of funds of that amount would be a voter-approved bond issue. On February 18, 1927, the trustees held a private meeting with the publishers of five San Francisco newspapers to test this idea. They described the situation, proposing that either the buildings be constructed piecemeal over an extended time as funds were raised or that the trustees bring a bond issue before the voters so that all construction could be done at once. The newsmen endorsed a bond issue, with the *San Francisco Examiner* editor Edmond Coblentz exclaiming that San Francisco already had enough "ruins."[13] A week later the board of supervisors approved putting the bond measure on the June ballot. The board also approved three other bond issues for the ballot, including one to buy the private Spring Valley Water Company water system and one to pay for expanding the San Francisco Municipal Railway. The four bond issues were packaged together as

Groundbreaking for the War Memorial on Armistice Day, November 11, 1926, with William Crocker and Charles Kendrick officiating.

Source: Courtesy of San Francisco History Center, San Francisco Public Library.

the "Progressive Bonds," and a citizens committee chaired by Kendrick campaigned for the entire group.

The city attorney, John J. O'Toole, insisted that the language of the War Memorial bonds conform to a state law authorizing bonds for veterans halls and meeting places rather than for general purposes. Thus, the measure presented to the voters stated that the bonds proceeds would be used to erect "permanent buildings in or adjacent to the Civic Center to be used as a Memorial Hall for War Veterans and for educational, recreational and other municipal purposes." There was no mention of an opera house or art museum, and this omission would cause trouble as time passed. While campaigning for the bonds, the mayor, supervisors, and other advocates spoke of the fine Opera House and Veterans Building that would result from the bonds' passage.[14] Merola, of the San Francisco Opera Association, said in a bond-endorsement interview, "I think that the plans for the War Memorial should bring special joy to all San Franciscans. Architecturally speaking, I do not think there will be anything more beautiful than those two buildings . . . the building for the veterans and the temple of music."[15] Some veterans were uneasy about how the bond funds would be spent. To reassure them, the board of supervisors passed a resolution on June

5, 1927, specifying that the board would not authorize the expenditure of any bond funds until the majority of veterans organizations were satisfied with the plans. As a result, the United Veterans Council endorsed the bonds and urged its thousands of members to vote for the whole package.[16] The voters approved the War Memorial bonds at a special election on June 14, 1927, with 70 percent. The other three major bond issues failed.

In 1927 Arthur Brown Jr. and John Bakewell, whose firm was overseeing the Veterans Building, dissolved their architectural partnership. With Drum's support, and although Lansburgh continued to play a prominent subordinate role, Brown assumed full control of both buildings of the War Memorial project. He set up a drafting office that at its peak had two dozen employees. By August 1927 the estimated cost of the entire project was $6.5 million. Despite the infusion of bond funds, the trustees found themselves $1 million short. They felt that they could not raise the difference in new contributions, so they asked Brown to further reduce costs. Over the next year, he made several changes to the plans, such as substituting terra-cotta for granite on the elevations of both buildings. In June 1928 he asked the trustees to approve narrowing both buildings by ten feet and substituting arcade windows for the expensive colonnades across the side façades.[17] Acoustical experts had recommended that the seating capacity of the original 4,000-seat opera house auditorium be reduced to 3,300 to improve sound quality. This change would make it easier to design slightly smaller buildings that would better frame the memorial court between them and widen the view of the City Hall dome from Fulton Street.[18]

Throughout 1927 and 1928 Brown and his office met with the United Veterans Council to discuss the Veterans Building. Brown's original scheme gave the veterans most of the first floor with additional meeting rooms in the basement. The art museum that was being designed within the building had a Van Ness Avenue entrance, a multistory sculpture court, and galleries on the second and third floors. After the passage of the bond issue, the veterans viewed the building as theirs alone and strongly opposed giving the art museum such prominence. They demanded an auditorium, and Lansburgh prepared plans for a handsome theater in the center of the building with a small stage and movable seating. Needless to say, the three-story theater space reduced floor space for other activities on the first three floors. As a result, the art museum was banished to the fourth floor with its own separate entrance on McAllister Street.[19] Soon other veterans came out in opposition to the auditorium and wanted a swimming pool, bowling alley, and club rooms instead, like those in an American Legion hall. The building design with the wide Van Ness Avenue frontage and recessed building behind upset some veterans, who felt that they would be getting an incomplete building. They created their own design advisory committee, which prepared its own critique of the plans: "The façade as set forth in the existing plans for the War Memorial is, in our opinion, poorly designed. It contains neither dignity nor detail and is inferior to a degree to the various public buildings now standing in Civic Center. . . . Particular criticism is directed to the lowest story, specifically the entrances which are weak and unattractive and give one the impression of entering a basement."[20]

The War Memorial bond election made no provision for the buildings' governance or a mechanism by which to combine city bond monies and private financing under the control of the regents in one fund. So on June 29, 1928, at the request of Kendrick and the trustees, a charter amendment was introduced to the board of supervisors to deal with these concerns. The amendment would create a War Memorial board of trustees within the city government to build, own, and operate the Opera House and Veterans Building. The board of eleven members would be appointed by the mayor and confirmed by the supervisors, with a special provision for veterans on the board. To add to the confusion, the attorney for the university regents issued an opinion on September 18, 1928, that, under the existing trust agreement, the trustees could not turn over donated funds to the board of supervisors or a city department; they could only place the funds in a new trust created by the supervisors that would be overseen by a new set of trustees.[21] Mayor Rolph and the supervisors quickly approved a charter amendment for the November 6 ballot. Veterans organizations claimed in the mid-twenties that there were 40,000 veterans living in San Francisco who could become a potent political force if organized, of which city officials were certainly aware.

Many veterans had lost confidence in the existing trustees, whom they felt were primarily concerned with the Opera House. They were particularly upset about the cost of the Opera House, which would be significantly more than the cost of the Veterans Building. They did not trust Mayor Rolph to appoint new trustees who would favor their interests. Just before the election, the American Legion and other veterans groups came out to oppose the amendment. Harold Hotchner, chair of the American Legion War Memorial Committee, told the board of supervisors, "This amendment will mean that the entire War Memorial project . . . will be in the hands of a group interested primarily in the opera house and art museum without regard to the wishes, desires, or needs of war veterans. The amendment was railroaded through the board of supervisors late at night before any public hearings." Veterans were particularly upset that the final wording of the charter amendment did not require that a veteran be appointed to the new board of trustees or, as they would have preferred, that a majority of the appointees be veterans. They blamed Kendrick—since he was involved with drawing up the amendment—and demanded that he resign as a trustee.[22] Their public opposition resulted in the charter amendment barely passing by 717 votes.

As a result of the tight election and the heated controversy, the trustees called a hearing on the War Memorial project on December 6, 1928, and asked Mayor Rolph, the supervisors, and the veterans groups to attend. Drum, still chair of the trustees, opened the meeting with a review of the past ten years. He pointed out that they had increased space for the veterans from 40,000 to 108,000 square feet. He said that their "plans favored no group. The War Memorial would be for all and be the finest and only one of its kind in the world." As an offering to the veterans, he recommended that the mayor nominate no trustees until the veterans were satisfied with his selection. Mayor Rolph chastised the veterans for causing "their dispute to hold up construction of the War Memorial buildings when the unemployed walked the streets." He also said, "We all feel cheap tonight to think that an attack could be made on public spirited citizens who have dug into their pockets to put hundreds of thousands of dollars into a project for the benefit of the whole community."[23]

Nearly nine months later, on August 25, 1929, Rolph announced his selection of eleven War Memorial trustees. He said that he had consulted with many groups but had difficulty getting "upstanding citizens" to serve. He had referred many names to veterans representatives and had disregarded those to which they objected. His final list consisted of five veterans (Lieutenant General Hunter Liggett; Frank N. Belgrano, state commander of the American Legion; Kendrick; former supervisor James L. Herz; and sitting supervisor Jesse Colman) and six civilians (Herbert Fleishhacker, banker and park commissioner; Robert I. Bentley, businessman and head of the San Francisco Opera Association; George T. Cameron, publisher of the *San Francisco Chronicle*; George Hearst, publisher of the *San Francisco Examiner*; Kenneth Kingsbury, president of Standard Oil of California; and J. W. Mullen, publisher of the *Labor Clarion*).[24]

The board of supervisors considered the mayor's nominations at a meeting on September 16, 1929. H. W. Glenson, of the United Veterans Council War Memorial Committee, spent almost an hour reading a statement expressing that group's views. He stressed that veterans should compose a majority if not all of the members of the board of trustees. He confirmed that they had met numerous times with the mayor but he had not appointed anyone from their lists. Liggett and Belgrano were acceptable, but Kendrick was not, because the veterans groups felt that he did not look after their interests nor was he responsive to them. Glenson reiterated that the veterans did not like the current plans.[25] He concluded by saying, "The veterans of San Francisco demand that the purposes for which the War Memorial Fund was created be carried out. The main purpose was to erect a building to house the veterans' organizations of San Francisco. Other uses and purposes were *incidental.* . . . If it is your intention to disregard the law and build an art museum and/or other buildings, leaving to the veterans such scraps of space as may be available . . . the best and most conclusive way for your board to manifest such intention is to confirm these appointments."[26] These remarks made a strong impression on the supervisors, and several criticized the mayor for not appointing a sixth veteran member. With the election looming in November, the board of supervisors rejected the eleven nominees 13 to 4.

Rolph was furious with these developments, and on October 13, 1929, he told the press that he would demand that the supervisors vote on each nominee individually, rather than vote on a list of nominees. "I can't see my way clear to remove any member from the board that I have named, particularly as I have been informed my selections would be acceptable to the private trustees who hold two million dollars in private subscriptions."[27] He again sided with men who could raise funds to keep the whole enterprise moving and not with veterans who desired a social hall.

The following day veterans groups sent an open letter signed by seven senior officers charging the mayor with bad faith in his appointments. They accused the existing trustees of gross mismanagement of the War Memorial since, after ten years, they had not started construction and the cost of the project kept growing. They stated that the mayor's current nominees included four of these trustees.[28] Rolph responded by saying that the veterans' letter contained "gross libelous" charges of dishonesty against upright citizens of San Francisco. He also pointed out that his nominees included only one current trustee—Fleishhacker. (He was in error; he had also nominated Kendrick.) However, in light of the upcoming election, Rolph said that he would wait before "forcing the issue."[29]

It was not until February 28, 1930, that Rolph reopened the discussion. He submitted a revised list of nominees with only one change. Fleishhacker had graciously withdrawn his name, according to Rolph, so he substituted Richard M. Tobin, a socially prominent banker, a founding member of the Music Association, and a former United States ambassador to the Netherlands. In December 1917, Tobin had joined the Navy as a lieutenant and had served in naval intelligence until 1920. While in Paris, he had cofounded the American Legion, and he was still active in a San Francisco post. The mayor's list now had a majority of certified veterans. The supervisors were eager to dispose of the matter, and unanimously confirmed the eleven nominees, regardless of whether they were acceptable to the veterans organizations. The *San Francisco Chronicle* reported that the veteran representatives sat in the board chambers silently "accepting the end of the matter with good grace." The mayor said that he was "mighty happy that the War Memorial question is out of the way."[30]

With the impasse behind them, the new trustees, the mayor, and the opera and symphony associations were eager to start construction. The 1929 stock market collapse had occurred only months earlier and economic conditions were worsening and unemployment was rising, and they thought that the project would boost morale. Using detailed plans that Brown had been developing for the past several years, work on both buildings was under way by January 1931. Signs affixed to supply trucks declared, "Hello Prosperity! Here Comes the War Memorial."[31]

On Armistice Day, November 11, 1931, cornerstones for the two buildings were laid with great ceremony. Patriotic speeches, 2,000 American flags held by veterans, and a military parade with marching bands were highlights of the day. Promptly at 11 a.m., two cornerstone boxes were positioned: Crocker oversaw placement for the Opera House, and Liggett oversaw placement for the Veterans Building. Each box contained a variety of souvenirs, including copies of the charter amendment that had created the War Memorial complex and a roster of the 65,000 people who had donated funds toward its construction. As had been done during the groundbreaking ceremony in 1926, the "Battle Hymn of the Republic" was sung, this time by the film actress Myrtle McLaughlin.[32] The veterans groups remained silent about any lingering resentment.

Construction proceeded rapidly, partly because the cost of labor and material had decreased at the start of the Depression and people were eager to work. The buildings adhered to the approved design, but there was little room for amenities, so the organ proposed for the Opera House was not purchased.

The two War Memorial buildings were dedicated on September 9, 1932. However, the real ceremony indicating completion was the opening performance of *Tosca* in the Opera House on Saturday, October 15, 1932, under Merola's baton. This was the ultimate social event of what had been a difficult year. The house was sold out, and the elegantly dressed attendees paraded their finery. The press gave it multipage coverage, with headlines featuring wealth and beauty. Needless to say, this was not an event for the veterans.

The San Francisco Museum of Art opened on the fourth floor of the Veterans Building in 1935 under the direction of Grace Morley, who curated several exhibits during the first year. To accommodate one of the veterans' demands, access to the museum was though a side entrance on McAllister Street, not through the main entry on Van Ness Avenue.

First performance in the new Opera House, October 15, 1932, Act 1 of *Tosca*.
Source: Courtesy of San Francisco History Center, San Francisco Public Library.

Because times were difficult, landscaping the memorial court between the two buildings was delayed until 1935, when it was designed by the well-known landscape architect Thomas Church, on Brown's recommendation. The work was completed the following year.[33]

After twenty years of struggle, San Francisco finally had a magnificent municipally owned opera house—the only one in the country. The final cost was four times the original estimate. The War Memorial complex expanded the Civic Center district across Van Ness Avenue and left the originally proposed opera house location on Larkin Street a desolate parking lot. The alliance of opera house advocates with veterans groups proved useful but highly frustrating, if not toxic, for both sides. The establishment veterans, most of whom had been officers, subscribed to the idea of art and music as a component of the memorial emphasizing life and the future. Most of the veterans organizations, however, were composed of enlisted men and people with more ordinary tastes who had desired a building to serve as a clubhouse for social events and veterans gatherings. Brown couldn't satisfy them with changes to the design of their building, which was not a typical American Legion hall: he could only offer them free office space and meeting rooms.

The veterans' ire had focused on Kendrick, the alliance's creator, who they felt had betrayed their interests in favor of the Opera House. Although they

The Veterans Building (*front*) and Opera House shortly after completion, circa 1933.
Source: Courtesy of San Francisco History Center, San Francisco Public Library.

had demanded his resignation as a private trustee and had asked Rolph not to appoint him to the War Memorial board of trustees, the mayor had appointed Kendrick and other veterans with similar backgrounds as trustees because he needed them to secure funds for the complex.

Crocker wrote, "More than any one person, Charles Kendrick was responsible for San Francisco's beautiful War Memorial Opera House and Art Museum."[34] The veterans most likely would have agreed heartily with that statement. The tension between the needs of the cultural elite and the veterans still affects the War Memorial. Nevertheless, despite the disputes regarding style and function, from this difficult alliance San Francisco received two extraordinary buildings in harmony with its imperial City Hall. For those who favored the buildings' style and final design, the Van Ness Avenue side of the Civic Center quickly became the area's high point.

Postwar and Modernism

The shadows of war had descended on San Francisco in the 1930s, and by spring 1941 newspapers reported daily disasters from Europe and across the Pacific. Although San Franciscans carried on in the lighthearted spirit of the previous two years, Bay Area military bases began preparing for the possibility of war. About 100,000 servicemen were on active duty in Northern California. Colonel Charles C. Commandy, commander of the 30th Infantry Regiment stationed at the Presidio, suggested to William Randolph Hearst, publisher of the *San Francisco Examiner*, that a hospitality center to assist and entertain servicemen on leave would be needed in San Francisco. Hearst and his newspaper took on the cause and contacted Mayor Angelo Rossi (who had become mayor after Rolph left office in 1931 to become governor of California), who pledged to provide the Larkin Street side of Marshall Square at Civic Center and $15,000 to cover the cost of materials for the project.[1] The city's Building Trades Council offered to construct the facility at no cost. Dodge A. Reidy, the city architect, designed a handsome one-story streamline moderne building to serve as the recreation center. The USO Hospitality House officially opened on August 9, 1941, and the *San Francisco Examiner* hosted a huge celebration featuring Hollywood stars, including Eddie Cantor and Linda Darnell; local bands and entertainers; and light shows employing army searchlights. Some 10,000 servicemen and 40,000 to 50,000 members of the public attended.

The attack on Pearl Harbor on December 7, 1941, would have a significant impact on life in San Francisco, and the grim results of warfare became very real when the ships bringing the dead and wounded from Hawaii arrived in the city a week later. After hearing rumors about Japanese aircraft flying over the city and confirming that Japanese submarines had attacked ships off the West Coast, San Franciscans rapidly geared up their civil defense. A control

This *San Francisco News* photograph was taken on August 21, 1943 from the State Building. The photo shows the completed temporary dormitories for servicemen built in just two days. Source: Courtesy of San Francisco History Center, San Francisco Public Library.

center was established in the City Hall basement, and the city prepared for blackouts. The largest rooms in City Hall were the north and south light courts with glass ceilings—spaces intentionally designed for flexible use as offices, meeting rooms, or exhibition areas as needs dictated. The public works department covered all of City Hall's skylights with a tar-like substance that darkened the underlying spaces day and night. On February 12, 1942, unidentified aircraft were reported over the city, and a blackout was declared. This was the biggest test of the city's civil defense to date. Most streets and buildings were dark; however, when the all clear was sounded, city officials found that lights on the second floor of City Hall had been left on.[2]

The city needed dormitory barracks to accommodate thousands of servicemen visiting the city and Hospitality House, and it was suggested that they be built in Civic Center Plaza. In 1943 Robert McCarthy, a local homebuilder, offered to construct two-story prefabricated structures. His offer was accepted, and he assembled the first of them in two days.[3] Nine dormitories were constructed in the plaza, offering 1,600 beds that could be occupied for 50 cents each per night. During the war, the US Navy had offices in the Federal Building, including an office for Fleet Admiral Chester W. Nimitz, commander of the Pacific fleet. By 1944 the navy needed more space, so it constructed a three-story wooden structure in the empty space behind the public library. In general, the war years were spent focusing on the troops and national needs, rather than on any civic improvement projects at home.

Postwar Development

Despite the travails of the wartime years, San Francisco rebounded after the close of war. The turn toward victory by the allies had boosted optimism in the city, and new ideas began to take shape for new civic works projects. Additionally, one particular event would have a special impact on San Francisco pride: on February 10, 1945, Mayor Roger D. Lapham—who had been elected in 1943 after Mayor Rossi largely lost the support of the city's business community—received a telegram from Secretary of State Edward Stettinius, informing him that President Roosevelt had announced at the Yalta Conference that the United Nations founding conference would be held in San Francisco in April. The news came out of the blue, but Lapham and the city's leadership were ecstatic—the momentous event would reinforce San Francisco's image as the most prominent city on the West Coast. Organizers were readily granted permission to use the grand War Memorial complex, and they began to prepare accommodations for 5,000 delegates, staff, and journalists for what was to become nine weeks of meetings. The business and social elite threw themselves into providing hospitality for world leaders. After victory in Europe was declared in May, President Harry Truman came to San Francisco on June 26, 1945, to sign the United Nations' founding agreement. San Franciscans basked in the glow of success, feeling that they were part of a new postwar world. Japan's surrender to the Allies two months later reinforced the city's desire for a fresh start.

Buoyed by the optimistic atmosphere as the war neared its end, Mayor Lapham appointed the Citizens Postwar Planning Committee on April 15, 1945, composed of prominent business leaders and a few labor representatives. The committee issued a report on August 20, 1945, stating, "We believe that San Francisco has become careless and allowed itself to 'run down at the heels.'" The committee called for a master plan to guide the city's development. Their primary concern was the lack of a modern airport, since an airport that had been planned at Treasure Island had never been built. The committee recommended that a $20 million bond measure to help pay for a new airport be placed before the voters. This bond measure passed on November 6, 1945. Also, as the city emerged from its wartime stance, in 1946 the military dormitory buildings that had been built at Civic Center Plaza were deconstructed and removed, and the Hospitality House was closed and turned over to the city's planning department for offices which remained located there for the next forty years. The navy's wooden building behind the library, known as 45 Hyde Street, dispensed with its military function and became city property in 1948, going on to serve as library office space for the next forty-five years.

In the post-war years, the tourism industry was eager to promote the city for visitors, so the San Francisco Convention & Visitors Bureau requested support from the Citizens Postwar Planning Committee for a new 25,000-seat convention facility. The committee, however, instead recommended spending $495,000 to remodel and expand the former Exposition Auditorium which had been built to accommodate conventions and meetings during the Panama-Pacific International Exposition (the engraved words *Exposition Auditorium* still graced the building.) After the Exposition, the old-fashioned hall with odd Turkish-style chandeliers and a painted-sky ceiling had become the Civic Auditorium and the city's major convention facility, accommodating 7,200 people. The Convention & Visitors Bureau, upset at the rejection for a new facility by the committee, approached the mayor and board of supervisors directly and persuaded them to put a $15 million bond measure on the November 1948 ballot for a new facility. But the voters defeated the measure, and the auditorium remained unimproved. Measures to help fund renovations would be proposed several times in the coming decades.[4]

Other improvements to the municipal buildings in the Civic Center were also promoted at this time. The Citizens Postwar Planning Committee recommended a new courthouse on the Marshall Square block to accommodate the civil courts then located at City Hall. When the new City Hall had opened in 1915, it had been expedient to locate the courts there, just as they had been in the pre-earthquake City Hall. No one thought this was ideal, but the city had lacked the time and resources to construct a new courthouse while preparing for the Panama-Pacific International Exposition. Rolph and others had proposed new courts before, but the idea never took hold. By 1945, court operational conditions were substandard, and judges and the rest of the legal community favored a new, dedicated building. In addition, City Hall was too small to accommodate growing government functions, so city offices were scattered among rental spaces and rooms in the Civic Auditorium. The committee recommended a $5.3 million bond issue for a new courthouse and a $904,000 bond issue to remodel City Hall for additional city offices. To reach this decision, the committee had consulted with Arthur Brown Jr., John Bakewell, and Frederick Meyer, part of the original design team for the Civic Center and City Hall. However, despite the need for the courthouse, the recommendation for the bond issue was ultimately not acted upon, leaving lawyers and judges to continue to advocate for a new courthouse for many years to come.

Following the war, San Francisco, like most American cities, was influenced by the ideas of modernism as espoused by such architects and planners as Le Corbusier and Mise van der Rohe. These ideas began to have an effect on the discussions to modernize and improve the Civic Center. On February 9, 1949, Sydney Williams, chief of the planning department's Master Plan Division, sent a memorandum to the planning commission and to Mayor Elmer Robinson, a former judge and the new mayor who succeeded Lapham in office, explaining that city, state, and federal agencies were growing and needed more space. He suggested this could be located in the Civic Center area if a plan were well conceived. The plan, Williams noted, needed to be based on "concise and accurate information including a survey of needs." New buildings should be "dignified architecture" to emphasize the vital role of San Francisco as a government center. Williams appeared to still be influenced by City Beautiful ideas. He recommended hiring eminent consultants with a proposed appropriation of $75,000 for a Civic Center master plan consultant. Nevertheless, when his memo finally reached the board of supervisors on February 27, 1952, it was unanimously rejected as a needless expense by the tightfisted supervisors. Supervisor Daniel Gallagher even called the proposal "a lot of foolishness."[5]

Undeterred, however, the city's planning commission did not take the rebuff as an end to the issue, and in May of that year it directed its planners to further study the Civic Center's current functioning within the government and city life. The resulting June 17, 1953, report stated, "The pressure and circumstances that create change [at the Civic Center] are at work; the need for added space, the need for new facilities, the problems created by traffic, and the problems created by dispersed and inconveniently located governmental facilities all demand solution, and all require that decisive steps be taken." Despite the initial dismissal, the plan and its component recommendation would gain traction in the upcoming years, taking the Civic Center in new modern design directions, ones which often departed from the its original Beaux-Arts design.

The report was "intended to indicate the possible form for future expansion" and recommended a detailed, definitive plan for development,[6] and it is particularly notable for being the first public announcement by San Francisco officials that indicated City Beautiful values no longer controlled Civic Center development. In the report's review of the 1912 Civic Center plan and building design, the authors pointed out that since there had been no domestic architectural style at that time, city leaders and architects had looked toward Europe and Paris and had adapted French themes and styles that emphasized control of all building elements and the expression of civic authority. The buildings, they wrote, had been "intended to impress and overawe." But the authors noted that style preferences had changed since that time, and they described design values in postwar San Francisco as "informal, [featuring] an absence of total authority and a tradition of laissez-faire." They suggested that new Civic Center construction use a "less paradoxical" style. They did emphasize, however, that "no one contemplates tearing down the existing palatial structures," but they suggested that more flexible, intimate, and utilitarian structures be built in the future. Prominent international architects of the time, such as Walter Gropius of Harvard, expressed similar, widely accepted views.

Expanding the Civic Center to accommodate current needs, the authors of the report pointed out, could not be accomplished by developing only the empty block of Marshall Square and other small parcels within the limits of the 1912 plan. They called for acquiring adjacent marginal properties to accommodate office needs within a compact layout. They were critical of City Hall as a functional city office building, pointing out the lack of space and the impossibility of expansion. They proposed constructing a new municipal office building to accommodate all city functions in one efficient building and converting City Hall into an expanded courthouse and home of the board of supervisors, a proposal that was contrary to the view of the 1945 Citizens Postwar Planning Committee report which had called for a new courthouse.

The planning commission report described a physical plan that encompassed the area from Golden Gate Avenue to Fell Street and from Market Street to Franklin Street. By combining the Marshall Square block and the adjacent triangular block on the south, thus eliminating the first block of Grove Street, the city could create a super block to house a municipal office building facing onto Market Street with two long parallel structures and a tall connecting tower. This was the report's most direct attack on the 1912 Beaux-Arts land use plan—although it retained its original eighty-foot cornice line for the new buildings proposed to house the health department, welfare office, police and fire headquarters, state and federal agencies, and arts and drama programs. To help address the need for space for large conventions, the report suggested the city construct an exhibit hall under Civic Center Plaza or a new facility closer to downtown hotels. All new buildings would be of "simple and straight forward design, using interesting and contrasting materials [to the historic architecture's Sierra granite]." In light of the traffic and parking needs of the post-war era, the report suggested a radical departure from the plan from 1912: raise the Civic Center Plaza several feet and build a large parking garage underneath. Polk and Larkin Streets would be suppressed to provide entrances to the garage, and pedestrian platforms would be built over both streets. The result would be a pedestrian mall from the steps of City Hall along the Fulton Street axis to the

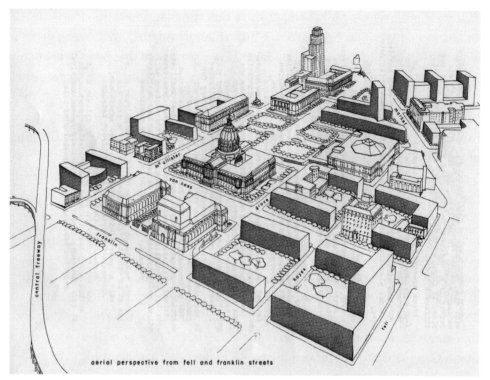

aerial perspective from fell and franklin streets

An aerial perspective from the San Francisco Planning Department's plan for the Civic Center, dated June 17, 1953. Note the super-block at Larkin and Grove with the 20-story municipal office tower and the other proposed public buildings in the area in excess of the original eighty-foot cornice line. Source: Courtesy of San Francisco History Center, San Francisco Public Library.

new municipal building at Market Street. Fulton Street from Larkin to Market Streets would be closed to traffic. In addition, Grove Street from Polk to Market Streets would be closed to provide pedestrian access to the Civic Auditorium.

Despite the board of supervisors' lack of enthusiasm earlier in 1952 for William's initial memo, there was nevertheless a growing consensus among the city's business and community leaders that the city needed to make improvements. Even before the report was published in 1953, Mayor Robinson had announced the formation of his own citizens planning committee, San Francisco Forward, composed of 166 businessmen and community leaders asked to assess the city's future needs. Its Public Buildings Subcommittee started work in late June 1953, when they received the planning department's Civic Center report. The subcommittee responded first to tourist industry concerns by recommending that the city refurbish Civic Auditorium to better serve conventions and build an adjacent underground exhibit hall below Civic Center Plaza. The recommendation for the underground exhibit hall was rapidly converted into a $3.25 million bond measure, which appeared on the November 3, 1953, ballot, but failed.[7] However, the board of supervisors put the same auditorium and exhibit hall measure on the November 2, 1954 ballot, and it passed.[8]

The subcommittee then turned its attention to the long-running issue of the Marshall Square block, the site of San Francisco's earlier City Hall that had been damaged in the earthquake and which still sat vacant as a parking lot fifty years later. The conversation specifically revolved around whether the city should build a new municipal building or courthouse. Thomas Brooks, San Francisco's chief administrative officer; John McDevitt, the city architect; and other city staff argued that office space in City Hall was inefficient because the rotunda, light courts, and decorative features created poor working conditions. They called for a large new municipal office building and for the conversion of City Hall into a courthouse with space for the board of supervisors. However, the city's judges, bar association, and legal community strongly supported a new courthouse, arguing that San Francisco was the only American city without a freestanding courthouse and that City Hall had never been designed to accommodate the courts. But to the legal communities' frustration, and in response to the subcommittee's request for a cost comparison, city staff reported that it would cost more to convert City Hall into efficient office space than to convert it into a courthouse. Their estimate included removing corridors and light wells and lowering ceilings. The historic value of City Hall was not part of their consideration, only the need for modern office space. In response to this cost estimate, at the subcommittee's final meeting on May 2, 1954, members voted unanimously in favor of a new municipal building and City Hall's conversion into a courthouse.[9] Despite this vote, city judges and lawyers were not deterred by the business-dominated citizens committee's rejection of a new courthouse. They organized a Court House Citizens Committee and sought support from Mayor Robinson and the board of supervisors, which unanimously endorsed placing a $13 million courthouse bond measure on the November 8, 1955, ballot. The business community, particularly the San Francisco Real Estate Board and the Building Owners and Managers Association of San Francisco, attacked the bonds, calling them impractical and costly, ultimately leading to the bond measure's failure.[10] The city did not, however, act on the recommendation to convert City Hall into a courthouse, leaving things more or less where they were before for another thirty years.

In a move indicative of the major shifts in the design and style preferences of this era, the city asked Skidmore, Owings & Merrill (SOM) and Wurster, Bernardi and Emmons (WBE), two of the most prominent modernist firms in San Francisco, to join forces and design an underground exhibit hall under the south half of Civic Center Plaza that had been previously approved by the bond

This *San Francisco News* photograph dated May 2, 1957, shows the construction of Brooks Hall exposition space under Civic Center Plaza, looking toward the Department of Health building. Source: Courtesy of San Francisco History Center, San Francisco Public Library.

measure in 1954. The project required more engineering than architecture. SOM had recently finished Lever House in New York and was working on the Crown Zellerbach Building in San Francisco. William Wurster had been the originator of the iconic Northern California regional residential style before World War II and his firm, established in 1945, embodied his aesthetic in projects of every sort, which were often completed in conjunction with SOM. The two firms could not have been more different from the City Beautiful–oriented designers of the previous half century. In July 1955 they issued their preliminary analysis for the underground exhibition space. Excavation began in September 1956, and the first convention in the new Brooks Hall opened in April 1958.

Following the recommendation of the city planning commission's report under Williams in 1953, the city also embarked on the underground Civic Center Garage on the northern half of the plaza in early 1959, about nine months after work was completed on Brooks Hall. The two underground structures would be independent and separate from each other, with a space between them for a water cistern. The garage would open for business on March 1, 1960.

At this same time, despite the new exhibit hall and its potential to host conventions, the renovations to the Civic Auditorium, funding for which had been rejected in the 1954 bond measure, remained an ongoing need. Walter Swanson, the general manager of the San Francisco Convention & Visitors Bureau, sent a letter on February 7, 1956 to Mayor George Christopher—another Republican businessman who had succeeded Mayor Robinson in January 1956—bringing his attention to the poor condition of the Civic Auditorium and stating that the city was having difficulty attracting conventions because of it. He called for modernizing the building; adding escalators; removing tenant city offices, such as the board of education; and creating a direct underground connection to Brooks Hall. The courthouse issue also remained of active concern to many, and simultaneously, judges and lawyers continued to aggressively advocate for a new courthouse.

In response to the many pressing needs at this time, in December 1956 the mayor and his administration commissioned SOM and WBE to prepare a Civic Center development plan to "fill present and future needs in a manner both enhancing the established traditions and utilizing the best contemporary technology, planning and design." The city also directed the same architectural and engineering teams to prepare new analyses and costs for building a courthouse on Marshall Square and remodeling City Hall into office space. The combined program was estimated to cost $22.15 million, and a bond measure for that amount, supported by the mayor and the city administration, was placed before the voters on November 5, 1957. Just as it had done two years before, the Building Owners and Managers Association and other real estate interests opposed the city's measure, calling for a new city office building and opposing a "monumental" courthouse, claiming that it was too expensive. The measure failed again. Feeling that the courthouse bonds were at a disadvantage during an off-year election, the courthouse proponents put the same measure on the ballot for November 4, 1958, a general election year with an active contest for governor. The Building Owners and Managers Association again opposed the measure and again it failed. On this ballot, the city also placed a $7.2 million bond measure to upgrade the Civic Auditorium based on an analysis prepared by SOM and WBE. It also failed, although there were no ballot arguments against it.[11]

The repeated failures of these bond measures are symbolic of the fierce reluctance among big property owners to support the Civic Center if it also meant the potential raising of the property tax. Various mayors seemed incapable of stopping the fighting between the property owners and the legal community over the need for a new courthouse building on Marshall Square. As a result, despite numerous efforts to develop a new courthouse and upgrade the auditorium, no progress would be made during this time.

The report that SOM and WBE had published in October 1958 (just before the November ballot measure), called the Civic Center Development Plan, acknowledged that San Francisco's Civic Center was "one of the most distinguished in the nation." Unlike the city planning department's 1953 report, theirs respected existing height and bulk limitations and the plaza's spatial layout "in a manner retaining the architectural quality and dignity of the surrounding buildings." Within these requirements, SOM and WBE recommended a new court building on Marshall Square in a contemporary design. City Hall would be remodeled to accommodate city offices, retaining light wells but not restoring first-floor light courts. Floors would be covered with vinyl tile, and acoustical ceilings would be suspended in office areas. A city government annex would be constructed opposite City Hall on McAllister Street, offering more office space. To accommodate conventions, and following previous recommendations, they recommended rehabilitating and modernizing the Civic Auditorium and creating an underground connection to Brooks Hall. They also proposed constructing a connecting meeting and exhibition facility on the block that contained the Department of Health building, which would be either moved across Van Ness Avenue or demolished. The new facility would include subgrade exhibition space connected directly to Brooks Hall. For parking, a new garage under the north side of the plaza would be paid for out of parking revenues, and other garages would be built on the periphery of the center. SOM and WBE used Douglas Baylis, one of the Bay Area's leading landscape architects, to design the center's plaza for the plan. In his report, Baylis proposed that the city restore the plaza in a manner that respected the historic design, with two identical pools and fountains and diagonal crosswalks, but using more intense landscaping divided into many planter beds and featuring a lawn running down the center. More interestingly, he proposed closing Polk and Larkin Streets to through traffic between McAllister and Grove Streets and turning them into esplanades, with ramps at each end of Larkin Street leading to parking garages under the plaza and the new courts building. In addition, Fulton Street from Larkin to Market Streets would be closed to traffic and made into a landscaped pedestrian mall. This plan would have significantly changed the character of the public realm.

Although the city did not seek immediate funding for the broader plan, the business community was desperate to improve the city's ability to host conventions. Using the SOM and WBE recommendations for improving the Civic Auditorium, they worked with Mayor Christopher and the board of supervisors to place a $7.575 million Civic Auditorium–improvement bond measure on the ballot for the November 3, 1959, election. The plan's recommendations for the Civic Auditorium had also included removing the painted ceiling and historic

Turkish-looking light fixtures and adding to the classic exterior "modern treatments creating features of beauty, utility and safety in conformity with the most advanced planning for public buildings." This report proved instrumental in helping the voters understand the need for these improvements and, as a result, this time the bonds passed with 70.4 percent.[12] This was a remarkable achievement considering how many times improvement measures for upgrading the auditorium had previously failed. The work on rehabilitating the Civic Auditorium would take a number of years and would be completed in 1964, nearly twenty years after the San Francisco Convention & Visitors Bureau had first requested the city to construct a new convention hall. However, in a disconcerting pattern of governmental inefficiency in San Francisco, the remodeled auditorium and Brooks Hall would soon be obsolete: seventeen years later, the city would open the new Moscone Convention Center in the South of Market area to accommodate the city's convention needs.

Civic Center Plaza Debacle

The Civic Center Plaza was originally designed for a gentile age of well-dressed people strolling or sitting and reading. By the 1950s many felt that it had not achieved what such an extraordinary public space should be. However, efforts to improve the plaza in the 1960s became a notable debacle when the city held an international competition to upgrade its design, functionality, and appeal.

When SOM and WBE first published the new Civic Center Development plan in October 1958, the plaza area was largely a construction site from the previous work on the underground Brooks Hall and the current work on the new underground garage. Baylis's first landscaping design for the plaza, which respected the historic plan, had been criticized by Mayor Christopher for being cluttered and lacking sufficient lawns. So Baylis submitted an entirely new design in February 1959 with no reference to the historic design. The new scheme contained a narrow rectangular reflecting pool running east-west across the plaza and olive tree groves in the corners.[13] To pay for the plaza construction, the city scraped together $450,000, which some said was a third of what should be spent. Baylis recommended that the new plaza be embellished with fountains and statuary. On July 31, 1959, Christopher invited senior city officials to a meeting to discuss the plaza, since work on the new garage was ahead of schedule. He directed that the plaza plans that Baylis had submitted be approved and that construction get under way as soon as possible. He also agreed to cover the cost of Baylis's embellishments with $250,000 from the city budget at a later date.[14] Two years later, when construction on Baylis's plaza design was nearly finished, Christopher held a meeting on March 1, 1961, where he pointedly critiqued the new plaza, expressing his concern that it was too barren, and he disliked the large expanse of pavement in front of City Hall. He was assured that the plaza would look better when the trees and other landscaping matured.[15]

But other critiques of the plaza design also flowed in. On May 29 the *San Francisco Chronicle's* design critic Allan Temko wrote a blistering column about the plaza, stating that "the poverty of design is painfully apparent." In mid-September editorials in both the *San Francisco Chronicle* and the *San Francisco Examiner* criticized the board of supervisors for not appropriating more money for plaza sculpture and fountains. The *San Francisco Examiner* wrote that the plaza had "too much angularity" and "an over abundance of stony planes." The newspaper called the rectangular pool's water spouts "piddling . . . looking like leaks that the plumber forgot to repair."[16]

By this time, Baylis had finished the project and was probably glad to be done with it. His papers, archived at the University of California, Berkeley, College of Environmental Design, contain no mention of any work on Civic Center Plaza.

To deal with the design controversy, the San Francisco Arts Commission decided on its own to propose plaza improvements and embellishments, so it

The new Civic Center Plaza, circa 1962, from the Mayor's Office balcony, highlighting the blank concrete space across from City Hall and rectangle pond without decoration.

Source: Courtesy of San Francisco History Center, San Francisco Public Library.

engaged an adviser, Donald Olsen, a professor of architecture at the University of California, Berkeley. In March 1962, Olsen proposed a revised pool shape, better fountains, and the addition of sculpture.[17] However, the following year, the Arts Commission decided on an entirely different course—a competition for a plaza design. In September the Arts Commission engaged Henry Schubart Jr. to administer the competition, which would be open to US and international artists and architects.[18] Schubart was a respected Bay Area architect with a strong modernist orientation. He had trained at Taliesin West, Frank Lloyd Wright's studio in Arizona. Schubart traveled to New York to discuss the competition with prominent artists and architects and assembled an eminent jury to select the winning proposal.

In fall 1963, congressman and labor leader John Shelley was elected mayor, succeeding George Christopher. This was the first time in more than fifty years that a Democrat had held the position. The Arts Commission and Schubart decided to delay the competition until the new mayor had made his own appointments to the commission. Indeed, Shelley appointed several people with strong modernist, rather than traditional orientation. On July 8, 1964, the Arts Commission approved the competition's final specifications, which challenged designers to aesthetically improve the plaza's central area through "augmentation, change or removal and replacement by a design element of the competitor's choice."[19] The jury of five members would include an architect, an arts patron, a sculptor, an art historian, and Thomas Church, a noted landscape architect, who would act as chairman. The plaza was the property of the recreation and park department, so it would be an equal partner when decisions were made about the plaza competition and remodeling.

The competition was finally announced in October 1964, with an open invitation to any and all ideas and an implementation budget of $270,000. Submittals were due on April 15, 1965. Schubart did his job well: 1,209 people from 45 countries paid $5 each to register, and the city eventually received 317 submissions. The jury consisted of Church, the architect Luis Barragán, the arts patron Moses Lasky, the sculptor André Bloc, and the art historian Sibyl Moholy-Nagy, whose husband, László, was a noted architect of the Bauhaus School. The jury met for several days in mid-May to consider submissions and select three finalists.

The jury report, prepared by Sibyl Moholy-Nagy, was presented to both the Arts Commission and the Recreation and Park Commission on May 25, 1965. They awarded first place to Ivan Tzvetin and Angela Danadjieva, two Bulgarian refugees living in Paris. Their design would replace the existing plaza with a series of overlapping 100-foot-square concrete terraces containing pools, fountains, lawns, and other landscaping. The jury reported that this design departed from the current plan so dramatically that it would create a new spatial and visual experience. The jury also stated that the design was a flexible contemporary solution that would accommodate painting and sculptural exhibitions on the terraces. The second prize was also contemporary, and the third retained the present design but placed a tall sculpture in the plaza's center.[20] The art commissioners were unanimously enthusiastic about the winning design, and Commissioner Jeremy Ets-Hokin exclaimed that it was "one of the most exciting and wonderful things ever offered to the City."[21] The recreation and park commissioners, however, were appalled. Commissioner James Kearny said, "It looks like a drying shed for apricots."[22]

A few days later, the *San Francisco Examiner's* art critic Alexander Fried wrote that the design was an exercise in "advance aesthetics" and undoubtedly would be controversial. He called it a "throwback to the neoplasticism of Mondrian."[23] Mayor Shelley weighed in, saying, "It looks like the display room of a linoleum store." With such comments from city officials, arts commissioner Tony DeLap resigned on May 27, 1965, accusing city officials of showing "an astonishing display of ignorance."[24] On August 13, 1965, the San Francisco Recreation and Park Commission voted to leave the plaza untouched. Schubart was bitter and told the press that he "was going to recommend to nationally prominent artists and architects never to participate in another competition in San Francisco."[25]

Walter Haas Sr., chairman of Levi Strauss & Co., was a longtime member of the Recreation and Park Commission and an ex-officio member of the Arts Commission. He had firsthand experience with the frustrating task of improving the plaza. Troubled by the lack of progress, he decided to resolve the problem himself. He asked Lawrence Halprin, a Bay Area landscape architect, to prepare a plaza design based on the historic scheme and offered to pay for Halprin's work. Halprin was willing, so Haas consulted with the two commission presidents, and they liked the idea. It probably helped that Halprin was a respected local professional working on several well-received Bay Area projects. At the Recreation and Park Commission's January 27, 1966, meeting, Haas presented his offer of $6,000 to engage Halprin, and it was approved. On March 2, the Arts Commission also approved the plan.[26]

As it turned out, someone else was also eager to make a statement about the plaza. At 1:20 a.m., on May 14, 1966, a loud explosion rocked the plaza. Police discovered that two sticks of dynamite had been placed on interior pool walls, shattering them and releasing water into the plaza when the bomb was detonated. It was not clear whether this was an aesthetic or a political protest.[27]

By fall, Halprin had finished his preliminary plaza redesign. He eliminated the rectangular pool, telling the Arts Commission at its December 5, 1966, meeting that "it seems to annoy everyone." He returned the original design's two circular pools on either side of the Fulton Street axis, and he proposed installing in each pool fountains with "great gushers of dense, heavy water that will not blow in the wind." He proposed replacing the four dense groves of olive trees at each corner of the plaza with tree-lined brick patios from which people could walk diagonally across the plaza. He would retain some pollarded sycamore trees on either side of the Fulton Street esplanade and intersperse them with flag poles. Both the recreation and park department and the Arts Commission were pleased with Halprin's plan and passed resolutions asking the board of supervisors to direct $231,000 left over from the competition to the new plan. However, at its July 9, 1967, meeting, the board's finance committee expressed concern that Halprin's plan would cost much more than $231,000. The finance committee voted to return the money to the general fund, and the board of supervisors directed the recreation and park department to prepare a detailed cost estimate and request a new appropriation.[28] The board may have tired of addressing plaza improvements, since the plaza had been the source of controversy for five years and remodeling it had no natural constituency. The recreation and park department never submitted a new appropriation request, and the issue faded away. The plaza would remain almost exactly as it was for the next five decades, with the exception of minor cosmetic changes in the late 1990s, encouraged by Mayor Willie Brown.

Civic Center BART Station

After Mayor Rolph left office in 1931 to become governor of California, the eastern side of the Civic Center along Fulton Street remained unchanged for three decades. Empty lots on Market Street at Fulton and Leavenworth Streets were eventually occupied by one- to five-story brick or concrete buildings of no architectural distinction. Even a gas station opened on Fulton Street. Fulton and Leavenworth joined at Market Street, providing a suitable entrance for parades transferring from Market to Civic Center Plaza for their final reviews.

On November 6, 1962, the voters of San Francisco, Alameda, and Contra Costa Counties approved the establishment of the Bay Area Rapid Transit District (BARTD) and the construction of a subway up Market Street with an underground Civic Center Station between Seventh and Eighth Streets as part of a three-county transportation system. This development would dramatically change the Civic Center's eastern edge. Engineering the subway called for digging a deep trench the length of Market and excavating under sidewalks where new stations would be built, as well as acquiring and demolishing all commercial buildings between Hyde and Seventh Streets, except for the Orpheum Theater and a small Methodist bookstore off of Leavenworth. Seventh Street would be extended across Market to connect with McAllister Street.[29]

The impending upheaval and disruption of Market Street prompted the city to establish the Market Street Development Project to plan and implement changes to the area's traffic patterns, pedestrian circulation, subway entrances, and other surface features. In June 1966 the city obtained a $20 million federal grant to help pay for designing and constructing new plazas at the Civic Center and at Powell Street stations.[30] Mario Ciampi and Associates and John Carl Warnecke and Associates were engaged as architects, and Halprin was selected as the landscape architect. They published their first report in November 1967, calling for four lanes of traffic on Market Street and wide red-brick sidewalks extending its length. For what now would be a huge plaza at the Civic Center Station at Fulton Street, they acknowledged the historic Federal Building but paid no attention to designs for Fulton Street in Howard's 1912 plan or the ideas developed under Rolph in the 1920s or the Orpheum Theatre's blank walls. They recognized Fulton as the ceremonial entrance way to Civic Center, but not as a street—only as part of a plaza. To integrate it into the new Market Street plans, they proposed extending the red-brick sidewalk to cover Fulton from Market to Hyde Street. They proposed a simple entrance to the Civic Center Station at the back of the Orpheum Theatre and decorative plaza sculptures.[31]

After the planners created estimates for work along the full extent of Market Street, the city determined that they needed additional funds. A special election was called for June 4, 1968, to authorize $24,500,000 in bonds to pay for improvements.[32] Voters approved the measure, and planning continued. At the same time, BART began digging the Market Street trench and demolishing buildings around Fulton Street.

The development project designers presented their revised proposal for Civic Center Station Plaza (now United Nations Plaza) to the Civic Design Committee of the San Francisco Arts Commission on December 21, 1970. The report called for an enormous pedestrian opening to the station south of the Fulton Street axis. Long escalators would transport riders to and from a deep open-air passageway, offering an experience similar to entering a cave or mine shaft. A large fountain designed by Halprin would be located on the north side of the Fulton Street axis, at the Leavenworth Street line. Halprin had developed an affection for Sierra Nevada views of water coursing through huge granite rocks, and he tried to bring that effect to his fountain by placing gigantic stacks of granite slabs around its outer edge up to twenty feet tall and smaller chunks of granite in the center, over which shot several spouts of water that eventually collected in pools. Visitors would be able to walk within the fountain itself. This would not be a Beaux-Arts experience, but one of raw nature.

When Halprin's plans were presented to the Civic Design Committee of the Arts Commission, the prominent architect and arts commissioner Ernest Born attacked them: "This is a flamboyant example of a designer's ego. . . . It's hypocrisy. Whoever designed this wasn't thinking of the people who are going to use it, he was only thinking about himself. Why does the thing have to be so vulgar?" The committee deferred a decision on the fountain pending further consultation with the design team.[33]

The proposed fountain was presented to the entire Arts Commission on May 7, 1971, where it was subject to another round of negative comments. Architect Thomas Hsieh said that "it is a very fine design for a shopping center, but it has nothing to do with Market Street and nothing to do with Civic Center." Noted sculptor Ruth Asawa called it "brutal. A very stark thing. It has no relationship to anything. . . . You have to design places in the city for people to sit on the grass, sit under trees, for flowers, for birds. The fountain accomplishes none of these objectives."[34]

The unfavorable comments delayed, yet again, the design approval while the fountain was reassessed. However, time was running out to begin construction on the plaza surface, and the plans already had the support of Mayor Joseph Alioto and other city officials. The commission met again on November 1, 1971, to consider a revised scheme. The fountain's dimensions were unchanged, as was its Sierra-inspired mix of granite and water. The primary change was a reduction of the height of the outer granite slabs to one closer to that of the inner stones, changing the scale. The commissioners approved the fountain with this alteration without mentioning their previous criticisms.[35]

The new United Nations Plaza was built according to plan, but it had little public appeal. The fountain, intended to represent the seven continents, continued to inspire derision. Temko called it "pretentious schmaltz . . . whose 'tidal pools' are supposed to simulate global oceanic action but rarely work and merely toss around empty muscatel bottles."[36]

In 1995, to commemorate the fiftieth anniversary of the signing of the United Nations Charter in San Francisco, private parties raised funds to embellish the plaza by embedding in the red-brick walkway granite plaques with specific references to the UN Charter and adding to the light posts lists of UN member nations. These adornments did not increase the plaza's attraction to visitors, but the installation of a twice-a-week farmers' market did. Several efforts to rethink the plaza and fountain were undertaken but without results, partly because of opposition by Halprin and his followers.

The Seeds of Historical Preservation

Despite the new artistic and design trends in the period following World War II, San Francisco's historical and largely neoclassical Civic Center survived the pressures of these interventions of the postwar modernist period. New buildings were proposed, such as the courthouse, but none had been built. Modern improvements were also proposed, but they were installed only in the Civic Auditorium. The only new construction was underground for the new exhibit hall and parking garage and on the plaza above it that was redesigned and rebuilt largely because of those excavations. But even these projects, after years of inept and hasty decisions, were widely disparaged by traditionalists and modernists alike. Although the Civic Center complex was generally respected by everyone who played a role in its development, few, if any, thought about preserving its historic integrity. They had practical goals—a successful convention industry, modern and efficient office space, and government service expansion. Ironically, what saved the Civic Center's historic integrity was the years of squabbling over issues such as a new courthouse and plaza aesthetics, the lack of strong leadership to initiate major changes, and the frugality of elected officials and taxpayers. Official parsimony also affected building maintenance. City Hall, in particular, suffered from inadequate plumbing repair, irregular painting, and other poorly conceived service. The city and the public were occupied by greater issues, such as neighborhood redevelopment around the city.

However, during the years of the Civic Center Plaza controversy, the seeds of historic preservation were planted. In 1962 the Junior League of San Francisco became concerned about the demolition of many of the city's fine old buildings and began a survey of historic resources in San Francisco, San Mateo, and Marin Counties. The results were published in 1968 in the seminal book *Here Today*,[37] which set the course for San Francisco's historic preservation. Consequently, the city established a Landmarks Preservation Advisory Board within the city government.

In 1978 the National Park Service placed San Francisco's Civic Center on the National Register of Historic Places. In 1994, Civic Center was designated a Historic District under the San Francisco Planning Code. These two designations have provided significant protection to the area and the Civic Center's buildings. They would encourage the public to take a deeper look at the Civic Center's importance to the city, something that would prove critical for galvanizing support for the funding of nearly $1 billion of extensive rehabilitation and upgrades to all the Civic Center's monumental buildings that was needed as a result of the damage they suffered from the 1989 Loma Prieta earthquake—a rehabilitation and restoration effort that continues to this day.

Late-Century Expansion:
Louise M. Davies Symphony Hall
and a New Library

By the late 1960s the principal buildings at the Civic Center no longer accommodated the uses for which they had been designed, and they were poorly maintained and generally ignored by the public. Wartime adaptations to City Hall, such as the concrete ceilings that had replaced light court skylights, had become permanent fixtures. Large areas were filled with wooden cubicles holding an ever-expanding city staff. The third- and fourth-floor courts were functioning over capacity, and court documents sat in piles in the court clerk's office. Decorative plasterwork discolored by time had not been cleaned or repaired, and even the drapes in the board of supervisors' chambers were frayed. Overcrowding in City Hall forced the city to rent office space in the surrounding blocks.

The neglect of City Hall and the Civic Center was the result of overly frugal politicians afraid to raise taxes, and a lack of leadership and a public concern for the municipal buildings. In a column dated December 13, 1965, *San Francisco Chronicle* columnist Herb Caen made this pointed critique: "On December 28, 1965, our beautiful City Hall—one of the finest examples of French renaissance in the land—will be fifty years old, and of course a gala celebration is planned. It is? Don't be ridiculous. NOTHING is planned. What are you, some sort of sentimental slob? . . . In the good old days, there would have been considerable festivities. The famous dome . . . would have been gilded for the Golden Anniversary. A new 'Avenue of Golden Lights' from Fulton to Market would have been dedicated—plus a new fountain in Civic Center. There would have been open house in the offices, a reception and music in the majestic rotunda. . . . But, these aren't the good old days. Happy 50th anyway, City Hall. And a quiet cheer for architects Bakewell and Brown, who cooked up a masterpiece."[1]

In addition to City Hall, another Civic Center building suffering from neglect was the San Francisco Public Library's main branch, which had reached its book storage capacity in 1944, forcing librarians to install bookshelves in hallways and reading rooms to handle the growing stock. Although the city continued to construct neighborhood branch libraries, the library system was never a high priority for city leaders. Thus, salaries remained low, staff were not profession-alized and included many part-time workers, cataloging was behind by several years, and books were organized in closed stacks. When periodic budget defi-cits occurred, the library was hit often with financial cuts and threatened with branch closures and fewer staff hours.

To overcome the library's low place among the city's priorities and to support its improvement, a group of ardent activists led by Marjorie Stern and Mary Louise Stong organized Friends of the San Francisco Public Library in February 1961. Founding sponsors came from the business and social elite. Shortly there-after, the Friends recruited several hundred members from across the com-munity and secured funds for its treasury. (They were able to afford a full-time executive director in 1967.)

The Friends of the San Francisco Public Library helped bring attention to the poor conditions of library system, an effort that would cause the elected officials to increase the budget to improve staffing, book buying, and storage. Nevertheless, the main library branch remained clearly inadequate. The library's 1962 budget included funds for a study of its problems, which was performed by local architect John Bolles and two national library experts. Their 1964 report concluded that expansion was necessary and could be accomplished in one of two ways: the existing building could be remodeled and expanded at the back, as had been the original plan in 1915, at a cost of $6.5 million, or a new building could be built at a cost of $12 million. The consultants favored a new building because even with improvements the existing building would be inefficient and difficult to operate. The San Francisco Public Library Commission endorsed the idea of a new building, and the Friends started to plan a campaign for a bond election in 1966 to finance its construction on Marshall Square. However, the will of the city's politicians to follow through was missing.

City Hall and the library were not the only Civic Center buildings to inad-equately accommodate their evolving occupants. The Veterans Building as a venue for the arts was becoming inadequate. The Museum of Modern Art on the fourth floor prospered and continually needed more space, often putting it at odds with the veterans groups that also used the building. In addition, the auditorium was considered dowdy and undesirable.

The War Memorial Opera House, too, could no longer serve its occupants well. The San Francisco Opera found it difficult to mount productions in repertory because the theater lacked sufficient space to store sets: for budgetary reasons, the size of the building had been reduced during the original design phase. As other arts organizations using the building matured, they wanted more room and a larger share of the Opera House calendar. The San Francisco Ballet, the oldest professional ballet company in America, had separated from the San Francisco Opera in 1942, and in 1944 it had begun the tradition of performing Tchaikovsky's *Nutcracker* during the holiday season. The company's skill and popularity grew, and by the 1960s the company wanted to use the Opera House for a full set of performances. The San Francisco Symphony also shared the building. It had originally relied on part-time players, but the symphony board wanted to retain full-time, career performers and launch longer seasons to improve the ensemble's quality and enhance its reputation as well as finances. In addition to Bay Area groups, national and international tour companies wished to rent the Opera House, which could accommodate them only a few days a year.

As early as 1960, leaders of the city's major arts organizations and the War Memorial board of trustees began to address their problems by proposing a "Musical Arts Building," or symphony hall, in a style conforming to the twin War Memorial buildings, at a cost of $10,750,000. The hall would be built across Franklin Street from the existing complex and would require the acquisition of several small residential and business properties between Franklin Street and the new Central Freeway. They also proposed building a 600-car garage under the new building. To tie together the two performance spaces, Franklin Street would be depressed and a platform built across it to connect the new structure to the Memorial Court. The two existing buildings would be rehabilitated, and the Museum of Modern Art would be expanded and upgraded. The total cost was $29 million, which was put before the voters in a November 2, 1965, general obligation bond measure. The bonds were supported by the mayor, board of supervisors, and labor, business, and community leaders. However, significant opposition arose from taxpayer groups led by the downtown property owner Louis Lurie, who argued that the proposed improvements were poorly planned and an extravagance to be enjoyed by the few and paid for by the many. The voters agreed, and the measure failed by a significant margin: 32 percent in favor, and 68 percent against. Three years later, the San Francisco Symphony musicians held a strike demanding full-time salaries and better working conditions, increasing pressure to build a performing arts center.

In January 1968, Joseph L. Alioto, a prominent antitrust lawyer and former chair of the city's redevelopment agency, became mayor of San Francisco. He had lofty aspirations for San Francisco not expressed since the time of Mayor Rolph's first term in office. Before he became chairman of the redevelopment agency, it had been mired with problems and poor leadership. As mayor, Alioto wanted to continue to move aggressively in what was then called slum clearance, demolishing whole neighborhoods and replacing the old structures with new modern housing, streets and parks. Also, unlike several predecessors, Alioto was a worldly man with a great love of arts and literature.

Sympathetic to the library's cause, Alioto appointed to the agency people he felt could raise funds. He also facilitated a federal grant to support a new study of the library's needs, which was conducted again by architect John Bolles and the Arthur D. Little consulting firm. They recommended a new nine-story main library building costing nearly $40 million in the report they released on January 19, 1971. Library supporters hoped to have a bond issue for that amount on the ballot in 1972, but the San Francisco Capital Improvements Advisory Committee raised the issue of priorities, considering that there were many other construction projects going on in the city at the time.

Alioto decided to shake up the system when the position of city librarian became open in July 1973. He nominated Kevin Starr, a San Francisco native with a PhD from Harvard who had recently published an award-winning book on California history, *Americans and the California Dream, 1850–1915.* Starr was spending a sabbatical from Harvard working on cultural affairs in Alioto's office. Although Alioto was pleased with himself for this radical move, the professional librarians and the Friends board were outraged because Starr was not a trained librarian. They were also put off by Alioto's nomination letter, in which he said, "Starr exemplifies the true spirit of what a San Francisco Librarian should be. He stands in sharp contrast to so many arid professionals who lose touch with the wonderful world of books."[2] Nevertheless, the library commission went ahead and appointed Starr, but only to the temporary position of acting city librarian. In response, Starr enrolled at the University of California, Berkeley, to obtain a library science degree at night, a move that did not placate his critics because they claimed he was getting on-the-job training. But the following July, after Starr finished his master's degree in library science, he was appointed city librarian.

While Alioto and library supporters pushed ahead with plans for a new main branch, the needs of the performing arts organizations were also being addressed. In 1968 Harold Zellerbach, retired paper company executive and longtime chairman of the San Francisco Arts Commission, directed the Zellerbach Family Fund to sponsor a performing arts center study by Vernon DeMars, a professor of architecture at the University of California and the architect of Zellerbach Hall on the Berkeley campus. On September 28, 1969, DeMars released a plan focused again on the west side of Franklin Street for a contemporary 2,700-seat multipurpose hall for symphony, ballet, and pop performances located on two blocks that included the Fulton Street right-of-way and a raised platform over Franklin Street. He also called for a large garage on the Grove Street portion of the south block. Mayor Alioto, on November 21, 1970, appointed twenty-five prominent citizens to the San Francisco Committee for a Performing Arts Center to officially study DeMars's proposal.

The committee quickly came to the conclusion that voters were unlikely to support any bond issue, so they would have to find other ways to raise funds. This also meant that they would have to lower the project's cost, so DeMars was instructed to prepare new plans for a center costing no more than $18 million, not including funds to expand the Opera House stage. On January 4, 1973, Alioto and the committee announced the new plan for the Performing Arts Center (PAC) on Franklin Street and asked the board of supervisors to set aside $1 million a year for five years from federal revenue-sharing funds as the city's contribution to the project. At the April 3, 1973, meeting, the board of supervisors' cultural affairs committee considered the pledge. A group of street artists and community cultural organizations led by Richard Reineccius, from the Julian Theater, appeared to oppose the Performing Arts Center concept and the city's contribution. Their protest was lively, and Joan Mankin, a member of the San Francisco Mime Troupe, threw a whipped-cream pie at a PAC supporter. They argued that city funds should be spent on neighborhood arts activities and that the Performing Arts Center should not take property from small businesses and housing from low-income people.[3]

Although the protesters did not block the Performing Arts Center project, they did succeed in some of their demands. At the supervisors' cultural affairs committee meeting on May 2, 1973, members went ahead and voted to provide $1 million for the Performing Arts Center as well as $500,000 for a neighborhood arts program, two projects that Supervisor John Molinari pointed out were not mutually exclusive.[4] The board of supervisors approved these appropriations on June 18, 1973. Alioto, concerned about the opposition to and controversy over the Performing Arts Center, decided that more vigorous leadership was required and arranged for Samuel Stewart, retired vice chairman of the Bank of America, to serve as the performing arts committee's chairman and Supervisor Ronald Pelosi to serve as vice chairman. The San Francisco Performing Arts Center, a parallel organization, was incorporated as a foundation to raise funds for the project.

Because of the controversy surrounding the Franklin Street site, the new leadership decided to try to secure a less controversial one at little or no cost. One option was the block directly south of the War Memorial Opera House, which the Opera House committee had bought in the 1920s but then sold to the school district after two blocks in front of City Hall were acquired. The school district used the block as a playing field for Commerce High School, and, when the school closed in 1952, the block became a commercial parking lot. But there were questions about the ownership of the school district block and how easily the district would give it up. The other obvious site was Marshall Square, where John Galen Howard's original Civic Center Plan had located the opera house. It was owned by the city and vacant, with the exception of the World War II–era hospitality building being used by the San Francisco Planning Department. Because the Marshall Square site seemed more clear-cut, the PAC sponsors began discussing this site with the mayor and other city officials. DeMars estimated the cost of a new building at that location to be only $15 million.

However, despite the fact that Marshall Square was legally more straightforward, this was the site the library supporters had been planning for years to use for the new library. In April 1974, Mayor Alioto called library commissioner Edward Callanan to his office and asked him what resources the library had to build a new building at Marshall Square. When Callanan said that they had none, the mayor introduced him to Stewart and the other members of the PAC committee and said that they did have resources and wanted Marshall Square for the Performing Arts Center. Despite Callanan's opposition to the plan, the mayor publicly endorsed the new PAC proposal on May 1, 1974.

When Friends of the Library learned of the mayor's decision, they were outraged and felt betrayed. They held a press conference on May 5, 1974, to protest and started organizing a petition campaign and creating a list of prominent writers and other library supporters. Starr was put in a difficult place by the controversy, but he strongly sided with the library against the mayor. On May 8, 1974, the library commission voted unanimously against using Marshall Square for anything but the library.[5]

The first battle over the decision to designate Marshall Square as the location of the Performing Arts Center occurred at the San Francisco Planning Commission meeting on August 8. Library supporters turned out in large numbers, and library commissioner Reverend Timothy McDonnell attacked the Performing Arts Center as a "playhouse for the privileged who live in Marin and Hillsborough." Starr said, "If the City takes Marshall Square away from the Library, it will be the latest in a series of indignities that the Library has suffered."[6] Nevertheless, on the recommendation of Allan Jacobs, the city's planning director, the planning commission voted unanimously in favor of the PAC use of the Marshall Square block.

The PAC sponsors kept up their fundraising momentum, announcing on October 10, 1974, that Zellerbach had pledged $1 million to the project. To add heft to their design team, they added Pietro Belluschi, a leader of American modernist architecture and the former dean of architecture at MIT. He was well-known in San Francisco, having worked on the Cathedral of Saint Mary of the Assumption on Gough Street and the Bank of America Center, a skyscraper located downtown. On November 26, 1974, DeMars and Belluschi published plans for a modern rectangular building at Marshall Square with a 3,000-seat fan-shaped auditorium. "What is hoped for," Belluschi said, "is a Civic Center in the full meaning of the term, with the new building giving no visual offense to the formal classical buildings surrounding it. . . . We can't produce a strong modern statement to confuse the current general concept."[7] The neighborhood arts activists continued to criticize the project and its use of city and federal funds.

When the board of supervisors' finance committee met on December 4, 1974, to consider the PAC proposal, they were faced with massive opposition organized by Friends of the Library. The Friends had focused their campaign on the board, assembling allies and gathering signatures on their petition, which boasted 15,000 names. Uncomfortable with all aspects of the controversy, the supervisors tentatively voted to give Marshall Square to the Performing Arts Center, but they asked Supervisor Pelosi to try to work out an acceptable settlement among the parties.[8]

Considering the passion and unwavering insistence on the part of the library supporters to use the Marshall Square block for the new building, Pelosi's only real hope to appease both groups would be to find a way to secure the school district block for the Performing Arts Center and leave Marshall Square for the library, something that that the PAC supporters had previously understood as being an unlikely option. However, boosting the possibility of this solution, Pelosi had recently obtained a game-changing opinion from the city attorney that the school district property had been originally bought with funds from city bonds, and therefore the city technically owned the property outright and could take possession of it immediately. Although realistically this would require some negotiations with the school district, the city was now in a much stronger position to decide how to use the properties.

Stewart and his colleagues on the performing arts committee made it clear they were amenable to this deal, but they wanted quick resolution since they were soliciting contributions and pledges from people who would not commit until they knew where the Performing Arts Center was going to be located. On January 14, 1975, library commissioner Callanan further raised the ante by threatening to organize a referendum if the supervisors granted Marshall Square to the Performing Arts Center.[9] After much give and take, with Stewart complaining frequently about delays, the city and the board of education approved an agreement on February 4, 1975, whereby the school district would convey their block to the city in return for the city waiving any rights to other district properties.[10] Library supporters were obviously relieved by this outcome, and with their petition now bearing 50,000 signatures, Starr quickly declared that the library would seek a bond election for a new main library in 1976.[11]

With a designated location and a green light, the PAC sponsors went to work. On June 30, 1975, they announced that Louise M. Davies had pledged $5 million to the project; therefore, the building would be named after her. On July 14 they publicly presented the preliminary design for a building with a square corner at Van Ness Avenue and Grove Street and a midblock entrance.[12] The new location prompted the PAC committee to decide to change architects to Skidmore, Owings & Merrill, adding the highly regarded local partner Edward Charles Bassett joining Belluschi. The two offices had worked together on the Bank of America Center. Bassett was a modernist who had begun his career working in the office of Eero Saarinen. The *San Francisco Chronicle*'s Allan Temko described him as a "leader in the efforts of younger modern architects to seek alternatives to the arid formulas of the International Style."[13]

In January 1976 George Moscone succeeded Joseph Alioto as mayor. Shortly thereafter Starr resigned as city librarian to write a sequel to his book *Americans and the California Dream*. Although Moscone ran as a progressive controlled-growth candidate as a reaction to Alioto, he supported the Performing Arts Center, and his administration obtained a federal grant to pay for most of the Opera House expansion that had also been included in the project's design.

On September 23, 1976, the proposed design of a modern, partially curved building containing a 3,000-seat auditorium with an entrance on Grove Street was released. Made of finely finished concrete, its color and refined rusticated base echoed the War Memorial buildings on the neighboring block.[14] The PAC sponsors continued fund-raising efforts, and by November they had collected $17.1 million in private contributions. On February 23, 1978, after nearly twenty years of effort, the city broke ground on Civic Center's newest addition. Temko wrote that Davies Symphony Hall "will be an extraordinary work of art, at once disquieting and brilliant, which would not be right anywhere but on this site just south of the Opera House on the great neo-classical Civic Center." It was "slavishly classical in concept . . . influenced . . . by the powerful presence of Arthur Brown Jr." and held an uneasy truce with modern design, Temko asserted. Furthermore, he reported that Bassett had reasoned that if the concert hall was to hold its own, it should share the monumental harmony found in Howard's Civic Center master plan.[15] The first performance of Davies Symphony Hall was in September 1980.

Louise M. Davies Symphony Hall opened in 1980 with round façade across Grove Street from the War Memorial Opera House. Source: Courtesy Wikimedia commons, https://commons.wikimedia.org/wiki/File:Louise_M._Davies_Symphony_Hall-San_Francisco.jpg, Photograph by Yair Haklai.

Meanwhile, during the years that Davies Symphony Hall was under construction, the block on Van Ness Avenue across McAllister Street from the Veterans Building became a candidate for another massive public building. The state had been considering constructing a new state office building in San Francisco and in his budget for the fiscal year 1978, Governor Edmund G. Brown Jr. had included $2.9 million to purchase a suitable site, with the likelihood that it would be on the Van Ness block. The block contained small commercial buildings owned by the San Francisco Redevelopment Agency and parking lots and an empty five-story building owned by the state of California. The redevelopment agency director, Wilbur Hamilton, told the press that the state was interested in the property, but, since the location was highly visible from Civic Center, it would not be good for "an institutional building, the way governmental buildings usually look."[16]

The state architect, Sim Van der Ryn, was sympathetic to Hamilton's design concerns, but he wanted a building that was energy-efficient. He selected the Davies Symphony Hall architects Skidmore, Owings & Merrill as the firm best able to design a building compatible with the Civic Center that would meet energy standards. The state and the San Francisco Redevelopment Agency set up a joint-powers agency to finance and build a structure that the state would lease from the agency. By the end of 1980, the design was ready, calling for a five-story building that covered the block, with the exception of an apartment house on the southwest corner. The new building had a round corner on McAllister Street, to echo the round corner of Davies Symphony Hall, and a grand staircase and entrance through the curved façade leading into a large inner courtyard lined with offices, which would benefit from good air flow and energy-saving opportunities. The base level was symbolically rusticated, and the top story sloped inward. The external surfaces were precast concrete and granite with a color and texture similar to other Civic Center buildings. On June 14, 1981, the state legislature approved construction of the $34.4 million building.[17] Work began in July 1983, and, on completion in January 1986, it was named the Edmund G. Brown State Building, after the governor's father. Over the main entrance was hung the Great Seal of the State of California, sculpted by the Californian artist Rosa Estebanez.

Creating sympathetic twin modern structures to bookend the twin neo-baroque War Memorial buildings was an extraordinary achievement, considering that all were conceived and constructed as public buildings. The critic Temko, however, reacted negatively to the new State Building, calling it a "Monument to a Mindless State." He started his column with, "The ghost of Mussolini would feel alive and well behind the crass, pseudo-classical façade at Van Ness and McAllister Streets. Not to worry. The massive curved front has been festooned with a giant fiberglass facsimile of the Great Seal of California, in Disneyish color, so that we will know we are not in a totalitarian state." He then lightened up by saying, "Considered only as abstract forms in the Cityscape, the new buildings succeed admirably. Their heavy massing, triple-tiered façades and swept-back copper roofs hold their own against formidable neighbors, composing a single symmetrical group four blocks long." Temko focused his ire on the architects, writing, "SOM tried to approximate a classical manner responding in scale, proportion and line . . . to the War Memorial and City Hall. It was a bit like staging *Julius Caesar* in modern dress, and under the circumstances was doomed to fail." He accused them of "being beyond their depth in a project of this order."[18] Ironically, he had praised the firm ten years before for the similar design of Davies Symphony Hall.

Despite the success of these two Civic Center projects, the bond issue to fund a new main library was thwarted by the economic downturn and city budget crisis of 1976 and 1977 and then stopped by state Proposition 13, which passed on June 6, 1978. This initiative was an anti-property tax measure put on the ballot by activists concerned about significant increases in property taxes and government spending. It was intended to uniformly limit the property tax rate statewide. One of its effects was to make unconstitutional local government issuance of new general obligation bonds, thus restricting long-term capital and infrastructure projects, such as building new libraries. (This limitation put such a stranglehold on local government improvements and developments that, on June 3, 1986, a constitutional amendment to allow for general obligation bonds was placed before the state voters as Proposition 46, and passed.)

Right around this same moment in San Francisco history, a tragic event cast a pall over the city in 1978. On November 27, after nearly three years in office, Mayor Moscone was assassinated in City Hall by a member of the board of supervisors. As president of the board, Dianne Feinstein became acting mayor, and then board colleagues confirmed her mayorship by election. Her immediate job was to stabilize the city, which she did so well that voters elected her as mayor in her own right in November 1979, the start of two terms in office.

It wasn't until 1984 that the library commission and the Friends of the San Francisco Public Library felt optimistic enough about the possible passage of a constitutional amendment to renew bond financing to begin plans for a bond campaign and a new library. The indefatigable library commissioner Stern invited civic activists and community leaders to her grand Russian Hill apartment in the fall to discuss the new effort.

Stern, my mother's childhood friend, invited me to attend, knowing that I had been involved in a number of community activities besides my legal practice. I agreed to join the effort, and in January 1985 I became a member of the board of the Friends of the San Francisco Public Library. My first task was to help persuade Mayor Feinstein, now in her second term, to pay attention to the project. She was a hard-headed, practical person who wanted to know all about something before she would support it. She had heretofore shown little interest in a new main library.

I had known and supported Mayor Feinstein since 1969, so I felt free to ask her by letter to consider a new main library building in the larger context of making it "part of a grand scheme for the cultural redevelopment of the east side of Civic Center." Besides calling out a new library at Marshall Square, I proposed turning over the old library building to the Museum of Modern Art, which desperately needed more space, and to several additional, smaller groups. I suggested that these projects "would be a wonderful and lasting achievement for your administration."[19] The mayor responded by letter saying that she had considered my ideas with great interest and had coincidentally convened a "Museum Consortium" of all the city's museums to consider their space needs. However, she cautioned that there was a lot of work ahead of us to obtain cost estimates and revenue projections.

As the efforts to figure out how to fund the construction of a new main library branch on Marshall Square continued, the questions remained about what to do with the old library. The old library was located on the block on the corner of Larkin and McAllister Streets just off the eastern edge of the Civic Center Plaza. It had been built in 1917 and held a prominent position within the Civic Center. While the movement to construct a major new main library continued, a future for the old library became an increasingly pressing one.

Meanwhile, the drive to secure funding for the new library building was ongoing. On May 8, 1985, Feinstein held a meeting to discuss a new main library with John C. Frantz, the city librarian; Stern and several other library commissioners; Supervisor Louise Renne; and a representative of the Friends. Frantz wrote to the library commission, stating that the mayor was focusing on the source of the money to pay for the project; he urged the commission to create a high-level committee of business people who could coordinate fund-raising. The mayor was "unenthusiastic about having the Library vacate the present building but acknowledged that more space was needed." She suggested a new multiuse building at Marshall Square that the library would share with others. Frantz concluded, "The mayor was not as sympathetic or as encouraging as we would have liked, but she clearly left open the door to more and better planning to solve the library's space needs."[20]

The mayor offered the opportunity, but she didn't promise resources; nevertheless, the Friends jumped in and started working. By then, the Friends had developed considerable resources, staff, and fundraising skills. First, they commissioned national consultants to do another study of the old main library, which was released on September 30, 1986, and concluded, not surprisingly, that the existing building was dysfunctional: Books were stored on the floors of the stacks; fire and safety hazards went unaddressed; and offices were cramped. They concluded that a new building at Marshall Square would eliminate the problems. Feinstein, true to form, was not about to espouse such an expensive project unless she knew that there was no possibility that the old library could not be rehabilitated and expanded. So the Friends raised more money and asked the consultants to study whether the needs of a modern library could be met by the old building. The Friends also commissioned Skidmore, Owings & Merrill to study the old library for alternative uses.

In the meantime, Feinstein's interest in the Civic Center grew from accommodating museums to completing and refurbishing the whole area. In early 1986, she asked Peter Henschel, her budget director and cultural affairs adviser, to convene a city task force to work with city agencies and the private sector on a new development plan that, as Henschel noted, involved a whole set of dominoes. "If we say 'yes' to the New Main [library], what do we do with the Old Main, what about the City's need for office space, about new courts?"[21]

On August 26, 1986, Feinstein's old political nemesis, Supervisor Quentin Kopp, went public with his own Civic Center development plan. Kopp was a rare conservative in San Francisco's political scene who for the next twenty years would take spirited aim at a succession of City Hall initiatives he deemed wasteful. Nevertheless, his Civic Center proposal called for a new main library on Marshall Square at a cost of $60 million, a new city office building on the corner of Polk and McAllister Streets at a cost of $50 million, and the reconstruction of the old main library as a courthouse at a cost of $30 million. He said that plans for such projects had been kicking around for years, and he intended to ask the board of supervisors to pass "an omnibus resolution to get something going." Kopp had no supporting studies on the feasibility or costs of these projects, leading Henschel to tell the press: "Kopp's move to immediate recommendations is a bit premature."[22] Ultimately, to get the votes necessary to pass his resolution on October 27, 1986, Kopp had to water it down to a request for planning and developing projects that would relocate the courts to a "suitable space."[23] In any case, his bit of mischief increased welcome exposure of Feinstein's and Henschel's efforts to complete a plan.

While Henschel and the city planning department worked on a draft report and waited for the Friends of the Library to complete their studies, the Urban Design Committee of the San Francisco chapter of the American Institute of Architects offered to undertake a design charrette and urban form study of Civic Center "to reawaken the public/civic spirit in the Civic Center Area." They cooperated with Henschel and other city staff and issued a report in October 1987. The primary recommendation was to "complete and restore the original 1912 Civic Center master plan in concept providing a formal Civic Center composition and character to the district." They emphasized that the Civic Center should be a district with a distinct character, not just a collection of buildings. To that end, they recommended constructing public buildings on Marshall Square and on the empty corners facing the plaza. The remainder of the twenty-page report dealt with pedestrian and vehicle circulation, streetscaping, and architecture.[24]

The city planning department's report and the mayor's recommendations continued to develop throughout the summer of 1987 while key pieces fell into place. The Museum of Modern Art informed the mayor that, rather than take over the old library building, it wanted to construct a new building at a location outside of the Civic Center on Third Street, in an area undergoing redevelopment with new hotels and the city's new convention center named after the later mayor George Moscone. Henschel then approached the Asian Art Museum to see if it would be interested in taking over the old library. The museum, which held the inestimable Avery Brundage Asian art collection, was located in an inadequate wing of the de Young Museum in Golden Gate Park and was eager to set up an independent identity and facility elsewhere. Judy Wilbur, president of the Asian Art Commission's board, responded positively to Henschel's inquiry, thus a suitable occupant for the building who might be able to get wide public support was found.[25]

Mayor Feinstein delivered her final State of the City message on October 5, 1987. Among many topics, she previewed her Civic Center proposal, calling the center "the jewel in our crown" and recommending a new main library on Marshall Square "to complete the original scheme." As for the old library, she suggested that it become a home for the Asian Art Museum or the courts, although she cautioned that the Hall of Justice might be the better location for the courts.[26]

The planning department's development report was finally completed at the end of October. Sixty-five pages long, it comprehensively discussed the Civic Center's seventy-five-year history; existing considerations and needs, particularly for city offices; development opportunities; and their recommendations. It did not deal with financing, which at the time was constrained by the city's fiscal deficits. Feinstein's accompanying Civic Center proposal used several aspects of the planning report and discussed financing in detail. In the report transmittal letter of November 3, 1987, Feinstein stated that the city's general fund could not be a source of support at that time. She also apologized for submitting her proposal so late in her administration, explaining that "once work began, it became clear that there were a large number of unanswered questions requiring detailed technical review. . . . We now have the necessary studies and consultants' analyses to proceed."

Her first and most significant recommendation was to build a new main library on Marshall Square, since "a key to our future is a great public library." After three years of work and studies, she had unconditionally accepted the library commission's and the Friends' point of view, a heroic achievement on their part. To finance this new major public building, she proposed securing $25 million from a state library bond issue proposed for the June 1988 election, $30 million from a city bond measure to be put on the November 1988 ballot, and $15 million from private funds. Second, she recommended that the old main library be turned over to the Asian Art Museum. To pay for the project, she proposed that the city include the seismic work in a proposed citywide seismic bond issue and that remodeling be covered by private funds. She admitted that the courts could be located in the building but at a high cost and with constraints on future expansion. An additional disincentive to placing the courts in the old library building was that remodeling could not begin until the library moved to its new home in 1995, requiring the courts to remain in cramped quarters at City Hall for another ten years. Thus, her third recommendation was to build a consolidated courthouse on Bryant Street several blocks away from the Civic Center adjacent to the Hall of Justice, providing San Francisco with a dedicated courthouse for the first time in its history. At that location, she argued, there would be space for the courts and ancillary offices as well as room for expansion. To finance the structure, she proposed raising court fees, using state bond funds, and taking advantage of rent savings. The momentum behind these projects at this point would finally result in both the new main library and courthouse being built and the old main library being converted into the Asian Art Museum, but it would be done at costs double or triple those estimated by Feinstein's administration, partly because of sharp increases in the cost of creating seismically safe structures.

Feinstein also pointed out in her proposal the need for more city-owned office space to reduce rental costs, but added that it was not a good time for new construction for this, which would be a charge against the general fund. Nevertheless, she suggested that the city reserve several underdeveloped parcels in the Civic Center area for that purpose and possibly acquire adjoining private parcels to yield large potential development sites for future city development. She concluded by supporting several "subordinate" elements from the planning department's report, including restoring Civic Center Plaza to its original 1913 Howard design, converting Fulton Street between the old and new library buildings into a "genuine pedestrian mall," and expanding the Civic Center Garage under Fulton Street. Although she did not mention it, the planning department report also recommended restoring the original historic City Hall floor plan, which would mean reestablishing the two light courts. She concluded her letter by writing "that implementation will require great effort and will offer major public improvements which benefit all San Franciscans."

To give her proposal and the planning department report official standing, Feinstein asked the board of supervisors to accept them in principle, which would not make them binding but would give them the status of official guidance. The judges were pleased that their miserable situation was being addressed and endorsed the plan, although they had mixed feelings about moving to Bryant Street, an industrial district where the criminal courts were located. The Asian Art Commission endorsed taking over the old library, and the library commission enthusiastically supported a new main library at Marshall Square. Mayor-elect Art Agnos commented that he had not yet had time to study the report, but had campaigned in favor of a new library at Marshall Square because he was well acquainted with the inadequacies of the existing building.

Temko wrote that Feinstein's proposal was much sounder after her staff had worked on it for more than a year, but the plan still left open questions about costs and design. He stressed that "the library must be a good contemporary building . . . with a fearless vision of democratic government, freshly minted for our time, but classical in essence so that it will live happily with the rest of Civic Center."[27] The only dissent came from former supervisor and now state senator Kopp, who wrote the following in a letter to the editor of the *San Francisco Chronicle* titled "Colossal Stupidity": "The mayor's Civic Center proposal is inadequate, imprudent and financially destructive." He called the proposal to build a new courthouse on Bryant Street unwise and accused Feinstein of "alarming negligence for not considering the School District property at 135 Van Ness for the courthouse." He pledged to oppose any of the proposed projects should bond measures be placed on the ballot.[28]

Feinstein's proposal was discussed at a special meeting of the board's public works committee on December 19, 1987. Several city officials and commissioners spoke in favor of the recommendations. On December 21 the board passed a resolution unanimously accepting the documents in principle, extended its appreciation to the mayor and her staff for doing such extensive work, and urged the city's chief administrative officer to implement the recommendations.[29]

Over the course of nearly three years, Feinstein was engrossed in the details of how to complete and enhance the city's great Civic Center, and she eventually espoused "a grand scheme," which became one of her legacies. Her plan's publication at the end of 1987 occurred precisely seventy-five years after Howard published the original Civic Center plan. No one in the intervening decades had given the original plan as much consideration as Feinstein had, and her work provided the benchmark for further developments over the next thirty years. However, as the planning department's report admonished, "A renewal of the spirit which created the inspiration for a grand governmental center is needed to accomplish the task."

Recent Decades and the Present: Building Toward Civic Center's Centennial

More than one hundred years have passed since the first buildings of the Civic Center were finished for the visitors to the Panama-Pacific International Exposition to see in 1915. Mayor James Rolph during his five terms as mayor oversaw the construction of additional buildings outlined in John Galen Howard's plan, including the magnificent City Hall, plus two more when the decision was made to expand the Civic Center plan west of Van Ness Avenue to accommodate the War Memorial cultural facilities.

It would not be until near the end of Mayor Dianne Feinstein's administration that the original Civic Center plan would be revisited with a goal to complete it. In these last three years Mayor Feinstein had prepared and left to her successors a new plan to finish off the Civic Center with a new library, court house and Asian Art Museum and to pull together and improve the whole district as one coherent place. Her plan provided the incentive to city officials as well as judges and library lovers to proceed.

The 1989 Loma Prieta earthquake damaged most of the Civic Center buildings and provided a second incentive to repair and restore them. All of this construction when done cost almost $1.5 billion, a significant portion of which the citizens of San Francisco paid for by authorizing the city to sell bonds. However, each new or rehabilitated building became its own single project with its own supporters. This meant that few if anyone was paying attention to what each renovation meant for the Civic Center as a whole. For example, the disputes that would erupt during this time over the remodeling of the old main library for the Asian Art Museum and Mayor Willie Brown's plans for the restored City Hall frequently ignored what was at stake for the grand scheme of the Civic Center. Additionally, despite the focus on the buildings, the plaza and public areas were being neglected, leading to a lack of visitors and activity. At times, they have appeared as homeless encampments. This has led to an unfortunate paradox of development over the last twenty-five years—massive construction on the buildings, but done so in a way that is ignorant or neglectful of the broader area's needs, thus leading portions of the general population to avoid the Civic Center.

Despite the many starts and stops along the way—often a battle between inspired leaders and bureaucratic dysfunction—the Civic Center remains the key site for all of San Francisco's city government. Even though the site has been neglected at various times over the last century, its original architectural and social philosophies inspired by the City Beautiful movement continue to influence how San Francisco imagines and advances its primary municipal and civic developments.

This chapter brings into focus the most recent efforts by the city and the community to improve or maintain the Civic Center, efforts that—although consistently less than this author would like to see—nevertheless demonstrate that central place that the Civic Center has within San Francisco's municipal and cultural operations. Although the Civic Center does not always receive the kind of attention that many of San Francisco's most famous international landmarks receive, for more than one hundred years, the Civic Center has been one of the defining design and social visions of San Francisco—and it deserves an enduring public recognition of the extraordinary place it has in the city's history.

The Courts and the Library

When Mayor Feinstein left office in January 1988, her Civic Center development plan fell into the hands of Rudy Nothenberg, the city's chief administrative officer she had appointed to the post in 1986. To follow through on Feinstein's recommendations for the library and courthouse, Nothenberg needed to work with the San Francisco Public Library Commission and superior court judges.

Housing the courts in San Francisco had never been easy. In 1916, placement of the city's courts on the upper floors of the newly constructed City Hall was considered a temporary measure. In the 1920s Mayor Rolph made several unsuccessful attempts to build an independent courthouse in the Civic Center. In 1938 voters defeated a bond issue to fund a new courthouse and did so several more times in the 1950s. Court conditions in City Hall deteriorated over the decades, much to the frustration of judges and the San Francisco Bar Association. To sidestep voter reluctance around the state to support courthouse bond issues, in the 1980s the state legislature allowed courts to exact filing fees and penalties to use toward constructing and repairing local civil courthouses. Thus, when Nothenberg and the judges began to plan a new courthouse, financing was now available. Feinstein's proposal had recommended building a new civil courthouse next to the criminal courts at the Hall of Justice on Bryant Street. But that location would have incurred significant costs and required the condemnation of private parcels. Furthermore, civil court judges did not want to leave the Civic Center, where they had been located since the days of the old City Hall and where they were close to the state appellate and federal courts. The corner property at Polk and McAllister Streets purchased in the original Civic Center land acquisition in 1912 had been slated to accommodate a police and fire department headquarters. Instead by the 1980s, that property contained a small antiquated city office building and a leased gas station on the actual corner. Other properties on the same block were an apartment house, which was not for sale, and a building belonging to the Society of California Pioneers, which Nothenberg and the judges agreed combined with the city property would be a suitable location for the new courthouse. The firm of Ross Drulis Cusenbery Architecture, specialists in designing justice facilities, was asked to prepare courthouse studies in 1989.

Meanwhile, as the discussions surrounding the construction of a new courthouse continued, the library commissioners, the Friends of the San Francisco Public Library, and other library supporters had been preparing their campaign for a new main library. Months before Feinstein released her Civic Center report in 1987, the Friends hired the community organizer Marilyn Smulyan to help strategize and plan a bond election campaign. The Friends also recruited John Molinari, a senior member of the board of supervisors, to sponsor the bond ordinance at the board's first meeting in 1988. John Frantz, who had succeeded Kevin Starr as the city librarian, had never been enthusiastic about a new building and he resigned in March 1988, allowing the library commission to recruit a new city librarian with the skills and enthusiasm to lead the project. They selected Kenneth Dowlin, then head of the Colorado Springs Library and noted expert in modern libraries.

Mayor Art Agnos strongly supported their drive, so Nothenberg was tasked with guiding their energy and enthusiasm through the city's bureaucracy to get a bond issue on the November ballot. Unfortunately, the city was suffering from financial hard times, and budget cuts reduced branch library service, causing some people to question their timing.

Before the board of supervisors could consider Molinari's bond ordinance, the city had to prepare a bond program report, drafted by outside architectural consultants. They assumed that the new building would cover Marshall Square and that its classical design and materials would be nearly identical to those of the old main library and other Civic Center buildings. The report was released on June 10, 1988, with a cost estimate of $120,468,000 for the new library building, which triggered much anxiety among library supporters and city officials, since San Francisco voters had never before approved a bond issue for more than $100 million. The main library served as a branch for only the central part of the city, and leaders from other neighborhoods started asking if any funds would be made available to upgrade their antiquated branch buildings. The supervisors struggled to come up with what they hoped would be a successful bond measure, finally voting on July 11, 1988, for one totaling $109,500,000, of which $5 million would be reserved to pay for branch upgrades, leaving $16 million less for the new building than the consultants had suggested. Regarding the use of the old main library should the bond measure pass, the supervisors had prepared a charter amendment for the November ballot that would create a city Asian art commission authorized to take possession of the old library to house the new Asian Art Museum.

The Friends and other library supporters were ecstatic about the proposed bond measure, in spite of the reduced funding, and quickly implemented their bond campaign, with Sherry Agnos, the mayor's wife, as chairperson and Dick Pabich, a well-known political consultant, as campaign manager. A *San Francisco Chronicle* poll indicated that 75 percent of likely voters supported the bonds.[1] A small but active opposition group led by Gladys Hansen, the city archivist,[2] and state Senator Quentin Kopp[3] argued that the new library building was an extravagance and that remodeling and expanding the existing building would be a more suitable approach. In the end, the Friends campaign committee convinced many well-known people and interest groups in the city to support their efforts, and the bonds passed with 76.2 percent. Voters also approved the charter amendment establishing the old library as the new home for the Asian Art Museum, endorsing the second proposal in Feinstein's Civic Center development plan. After more than twenty years of struggle, Marjorie Stern and her library supporters finally had San Francisco on track for a new main library on Marshall Square, which had been a blank space in Howard's Civic Center plan since the demise of the original opera house scheme more than eighty years earlier.

The library commission, awed by the heavy responsibility of building a new library within the historic Civic Center, reached out to Ada Louise Huxtable, the former *New York Times* architecture critic, to oversee an architectural competition for the new building. In February 1989 the general specifications for the competition were published. Although the bond report gave the public the impression that the new library building would replicate the French neoclassical style of the old library, the specifications called only for a building with a mass comparable to the old building, along with base and cornice lines similar to those set by Howard in his original Civic Center plan. Allen Temko, the design critic for the *San Francisco Chronicle*, commented, "Granted, the new library must have a classical presence. It must live happily beside its venerable neighbors, but it must speak to the future at the same time. It can be a building of surpassing beauty and exhilarating freedom, worthy of a postindustrial era, within the classical humanist tradition."[4] Many prominent US and European architecture firms entered the competition. On June 15, 1989, Nothenberg announced the unanimous decision: James Ingo Freed, of the New York firm Pei Cobb Freed & Partners, and the local women-owned firm Simon Martin-Vegue Winkelstein Moris were selected to design the library. Pei Cobb Freed & Partners was well-known for its design of the east wing of the National Gallery of Art in Washington, DC, and the pyramid and underground areas of the Louvre in Paris. The decision was well received in San Francisco, and Temko wrote that the selection "was a victory for architectural excellence and affirmative action."[5]

An Earthquake Interrupts

At 5:04 pm on October 17, 1989, an earthquake measuring 7.1 on the Richter scale shook San Francisco's dynamics and well-established routines. The third game of the World Series was about to begin at Candlestick Park, and the commuter rush hour had begun. Several elevated freeways and a section of the Bay Bridge collapsed or were damaged. Isolated fires broke out in the Marina District. In areas south of Market Street, small wooden structures collapsed because of unstable soil conditions. Sixty-three people in the Bay Area died, but most San Franciscans experienced only inconveniences and short-term disruptions to their lives and were able to return to their normal lives within a few days.

All of the Civic Center buildings, with the exception of the newest, Davies Symphony Hall, suffered damage. The California State Office Building and Supreme Court and its annex from the 1950s were seriously weakened and were closed to further use. Before the earthquake, the state had already recognized the vulnerability of the building complex and had been preparing a seismic retrofit and upgrade.[6] The north wing of the main library suffered damage, but the most immediate problems were the cracked glass floors of the library stacks and the more than 100,000 books that had fallen from the shelves. They created a dangerous work environment, but, despite the serious risks, many library staff members volunteered to clean up and restore order and the main library reopened in three months.

City Hall and other Civic Center buildings suffered from cracked and falling plaster and required shoring up before being returned to public use. The War Memorial Opera House was one of these, but the San Francisco Opera had begun its fall season and could not afford to have its venue closed for long, so a screen was placed under the auditorium ceiling to catch loose debris. The underlying structure of all of the buildings in Civic Center, including City Hall and its grand dome, held up well—a testament to the engineers who had helped design them. However, further studies showed that they could be vulnerable to another earthquake of a comparable magnitude, and all of the buildings would have to be retrofitted and upgraded at great expense. Nothenberg quickly directed city staff to organize the enormous effort to construct, repair, and upgrade the Civic Center buildings. They prepared a program estimated to cost $332 million and submitted it as a bond measure to the board of supervisors on January 22, 1990, for the June 5 ballot. The voters passed the measure with an overwhelming 78 percent. Nothenberg told the public that, because of the deferred maintenance of Civic Center structures, "it is a big measure, but I think it's a more honest way to say that this is what it is going to take."[7] The estimate turned out to be very low, and additional bond measures had to be passed and other funding sources including the Federal Emergency Management Agency (FEMA), had to be secured over the next twenty-five years so that the city could complete the job.

Buildings had to be empty during seismic upgrades and repairs, which created complex logistical problems as organizations jockeyed for operating space elsewhere. While City Hall was repaired, the upper floors of the Veterans Building could temporarily accommodate the mayor, supervisors, and their staffs. But they would have to wait until after the San Francisco Museum of Modern Art moved out of the fourth floor and into its new Mario Botta–designed building on Third Street, scheduled for 1994. The San Francisco Opera could use the Civic Auditorium for performances during the eighteen months the War Memorial Opera House would be closed: the company had used the auditorium before and knew its assets and limitations. But work on the auditorium would have to be completed before they could move into the temporary venue. Before the Asian Art Museum could move into the converted old main library, the new library would have to be built, further complicating Civic Center occupancy. Many organizations, including the courts, used rental space throughout the city for several years.

The Courts and the Library, Resumed

While the library was being developed, work on the new Civic Center Courthouse on the corner of Polk and McAllister Streets proceeded apace. Judge William Cahill and his committee of judges had decision-making authority regarding the building's design, the complex financing, and the purchase of an adjacent private parcel, and their deliberations weren't completed until spring 1993.[8] That summer, Mark Cavagnero Associates and Ross Drulis Cusenbery Architecture were engaged as designers. Mark Cavagnero had worked for New York architect Edward Larrabee Barnes, who had designed many institutional buildings and was a finalist for the new main library.

Civic Center Courthouse, designed in a compatible style to the original Civic Center Buildings, opened in 1997. Source: Courtesy Mark Cavagnero Associates Architects.

Cavagnero had a joint office with Barnes in San Francisco, and this became his own office after he was selected to design the courthouse. Although a modernist in training and background, Cavagnero was sensitive to the Beaux-Arts Civic Center plan, the existing buildings, and the role the plaza's corner lots played in the overall plan. Cavagnero proposed a four-story monumental building with a chamfered corner, arched windows referencing those in the adjacent California State Supreme Court Building, and a cladding of Sierra White granite from the Raymond quarry, which had supplied granite for City Hall. The judges wanted a ceremonial courtroom, which was accommodated by placing a conical structure above the top floor that was visible from the plaza. Some viewed this addition as a controversial decision.[9] However, construction of the $83 million Civic Center Courthouse was unimpeded, and the new structure opened on December 8, 1997.

With similar momentum, the library project also moved ahead. After winning the library competition, the architect James Ingo Freed and his local partners from the firm Simon Martin-Vegue Winkelstein Moris needed to understand the library in light of important new issues: the rigorous seismic engineering requirements demanded after the 1989 earthquake, the bond report's building description, and the constrained budget, which required eliminating one floor in the proposed multistory basement.

The bond report called for the Pioneer Monument, originally installed in Marshall Square in 1894 in front of the old City Hall, to remain at the corner of

Hyde and Grove Streets, tucked into a curved cutout in a corner of the new library. The monument comprised a central statue of Eureka, representing California, on top of a column and four auxiliary piers supporting bronze sculptures of pioneer tableaux. Freed concluded that leaving the statues in place would reduce the building's useful square footage, possibly eliminate the lower-level auditorium, and reduce the size of the mezzanine-level children's section, as well as obscure the view of at least one side of the statuary group. It would also require more complicated construction, which would increase costs. The architect team and the library commission concluded that the best course would be to move the monument to the middle of Fulton Street, between the old and new library buildings on the City Hall east-west axis, where the work could be viewed on all sides.

Freed proposed that the new library have two façades—one facing the Civic Center, echoing the classical façades of the other buildings, and the other appearing on the Market Street side of the building, sporting a modernist approach. Although representations of columns and cornice lines appeared in the classical façade, the surface was nearly flat, not articulated. This change from tradition was the architect's intent, but it was also driven by budget constraints. The whole building would be covered in Sierra White granite from the Raymond quarry to match other Civic Center buildings. The building's interior would include several light courts, bringing natural light deep into the building. The central atrium, covered by a glass skylight resembling a nautilus, would give the interior an elegant quality.

Word of the architect team and library commission's design decisions reached the public in spring 1990. Soon the preservation group California Heritage Council organized opposition to moving the Pioneer Monument.[10] They claimed that the monument was the last vestige of the Victorian City Hall and should be retained. Of course Howard's 1912 Civic Center plan ignored the Victorian building arrangements. The board of supervisors debated whether to save the Victorian Hall of Records which conflicted with the new plan and made the decision to demolish it. Thus, the preservationists wanted to retain the monument in derogation of the plan. The following spring, Kopp dispatched letters to city agencies expressing his opposition to the move.[11] The civic group San Francisco Tomorrow weighed in against relocating the monument and also expressed concern about the building's façade.[12] This unexpected controversy put into question whether the planning commission would support the library commission's desire to relocate the monument. No formal decision could be made until the project's environmental impact report was certified in fall 1991, but in the meantime the controversy made library planning difficult. Therefore, the planning commission scheduled a library workshop for June 6, 1991, for people concerned about the fate of the monument.

In an effort to support the moving of the monument, Pabich, the library bond campaign manager, and I contacted Bobby Castillo, a Native American leader with the International Indian Treaty Council. One of the statues within the monument—called *Early Days*—was controversial, as it portrayed a Franciscan father and a Mexican vaquero standing over a supine Native American in a way that was offensive to Native Americans groups in California. Castillo came to the planning commission library meeting and was the first person to present his views, denouncing *Early Days* as depicting "genocide being committed on our people." He said he would personally like to "take that monument and dump it in the ocean," but realized that this was not possible, so he urged that it be moved so that a great public library could be built for everyone, including his young son, whom he had brought with him. After his presentation, the opposition meekly presented its viewpoint. All but one planning commissioner supported moving the monument, which eliminated it as an architectural design issue.[13] Yet the commissioners still expressed concerns about the façade design, which remained a negotiating point for several months.

The environmental certification was approved on February 27, 1992, allowing the project to proceed.[14] However, the site still contained the temporary 1941 Hospitality House that had been used as planning department office space since the end of World War II. The historic streamline moderne building generated much sentiment, but the city had no use for it, and it was finally offered to the public for one dollar, with the requirement that it be removed immediately from the property. The offer remained open for ninety days, but with no takers. So, on April 11, 1992, a brief ceremony was held by representatives of the San Francisco Building Trades Council, which had originally built it at no cost, and the council demolished it without charge as their contribution to the library project.[15]

By now, the new building was a $142 million project that needed $37 million more in private donations to furnish the interior which could not be paid for by the bond funds.[16] Funds of that magnitude for public libraries had never been raised in San Francisco, and fundraising consultants questioned whether it could be done. Stern was not deterred, however, and organized the Library Foundation, separate from the Friends, comprised of people adept at raising large sums. They secured a number of large contributions, but they also wanted broad participation. By the time they were finished, 17,000 people had contributed to the project, 12,000 of whom had pledged $1,000 or more. More than $37 million was raised—a grand testament to the private support of public libraries.

A festive library groundbreaking took place on April 23, 1992. As the excavation was underway, the workers uncovered old City Hall foundations and corpses, probably from the Yerba Buena Cemetery, so archaeologists and other

Moving the 1894 Pioneer Monument from its original location at the corner of Grove and Hyde Streets to the middle of Fulton Street to accommodate the construction of the new main library.
Source: Courtesy of San Francisco History Center, San Francisco Public Library.

specialists oversaw the work.[17] A number of artifacts were uncovered, including parts of a jail that had been located in the old City Hall basement.

On July 10, 1993, the 850-ton Pioneer Monument was raised by hydraulic jacks, placed on heavy-duty dollies, and slowly moved to the center of Fulton Street to make way for library construction. Months before the new library's grand opening in 1996, and without discussing its decision in a public hearing, the San Francisco Arts Commission proceeded to prepare a plaque to be placed in front of the statue to clarify its context. The arts commission sent the following statement to a foundry to be cast in bronze:

> The three figures of "Early Days," a Native American, a mission padre, and a vaquero, were created to represent the founding of California's missions. In 1769, the missionaries first came to California with the intent of converting the state's 300,000 Native Americans to Christianity. With their efforts over in 1834, the missionaries left behind about 56,000 converts—and 150,000 dead. Half the original Native American population had perished during this time from disease, armed attacks, and mistreatment.

The wording said, in effect, that Franciscan missionaries murdered half of the Native American population. The media soon picked up the story. The text brought forth furious responses from the Catholic Archdiocese of San Francisco, the Spanish consul general, several prominent historians, and, especially, the Franciscan friars who ministered to the poor and needy in San Francisco's Tenderloin District through St. Boniface Catholic Church. Brother Kelly Cullen called the plaque "unnecessarily negative." The media attention also stirred up Native Americans, who took the opposite view and further criticized the statue. Mayor Brown was quoted in the *San Francisco Chronicle* as saying, "Oh, sh—. I don't need another problem." He ordered the arts commission to revise the plaque.[18] The commission met on May 6, 1996, and heard from grieved parties on both sides of the argument. Brown showed up in person to urge the commission to resolve the matter. It did so by deleting "—and 150,000 dead" and beginning the final sentence with "As a result of the colonial occupation." Bobby Castillo, whose speech before the planning commission had been so influential to moving the monument, endorsed the compromise but said he would still prefer to have the offending statue removed.[19]

Building the library was a massive construction project requiring the excavation of a full city block eighty feet below the surface. The Brooks Hall convention center entrance ramp began on Fulton Street, where the new library entrance was going to appear, so it had to be moved out of the way by extending it to Hyde Street. By this time the hall was rarely used because Moscone Convention Center in the South of Market area, which had opened in 1981, drew most of the convention activity away from the Civic Center. Rebuilding the Brooks Hall entrance and closing the Civic Auditorium for seismic reha-

The new main library opened in 1996. Source: The Jon B. Lovelace Collection of California Photographs in Carol M. Highsmith's America Project, Library of Congress, Prints and Photographs Division; Gift; The Capital Group Companies Charitable Foundation in memory of Jon B. Lovelace; 2012; (DLC/PP-2012:063).

bilitation in 1994 finished off commercial use of the underground exhibition space, and it became the city's storehouse, prompting persistent discussion as to what its future should be.

The huge library building was completed in four years and had a lively dedication on April 18, 1996, the ninetieth anniversary of the great earthquake and fire of 1906.[20]

Seismic Repairs and Renovations of the Old Buildings

While new buildings rose in the Civic Center, the city began extensive seismic rehabilitation of preexisting structures. The first to undergo restoration was the Civic Auditorium, which had been renamed the Bill Graham Civic Auditorium in 1992, after the rock-concert impresario who had died the previous year.[21] The building closed for renovation in the summer of 1994. The Loma Prieta earthquake had damaged the interior plaster, and a large piece had dropped onto the Exposition Organ. After World War II, organ concerts had fallen out of favor and the huge instrument was played less frequently and poorly maintained. By the 1980s, it was inoperable, and damage from falling plaster only made matters worse. The city sent 11,000 pipes and other major organ components to the Austin Organ Company, the original builder in Hartford, Connecticut, for rehabilitation. The city decided to repurpose the organ's original auditorium location for general use, so when the organ parts returned to San Francisco in 1996, they were placed in storage in Brooks Hall, where they remain to this day. The auditorium was revamped at a cost of $25.5 million, which covered strengthening foundations, improving structural shear walls, and adding new lighting and access for people with disabilities. The building reopened on March 19, 1996, and was soon occupied by the San Francisco Opera while the War Memorial Opera House was closed for seismic work.[22]

Renovation and repair to the other Civic Center buildings kept apace. After the earthquake, the state of California decided not only to restore the Civic Center's original renaissance-style State Building, designed by Bliss and Faville, but also to remove the old annex and build in its place a large new office building in which to house several of its agencies. The California legislature authorized the project, which had an estimated cost of $250 million, and the governor approved it on September 21, 1993.[23] On August 13, 1994, the state announced that a novel design-and-build team would take full responsibility for the structure: Hines Interests (developer), Skidmore, Owings & Merrill (architects), and Hyman Construction Group (contractor). A controversy arose over the suitable height of the building, somewhere between twelve and sixteen floors. Susanna Montana of the San Francisco Planning Department said, "We don't mind tall buildings [at Civic Center] if they are handsome and contribute to the integrity of the area. . . . It might be beneficial to mask the ugly Federal tower [behind it, at 450 Golden Gate Avenue,] with a handsome new building."[24] The final height was a compromise of fourteen stories. The building complex was dedicated on December 10, 1998. The meticulously restored state Supreme Court building, now named after Earl Warren, former California governor and chief justice of the United States, was connected by a great interior court to the new state office building, a muted but graceful presence in the area named after Hiram W. Johnson, also a former governor as well as a US senator. Chief Justice Ronald George declared the buildings "spectacular in both beauty and utility."[25]

Also damaged in 1989, the great City Hall needed rehabilitation, so the city had the building surveyed and found the steel frame sound but many walls and ceilings cracked. The 90,000-ton dome had twisted about two inches and had weakened, but the fact that it had not collapsed was a testament to the skill of the building's engineers. Tony Irons, the city architect responsible for the project, said, "It has a magnificent building design. The main floors were meant to take the earthquake forces. The building did what it was supposed to do, but it won't do it again." Forell/Elsesser Engineers, which specialized in seismic and innovative methods, was called in as consultant and recommended that the building be retrofitted using the base isolation technique. The method, developed in Japan, calls for a base isolator beneath each vertical structural beam. The isolators are made of laminated steel and rubber and absorb and dissipate much of an earthquake's kinetic energy. The building is then strengthened and made more rigid so that internal structures don't move against each other. Finally, a twenty-inch "moat" is constructed around the building's perimeter to allow forces moving the isolators to dissipate. All told, City Hall would need 568 isolators and would be the largest building to utilize the technique to date.[26] The task would require digging out the building's foundations and underpinnings and carefully securing each vertical column by cutting off its base and installing an isolator underneath—a time-consuming and expensive process. FEMA's initial reaction to the proposal was to favor a more traditional foundation. FEMA officials finally agreed to the isolator plan, but the agency would provide only their estimated cost for a traditional approach, $104 million. The city estimated that the total cost would be $181 million and committed funds from the 1990 bond measure to make up the difference.[27]

As the city dove deeper into seismic retrofitting, repair, and modernization of the various Civic Center buildings, it became clear that the 1990 bond issue would not cover all costs. In 1993 a bond issue was prepared to provide for the seismic upgrade of the old main library and its conversion into the Asian Art Museum. City

During the seismic reconstruction of City Hall, all the vertical structural beams in the basement were held up by huge jacks and the bottom few feet cut off (*right side*). Then two base isolators were placed under the beam and the jack lowered (*left side*).
Source: Courtesy of the San Francisco City Hall Building Management Office.

officials believed the bond issue needed broader appeal to be successful with the voters, so they included a request for funds to rehabilitate the Steinhart Aquarium in Golden Gate Park, the Palace of Fine Arts in the Marina District, and five neighborhood arts and cultural centers, as well as construct a new lesbian and gay community center, bringing the total to $98 million. The range was inclusive, but the size of the bond issue drew taxpayer and property-owner groups into opposition. Senator Kopp, on behalf of his San Francisco Taxpayers Association, said, "Proposition A is a Christmas tree. There is something for everyone. But before we go into debt for non-essential projects, we need a new hospital for the sick and elderly and a new jail."[28] The measure needed two-thirds support to pass: at the November 2, 1993, election, the supporting vote was only 61.1 percent. The defeat taught Nothenberg and other city staff that they needed to change their strategy before proposing future Civic Center bond measures.

In 1994 the Asian Art Commission itself submitted a bond measure for $42 million dedicated to seismic work on the old library and carefully developed and funded a broad-based campaign. Senator Kopp agreed to support this measure, claiming it was common sense to reuse the vacant building and move the Asian Art Museum out of Golden Gate Park.[29] Without taxpayer- and property-owner opposition, the measure passed on November 8, 1994, with 71 percent approval.

City Hall and Mayor Willie Brown

In November of 1995, former speaker of the assembly Willie L. Brown Jr. won the election for mayor of San Francisco. As speaker, Brown had overseen the 1874 State Capitol's upgrade and seismic retrofit, in which he had taken intense personal interest and delight. He was excited about taking a similar commanding role in the work on City Hall. Within days of his election, he asked Irons, the city architect, for a briefing during which he was told about the complex needs the building currently had.[30]

The city had crafted the previous year a $38 million bond issue to cover restoring City Hall to its original condition, including converting court space into city offices and installing modern electrical and fire-prevention systems. No campaign nor compelling argument supported this bond measure, other than expressing the need for timely repairs, and it failed. With work under way on City Hall, the lack of additional funds put complete rehabilitation in a bind— after the seismic work was finished, the building would be strong but in poor condition and ill-equipped for modern office use. The argument was also made that without an up-to-date fire-protection system, the city fire marshal might not let city offices return to the building. After much internal discussion, Louise Renne, the city attorney, agreed to take the lead for a new bond campaign, and I agreed to organize a campaign committee and serve as its treasurer. With the addition of several more building improvements, including the historic preservation of all aspects of City Hall, the board of supervisors placed before the voters a $63.5 million bond issue. The bond campaign emphasized two points: first, the rehabilitated space would accommodate more city staff than before, thereby saving money spent renting other facilities; and, second, without funding, the building might stand empty. Campaign supporters obtained endorsements and mailed campaign literature and met no organized opposition. The voters approved the measure on November 7, 1995, with 70 percent.

Although this bond measure called for restoring historic conditions and modernizing building systems, detailed plans had not been developed yet, giving Brown a free hand to guide the finished project. He spent a great amount of time during his first year in office involved with all aspects of preparing the final plans and design for City Hall. At the same time as he immersed himself in these issues, he was engaged in improvement projects on the Civic Center more broadly, directing the San Francisco Department of Public Works to shape up Civic Center Plaza by replacing the leaky rectangular pond with grass, removing several thick groves of olive trees (which were dense, felt threatening, and attracted rats), improving lighting, and adding another playground on the Larkin Street side. He even tried to get involved with the final design of the Civic Center Courthouse, but he was rebuffed by the judges.[31]

As Mayor Brown got deeper into the plans for City Hall, he envisioned the structure as something akin to a presidential palace rather than simply a municipal office building. He wanted the building to accommodate on the second floor an expanded mayor's office, the city administrator (a new position created by a recent charter amendment), and the city attorney; and on the third floor the board of supervisors, each member of which would have a suite of offices with their own private bathroom. The nearly three-acre ground floor would be devoted to public meetings and exhibits. Arthur Brown's light courts would be restored as flexible spaces, but the architect's carefully conceived offices on the north side of the building for the recorder and assessor and on the south side for the treasurer and tax collector would be emptied with those functions banished from the building. They provided services to ordinary people such as places to pay taxes or to obtain a marriage license and be married under the grand dome. Instead the ground floor would be converted into meeting, exhibit, and banqueting spaces. A restaurant-size kitchen was even suggested to cater banquets. In total, the building would hold only 750 city employees, as opposed to some 1,300 before closure (although about 200 of those had been court employees who would be accommodated in the new courthouse).[32]

Irons was dispatched to the April 10, 1996, meeting of the supervisors' finance committee to present the plan and secure the release of the $63 million in bond funds. Committee chair Tom Hsieh commented, "The mayor's vision borders on extravagance and makes me very uncomfortable. . . . I think it will enrage the voters." Supervisor Barbara Kaufman said that, when approving the recent bond measure, the voters had expected the city to consolidate several departments in the building and save money on rent. The committee members voted to continue the matter for two weeks and gather more details.[33] In a follow-up letter, Irons admitted that the plan could cost up to $2.7 million more in rent.[34] The media started talking about Brown wanting to turn City Hall into a Taj Mahal—which soon morphed into the "Taj Ma-Willie."[35]

At the finance committee meeting on April 24, 1996, the mayor personally made the case for his plan. As John King, reporter for the *San Francisco Chronicle*, wrote, "For 25 minutes he cajoled, implored, flattered, and sought to pull the committee his way through sheer force of eloquence." Brown proclaimed,

"We must be prepared to be bold, to show courage. . . . Small-minded people weren't on the library board. It has the magnificence of dreamers. City Hall can be an equal facility." He defended the use of the ground floor as a ceremonial space, saying it was needed for use by "visiting dignitaries who come by regularly." The supervisors found themselves in an uncomfortable position, as they were his allies and friends, and Brown was very popular. Supervisor Hsieh thanked Brown for his presentation and remarked, "Now I know why you were so successful as Speaker." The three committee members then voted to extend $5 million of the bond funds for further planning and asked for a revised plan in two months.[36]

Irons faced the task of mediating between Mayor Brown and the committee members on a proposal that would satisfy both parties. At the July 17, 1996, committee meeting, a harmonious arrangement was approved. The second floor would contain the mayor's office, the supervisors with only modest suites, and the city attorney. The third and fourth floors would be office space for unnamed city offices. As a concession to Brown, the ground floor would contain public exhibit and meeting spaces built to be converted easily into offices. The full kitchen would be redesigned as a pantry or catering preparation room. Irons suggested that ground floor space would be prime event space and could generate $1 million or more in annual rent. But services for ordinary citizens would still be banished from the building. The number of employees who could be accommodated in the renovated building grew to 825. Irons pointed out that under the current fire, safety, and disability codes, there was no space for the 1,300 employees who had been jammed into the building before it closed. The building now had a legal capacity of approximately 1,100 employees. Hsieh approved the new plan, saying, "I want everyone to hold back their critical comments and give the benefit of the doubt to what Mayor Brown has in mind. Maybe something really exciting can be developed."[37] Renovation proceeded with sensitivity to the building's historic fabric on the one hand and the need for state-of-the-art electronic services on the other. Reopening was scheduled for January 1999.

But problems, perhaps inevitably, persisted. On October 28, 1997, Brown publicly confirmed the rumor that the project was $30 to $40 million short of funds because of the increased cost of the isolator structural system and FEMA's reluctance to cover it. He placed the blame on Nothenberg, the former chief administrative officer, for not negotiating a better deal with FEMA and indicated that he had been in touch with President Bill Clinton about getting FEMA to increase its support.[38] Although Brown would eventually later get those funds, the news drew out longtime Civic Center critic and Brown arch-political nemesis,

Senator Kopp. On December 8, 1997, Kopp held a press conference in front of the City Hall scaffolding to announce that he would be collecting signatures on an initiative for the June 3, 1998, ballot to require that all city departments that had resided in City Hall before it closed be accommodated there when it reopened. "City Hall is for city business," Kopp stated. "It is not an entertainment center. We have plenty of entertainment centers." Brown commented on Kopp's initiative by saying, "It is a crazy thing to do."[39]

The need for additional funds was acute, so Irons asked the board of supervisors' finance committee to transfer to the project $25 million in bond funds that had been set aside to seismically retrofit the Civic Center's Department of Health building on Grove Street. At its December 22, 1997, meeting, the committee approved the transfer after extracting from Irons and Brown a commitment that an additional 200, or even 300, employees would move back into City Hall.[40] This meant that the departments traditionally located on the ground floor would return to their customary places and the building would be restored to what Mayor Rolph called "The People's Palace." However, the light courts would be restored and left free of office cubicles. Although the supervisors were Brown's allies, they acted in the face of a strong public reaction to cost overruns and Brown's grandiose intentions. Brown acquiesced by saying he would "sign on to whatever Tony Irons recommends." Kopp was not placated and would not withdraw his initiative. Babette Drefke, his spokesperson, said, "We've learned that you can't trust anyone's word. It has to be down on paper."[41]

Vigorous campaigns were run for and against the initiative, known as Proposition F, which Kopp said was needed to keep Brown and the supervisors from returning to their Taj Ma-Willie ways. Brown and the supervisors argued that the measure was unnecessary since City Hall would be full of city workers when it reopened, and it would jeopardize the restoration of the historic fabric of the building. Brown organized hard-hat tours to show the public what was actually going on within the building.[42] At the June 2, 1998, election, the voters supported Proposition F with 59 percent, clearly a rebuke to Brown and his expansive ideas for City Hall. Brown declared that nothing would change, since everything that had been done on City Hall was consistent with Proposition F. Kaufman, president of the board of supervisors, had an ordinance prepared confirming that statement and approving the removal of several small city departments from the roster of those returning to City Hall.[43] Kopp objected and said that he wanted to bring in an independent review committee of architects to examine the situation. He suggested that the historic light court might be better used as before—filled with office cubicles. On June 22, 1998, the supervisors voted 10 to 1 in favor of Kaufman's resolution, in effect "sticking their fingers in Kopp's eye," as a *San Francisco Chronicle* reporter commented.[44]

Most of the City Hall design issues had been resolved by fall 1997, except for the dome's appearance. In 1915 the City Hall architect, Arthur Brown Jr., had modeled the dome after that of the church at Hôtel des Invalides in Paris, with a dark leaded base over copper sheeting decorated with gold leaf. The dome's lead base and gold leaf had weathered so badly so that by the 1950s the public view of the dome was of copper sheeting transformed by a lovely green patina. Almost no one remembered the original decoration. Irons and his design team therefore had to confront the dilemma of whether to restore the dome to its original condition, as orthodox preservation would prescribe, or leave the dome's green patina.

In January 1998 Irons and his team called several meetings of City Hall consultants, engineers, preservationists, myself, and even Arthur Brown's son-in-law, Roland Jensen, and his biographer, Jeffrey Tilman. The metallurgists discussed the copper's condition and reported that a urethane surface covering made by Tnemec would serve as a suitable coating in lieu of lead. All agreed that the best approach would be to restore the original decoration. However, some people, including the Arthur Brown representatives, had an affinity for the green patina and suggested that the gold leaf be restored without the dark base.[45]

A construction fire between the walls of the dome in the late afternoon of February 12, 1998, forced the decision. The four-alarm fire took three hours to extinguish. Firefighters had to cut into and remove fifteen percent of the dome's external copper sheeting.[46] Replacement sheeting would be new copper, and the metallurgists reported that there was no way that a uniform green patina could be developed. Thus, Irons sent a letter to the mayor and board of supervisors on February 17, explaining that the dome would need to be restored to its original condition.[47] The issue of restoring the gold leaf had been a longstanding cost dilemma for the city. As far back as 1938, after twenty-five years of weathering, the dome's gold leaf decoration had become so tarnished and worn that it was barely visible. At the time, the members of the board of supervisors suggested restoring the gold leaf before the Golden Gate International Exposition, but when they received the restoration estimate of $40,500, they quickly dropped the idea.[48] Sixty years later, costs were even worse and in 1998, the cost would be $500,000 with the installation. Because of city budget problems, Mayor Brown indicated that no taxpayer monies would be spent on gold, giving the impression that he would raise it from private sources. However, Brown came up with a quicker and easier strategy. In 1988 the city had enacted a downtown zoning plan calling for developers to provide for public art in new buildings or pay into a "downtown public art fund." Ten years later, the fund had a substantial balance. Since the downtown plan district boundary extended up Market Street to Van Ness Avenue, the Civic Center adjoined it. Brown had the supervisors amend the rules for the funds to allow for public art expenditures to be made on public properties adjacent to the district, thus making public art funds available to pay for the dome's gold leaf. The public's reaction to this sleight of hand was surprised, but positive. Irons commented, "Actually, I thought it was a pretty clever solution."[49]

City Hall reopened on January 5, 1999. Taking into account the grandeur of the building and recent controversies stemming from its rehabilitation, Brown decided to forgo an extensive rededication ceremony, but rather allowed people to see the building for themselves. However, he could not restrain himself, and he spoke outside for half an hour before letting people inside. The board of supervisors held its regular weekly meeting at 2:00 p.m., where they praised and honored Irons. The public swarmed into the building to see what the millions had produced. Most were delighted by the polished and glittering building with natural light shining through the restored skylights. Those who remembered City Hall's previous dingy condition expressed amazement.[50] Retired *San Francisco Chronicle* design critic Allan Temko exclaimed, "I love it. I love the gold, the old oak furniture, the restored light courts with their sky lights. . . . It is a great achievement of the bureaucracy."[51] The final accounting for the building restoration and move-in came to $345 million, $45 million more than the original estimate. The building was designed to hold 1,071 city employees, just less than the 1,100 allowed by the current fire codes. But that did not satisfy Senator Kopp, who groused, "So we must continue to pay out taxpayer money [for rent], a circumvention of promises to the voters."[52]

A week or so later, a reporter found Mayor Brown, dapperly dressed as usual, closely examining a stain in the marble floor which he said he wanted removed immediately. Brown was known for perpetually prowling the building and checking that things were neat and tidy (one newspaper called him the City Hall fussbudget).[53] He was told that the stain was from long ago, and the discoloration had seeped into the stone and could not be removed. In general, Brown's interest and concern for the building were sincere. Although federal, state, and local preservation regulations called for the building to be restored to its original condition as reasonably as possible, he made sure that the highest standard was always met. He had also brought drama and controversy to the project, consuming many people's time and energy. As a result, he suffered a rebuke from the voters. Did he add value to the restoration? Probably, although Irons is the one who guided the project through difficult times and made it happen. Brown was right about how the restored rotunda and light courts would attract weddings and corporate and charitable events and generate funds for building maintenance. For example, approximately 8,000 marriages and 750 events took place in City Hall in fiscal 2015–2016, generating $2,981,000. Brown wrote of his City Hall restoration experience in the autobiography, *Basic Brown*: "Politically I could have passed the buck on the restoration while focusing on other issues. I could have left the task to a commission or committee, but I believed in it, and I believed that the grandeur of City Hall was worth protecting. And the only way to do that properly was to become personally involved. I spent immense amounts of time on the project. I became the restoration manager."[54]

The War Memorial Opera House

In the summer of 1996, the same year Brown was inaugurated to his first term, the War Memorial Opera House closed for seismic retrofitting and rehabilitation, which lasted twenty months. The War Memorial board of trustees is an independent body over which the mayor has no control, so Brown could only offer support from the sidelines. The estimated cost was $86.5 million, and the city's 1990 bond provided $49.7 million; FEMA, $7 million; and private contributors organized by Charlotte Mailliard Swig (later, Shultz), the remainder.[55] The San Francisco Opera spent $2.5 million to upgrade the Bill Graham Civic Auditorium to house its opera performances during the War Memorial closure. The company had used the auditorium during the 1920s.[56] Large productions, including a spectacular *Aida*, by Giuseppe Verdi, were held in the Civic Auditorium; more intimate productions, such as Giacomo Puccini's *La Bohème*, were presented at the Orpheum Theatre. The San Francisco Ballet used the Palace of Fine Arts theater and other venues. Work on the Opera House, including modernizing and upgrading its building systems, was smoothly overseen by Tara Lamont, of the city's bureau of architecture, assisted by Skidmore, Owings & Merrill.

The Opera House reopened on September 11, 1999, with a production of Verdi's *Un Ballo in Maschera*. Many people thought the building outshone the production, with the gleaming monumental auditorium chandelier, reupholstered red-velvet seats, and expertly restored gold leaf. It was a great indicator of how beautifully all of the Civic Center buildings could be renovated and restored to their original grandeur as buildings for all of the public.

The Asian Art Museum

Converting the old main library into a new home for the Asian Art Museum did not proceed as smoothly as the Opera House's renovations. With the 1994 bond funds in hand and the old library building scheduled to be turned over to the museum in mid-1996, the Asian Art Commission spent two years raising private money for the project and choosing an architectural team to oversee the work.

On December 3, 1996, the commission received a report that the architectural competition committee had selected Italian architect Gae Aulenti to design the museum, assisted by the San Francisco firm Hellmuth, Obata, and Kassabaum. Aulenti appeared to be an inspired choice: she had overseen the conversion into museums of the historic Gare d'Orsay train station in Paris, the Palazzo Grassi in Venice, and the Palau Nacional (national palace) in Barcelona. At her introductory press conference, she said, "It will be a challenge to integrate the Asian art collection with a European-style Beaux-Arts building. The cultural roots are so different. I hope to find a poetic way of making this synthesis."[57] While Aulenti worked on her plans, a furor erupted over the fate of several murals that were mounted along the loggia at the top of the main staircase of the old library. Gottardo Piazzoni, a prominent North Beach artist who painted excellent tonalist landscapes, had been commissioned by private subscription to paint fourteen murals for the outer walls of the loggia. Ten were installed in 1931 and 1932, and the remaining four were added much later, in 1974. They were attached to the brick walls of the loggia and artificially lit. Because they were hard to view in this cramped location, most people paid them little attention, and they were poorly maintained.

The Asian Art Commission met on February 25, 1997, to consider a resolution to remove, conserve, and store the murals and other artwork during reconstruction. However, the plan did not indicate the murals' future. Emily Sano, the Asian Art Museum's director, thought that the murals had no place in the new museum. A number of local art experts and preservationists challenged Sano's view and argued that, when the Asian Art Museum accepted the old library building, it took everything that came with it, including the murals.[58] The board of supervisors intervened in April and established a panel of three experts, including Aulenti, to prepare a report on the condition of the murals and the feasibility of removing them or remodeling the building while they remained on the existing walls.[59]

Aulenti revealed her design for the new Asian Art Museum before the Asian Art Commission on July 15, 1997, a plan that included removing the murals and changing other historic elements of the building. "We're preserving the building but giving it a new heart," she declared. "Before, the building was dark, somber. The concept is to open everything up, to bring in more light." To accomplish her objective, she proposed opening the two existing light courts to ground level, covering them with V-shaped skylights. Visitors would enter through the original foyer and then continue either left, to the temporary exhibit space on the ground floor, or right, to an escalator leading to the permanent collection upstairs. The right side of the ground floor would also contain the restaurant,

gift store, and other visitor services. The existing grand staircase would be retained, but it would lead only to the original book-delivery room, which would
now serve as a meeting and entertainment space. The loggia would be opened
to light by removing the Piazzoni murals and walls and inserting exhibit cases
for small precious items. It would also serve as a secondary entrance to the
permanent collection. The large reading room on the south side of the building
contained such a high ceiling that Aulenti proposed inserting a new third floor to
accommodate more of the permanent collection. The challenge was to transform
a building "where people go to sit in one place and study into a building where
people go to visit the collection, to walk through the building." They will "discover
at once they're in a museum of Asian Art," Aulenti explained.[60]

However, during the same meeting, David Bahlman, executive director of
the Foundation for San Francisco's Architectural Heritage, criticized Aulenti's
design for changing the historic fabric of the building.[61] The previous day,
Susan Brandt-Hawley, Heritage's attorney, had transmitted to Sano a letter
"requesting a design that protects the integrity of the interior spaces and re-
tains the murals *in situ* as required by law." The interior space covered by the
letter included the grand staircase, the loggia, the book-delivery room, and
several reading rooms.[62]

The panel of experts commissioned by the supervisors to study whether the
murals could be removed safely from the library walls before construction delivered its report on July 30, 1997. Two of the three committee members concluded
that the murals could and should be removed, and one member took the opposite view.[63] On December 15 the full board of supervisors voted 9 to 2 favoring a
resolution to remove the murals.[64]

On August 12, 1997, the Asian Art Museum gave a tour of the building to
preservation and related government staff to help them understand the new
plan. Cherilyn Widell, the California state historic preservation officer, and
David Look, from the National Park Service, followed up with written comments
on September 8, in which they expressed "grave concerns" about the project,
which made "changes to the significant historic interiors of the former library
building, particularly the loggia, second floor reading rooms, and the great hall
[former book-delivery room] and removal or alteration of significant historic
fabric, including fenestration of the light court walls and Fulton Street elevation,
the murals, statuary over the front entrance and interior elements which will be
affected by the seismic alterations." The letter indicated that all of the changes
would violate federal regulations.[65] Widell and Look informally indicated that
changes could lead to the removal of the building from the National Register
of Historic Places, something that would nevertheless have little financial

consequence, as no federal funds were involved. But the point they were making was clear—the Asian Art Museum should restore the building to its 1917 condition and then fit the new museum into it as best as it could. Sano, Aulenti, and others were shocked and outraged by the letter and, based on the advice from their preservation consultants and lawyers they were not about to make major changes to their plans.

By this time, I had a lot of experience with the Civic Center and historic preservation, including five years' service as President Jimmy Carter's appointee on the federal Advisory Council on Historic Preservation. On September 25 I sent an eight-page letter to Look and Widell, pointing out "the narrowness of [their letter's] approach and its cavalier objections to the conversion plans" and the omission of any reference to the remarkable City Beautiful Civic Center design and values. I asked them to think about what the Civic Center really was and reconsider their comments.[66] Their response was, however, dismissive of those concerns.[67] I then solicited opinions about the museum conversion project and the views of state and federal officers toward it from two noted experts on the City Beautiful movement and civic centers: William H. Wilson, professor of history at the University of North Texas, and Joan E. Draper, associate professor of architecture at the University of Colorado. They suggested remaining flexible while adapting the library. Draper was writing a book about "reinterpreting" significant American structures and observed, "Only a few . . . places can and should be restored or preserved as they once were at a single moment in time; perhaps Mt. Vernon is one of those places. However, the San Francisco Civic Center is not Mt. Vernon."[68] Bahlman, of the Foundation for San Francisco's Architectural Heritage, reacted to my correspondence by accusing me of interfering in the official process and dismissed the professors' letters as being irrelevant.[69] However, the San Francisco Examiner liked Draper's Mount Vernon observation so much that it was quoted the following year in an editorial to support the museum project.[70]

The Asian Art Museum could not make final design decisions until fall 1999, after required environmental reviews were complete and the planning commission had voted on the plan. Meanwhile, on September 2, 1998, the Landmarks Preservation Advisory Board, by a vote of 5 to 2, recommended that the project not be approved because it included interior changes, among them, removing the Piazzoni murals.[71] The planning commission did not make its decision until December 10, 1999. After five and a half hours of emotional testimony, the commissioners voted 6 to 1 in favor of the Asian Art Museum's plan. Steade Craigo, from the State Office of Historic Preservation, repeated the objections his office had put forth for months, and it was again suggested that changes to the building might jeopardize its status on the National Register of Historic Places.[72] Senator Feinstein sent a letter to be read to the commission endorsing the project's goal to create a world-class museum. She had previously sent a letter to the US secretary of the interior, Bruce Babbitt, complaining about the threat to remove the building from the national register.[73] Opponents of Aulenti's plan appealed the decision to the board of supervisors, which, to no one's surprise, denied the appeal on January 25, 2000 by a vote of 8 to 3.[74]

The Foundation for San Francisco's Architectural Heritage filed a lawsuit on February 17, 1999, to overturn the decision.[75] The suit did not stop the Asian Art Museum from holding its groundbreaking ceremony on May 7, 1999 attended by its major donor, Chong-Moon Lee, after whom the building would be named.[76] By this time, the murals had been carefully removed from the walls and sent to several conservators around the country. Superior Court Judge David Garcia ruled against the Heritage Foundation in all respects on June 4, 2000, and the group chose not to appeal.[77] I wrote an editorial opinion for the *San Francisco Examiner* where I suggested that it was time for historic preservationists to rethink their purpose and methods in light of the extraordinary nature of the Civic Center.[78] Since then, they have shown no further interest in the issue. On October 1, the Asian Art Museum and the Fine Arts Museums of San Francisco announced an agreement whereby the de Young Museum would take ownership of the Piazzoni murals and install them in the Family Room on the ground floor of the new museum in Golden Gate Park, where they could be enjoyed in a larger space.[79]

The Asian Art Museum at the Civic Center opened to the public on March 13, 2003, seven years after receiving the old main library building and thirteen years after it had been offered by Mayor Feinstein. The museum used Aulenti's design, and the work cost $161 million. Its permanent galleries could show more than 2,500 pieces from its vast collection without being disrupted by temporary exhibits. Harry Parker, the director of the city's Fine Arts Museums, said, "They successfully converted the old Main Library into a functioning and beautiful art museum. . . . It certainly gives the Asian Art Museum the kind of prestige and stature to which it has aspired."[80] John King, now the *San Francisco Chronicle*'s urban design critic, wrote that the museum "excels as a work of restoration and as home for objects as much as 6,000 years old. . . . What counts ultimately is that one venerated landmark has been renewed for an entirely different purpose by another venerated institution. Cities change— in this case for the better."[81]

Reviving the Federal Building at UN Plaza

Like several Civic Center buildings after the Loma Prieta earthquake, the federal office building located at 50 United Nations Plaza was damaged but still usable. Nevertheless, the federal General Services Administration (GSA), which controlled the building, gave little attention to the damages because the agency was preoccupied with constructing a new office building outside the Civic Center area at Seventh and Mission Streets. Begun in 2003, that new building—a controversial eighteen-story, environmentally sensitive building in a stark modern design by Thom Mayne, a founder of the Los Angeles firm Morphosis—was finished in July 2007 and thereafter occupied by many agencies formerly housed at 50 UN Plaza.[82]

During the early 2000s, the GSA's Republican administrators contemplated declaring Arthur Brown Jr.'s historic federal office building surplus and leasing it to a developer to convert into apartments. With this in mind, they vacated and closed it after the new Mayne-designed Federal Building was completed. When San Francisco congresswoman Nancy Pelosi became speaker of the House of Representatives, however, she had that decision rescinded because the federal government still leased more office space in San Francisco than it owned. The rehabilitation and reuse of the building for federal offices would correct that problem and retain a historic building as federal property. The GSA duly prepared a plan with an estimated cost of $121 million to cover the building's seismic work, rehabilitation, and modernization. There was, however, concern about whether Congress would appropriate funds for such an expensive project in San Francisco. While in Washington, DC, in January 2009 for the inauguration of President Barack Obama, I contacted Speaker Pelosi who put me in touch with Susan Brita, a senior staff member of the subcommittee responsible for oversight of public buildings in the House Committee on Transportation and Infrastructure. I made the case to her about the importance of the building and its compromised condition. With the support of Speaker Pelosi, Brita acted on my request. When the anti-recession American Recovery and Reinvestment Act was signed by President Obama on February 17, 2009, it contained $121 million for 50 UN Plaza.[83]

The GSA prepared a detailed, beautiful, and practical plan to restore the building to federal office use, and the reconstruction was completed in 2013. The building's drab and lifeless inner courtyard was turned into an award-winning landscaped plaza for employees. Unfortunately, because of government security, few people are allowed to see the inside of this great Arthur Brown Jr. building.

Civic Center Plaza

During his first two years in office, Mayor Brown had been interested in everything Civic Center. At the time, the city government was flush with funds and he gave the department of public works $200,000 to commission a new plan for the tired Civic Center Plaza and adjacent streets. Several years earlier the city had unsuccessfully attempted to obtain funding for plaza upgrades through bond measures without preparing a plan first. In 1992, as a member of the board of the Friends of Library focused on the new main library project, I had convinced the city administration to place several Civic Center improvement measures from Feinstein's report on the June 2, 1992, ballot, with the most important being a $26,700,000 measure to restore and upgrade the plaza and convert Fulton Street between the new and old library buildings into a mall. However, the weak endorsement from voters at that time for the measures indicated that the city as a whole had not yet bought into the vision of a thriving and functional Civic Center.

But Brown's energy and focus on the Civic Center and its plaza would help bring a renewed attention to the plaza's needs and, in 1997, the department of public works requested proposals from firms around the country for a new plan for the Civic Center Plaza. The accepted bid came from the Olin Studio of Philadelphia and Simon Martin-Vegue Winkelstein Moris (SMWM), the San Francisco firm that had worked with James Ingo Freed to design the new main library. Laurie Olin was one of the most prominent landscape architects in the United States, having revived Bryant Park in New York and designed the gardens at the J. Paul Getty Center in Los Angeles. SMWM, in addition to having been associate architect on the new main library, had an active national and Bay Area planning practice. The team began work in early 1998 and held several community workshops during the summer. They concluded that the original Howard plan should be restored, with two round ponds on either side of the east-west axis and four small gardens, or "rooms." Their recommendations also included narrowing the wide streets around the plaza and rebuilding ramps to the garage to allow pedestrian passage through the plaza from all directions. Their plan also described how to program and manage the space. They finished the draft report for public review at the end of 1998.[84]

In January 1999 the public works department began to prepare for the report's release with presentations and workshops for individuals and community and civic groups. After several months, however, the mayor's office said that the whole project would be put on hold. Brown was up for reelection that fall, and his administration had generated controversy from projects such as the City Hall restoration, and the opposition resulted in a number of candidates running against him. One such candidate was Clint Reilly, Kopp's colleague in the City Hall ballot measure. The mayor's political advisers did not want anything regarding the Civic Center to remind the public about the Taj Ma-Willie. In the November 2, 1999, election, Brown received only 37 percent of the vote, forcing a runoff election on December 14, which he won handily. However, this experience cooled his ardor about improving the Civic Center.

During Brown's second term, I repeatedly tried to convince him to release the report and prepare for its adoption, but he refused to do so or to move forward with any permanent rehabilitation plan for the plaza and other Civic Center public areas during the rest of his time in office. Regrettably that plan was never officially released.

When Gavin Newsom became mayor in January 2004, he was also interested in a number of issues related to the Civic Center, including the condition of the plaza. An important contribution he made during his time in office was the creation of a Community Benefit District (CBD) to oversee the Civic Center area upkeep and improvement. Since the 1989 earthquake, more than $1 billion had been spent in the construction of two new buildings and upgrading five older public buildings. However, nothing had been done to improve the plaza and adjoining streets, which many people thought were unsafe and inhospitable. I spoke with Mayor Newsom several times about publishing and completing the 1998 plaza report. He was constrained by two factors: the city was in a fiscal recession, and therefore no funds were available; and the city's recreation and park department, which had jurisdiction over the plaza, was going through a wholesale reform, led by Isabel Wade of the nonprofit Neighborhood Parks Council. Wade decreed that the department should focus only on parks that served neighborhoods; the city's plazas and squares should be another department's concern. This view was odd, because the plaza had two playgrounds that served the surrounding Tenderloin neighborhood. Nevertheless, the San Francisco Recreation and Park Commission refused to take an interest in the plaza report or allocate funds for its completion and approval. Newsom did go ahead and ask the city administrator, Edwin Lee, to come up with a way to complete the report and develop a plan to improve the plaza. But Lee was unable to make any progress.

In the spring of 2005 I suggested to Mayor Newsom that he organize a gathering of Civic Center stakeholders to discuss area conditions. He agreed, as long as I did the organizing. This resulted in a meeting of approximately 125 people in the Green Room of the Veterans Building on May 22, presenting to Newsom in person their ideas for the plaza that I then compiled and delivered as a memorandum to the mayor.

For several years, in my role as convener of the stakeholders group, I prepared yearly memorandums for the mayor on the status of key issues, including crime and security, cleaning and maintenance, homelessness, parking and transit, the plaza's condition, the area as a neighborhood, and the area's promotion. Over time, however, it became obvious that I could not track all of the issues alone, and I asked Mayor Newsom to create a CBD in the Civic Center area. California law authorizes property owners to establish and operate Business Improvement Districts (BIDs) and CBDs for which the property owners can assess themselves and provide additional funds for area maintenance, security, promotion, and so forth. In 1999 the Union Square merchants had established a BID, which provided additional cleaning, problem-solving personnel on the streets, and promotion, and it had a board of directors to voice their concerns. The district's success inspired other areas to create their own neighborhood organizations.

In spring 2006 Newsom responded positively to my request to create a district. This would be tricky, because nearly half of the properties were government owned and would be subject to assessments paid for by individual agencies from their budgets. It took four years to develop a plan and obtain agency and property-owner support. In December 2010 the board of supervisors considered the district proposal. It was opposed by city employee unions and several citizens who did not seem to appreciate the poor conditions in the area and argued that the district would "privatize the public space." On January 4, 2011, the supervisors voted 6 to 5 in favor of creating a district: Supervisor David Chiu, the board president, provided the key vote. Mayor Newsom signed the legislation to create the Civic Center Community Benefit District on January 9, 2011, his last day in office before becoming lieutenant governor of California. For the first time, the Civic Center area had an organization with a board of directors of fifteen people focused on area conditions and with resources to try to improve them. The district provides extra cleaning and graffiti removal, employs ambassadors to assist tourist and the homeless, and organizes events to enliven what can sometimes be a desolate place.

When Ed Lee succeeded Newsom as mayor in January 2011, he was already familiar with Civic Center issues, but he led a city government with financial problems. He turned over the plaza problems to Phil Ginsburg, the general manager of the San Francisco Recreation and Park Department. Ginsburg, a longtime city official, was concerned about the condition of the plaza and took responsibility for it, making cosmetic improvements and bringing activities and programs into the space. As far as resurrecting planning for the plaza and adjoining areas, however, Ginsburg was sympathetic but lacked funding. As a result, Ginsburg thought that a nongovernmental agency might be better at creating a plan for the plaza. The plan from 1998 that Brown had commissioned was no longer current enough to be useful so in the summer of 2013, he contacted Gabriel Metcalf, president of SPUR, an established research and planning organization in San Francisco. SPUR had taken an interest in the Civic Center in the 1990s and had even created a special committee to study and work on the Feinstein plan, but that committee had been long dissolved. After considering the project for several months, Metcalf said that SPUR would undertake it for $500,000, but only if $50,000 were delivered up front before further discussion—that was a nonstarter.

In 2013, the frustrated Ginsburg received a phone call from the philanthropist Helen Diller, who had already supported the renewal of other city parks and recreation areas. Noticing the rundown condition of the two plaza playgrounds, Diller offered to fund their upgrade by using the Trust for Public Land (TPL) to oversee the work. Her offer was enthusiastically accepted, and the TPL began the complicated job of designing relevant new playgrounds in a historic plaza. The TPL was pulled in two directions by the historic development of the plaza— whether to use Douglas Baylis's aborted design from the 1960s or Howard's 1912 plan as the starting point. In the end, the trust developed a final playground plan that not only respected the earlier plans but also provided new, exciting play spaces for children of the Tenderloin neighborhood. The project's cost grew to $10 million, and the playgrounds opened in 2018.[85]

By 2014, with the extraordinary and ongoing growth of the city's economy because of tech industries, San Francisco's coffers were growing and the city had discretionary funds again. Despite the notable work on the two playgrounds, however, there was no improvement on the other areas of the plaza or the adjoining streets. In a conversation I had with Mayor Lee, I described the lack of progress and frustration that Ginsburg and I were confronting with getting the area planning underway. Mayor Lee responded quickly to this message, directing the planning department to include funds for a Civic Center Public Realm Plan in its upcoming budget to help address this. This plan, when it is released in the winter of 2019, will provide a much needed new vision for the renovation and revitalization of the plaza in the future.

New Civic Center Building for the SFPUC

In addition to Newsom's contribution to the welfare of the Civic Center area by instituting the Community Benefit District, another important improvement project undertaken during his time as mayor was the construction of a new headquarters for the San Francisco Public Utilities Commission (SFPUC).

Children playing at the new Helen Diller Playgrounds, opened in 2018, with City Hall in the background. Source: Courtesy The Trust for Public Land, photograph by Lindsay Upson.

Newsom (who was twice elected lieutenant governor and then elected governor in November 2018) had been particularly interested in environmental issues and wanted sustainable water and power for San Francisco. The SFPUC had needed a new headquarters for some time, so the mayor initiated a discussion about building the most advanced sustainable office building in the country on property on Golden Gate Avenue which had been dropped from the original Howard plan acquisition list for lack of funds.

The state of California owned a nondescript building on this property on the corner of Polk Street and Golden Gate Avenue, across from the original State Building annex. Severely damaged by the 1989 earthquake, this building was closed and had remained unoccupied for fifteen years. When Brown was mayor, he had talked the state into selling the building to San Francisco for a dollar.[86] Brown had originally contemplated building offices there for city employees relocated from City Hall under his grand scheme. However, funding was not to be found, and the state's building remained derelict. The SFPUC could take over the site and clear it using funds from the sale of an old small office building in its possession, but the question for Newsom and the board of supervisors was whether a new fully sustainable building could be designed and built for less than renting office space from private owners. The financial analysis was close, but they took a risk and supported a new building because they believed it would be a good addition to the Civic Center, filling in an empty space and adding more employees to the area.[87] Construction began in September 2009 and was completed in July 2012 at a cost of $202 million. KMD Architects designed the new building in a restrained modern style compatible with the nearby San Francisco Civic Center Courthouse and the Hiram Johnson State Office Building. It was touted as the greenest office building in North America.

War Memorial Veterans Building

One of the major buildings in the Civic Center that had still not yet been seismically strengthened and upgraded twenty years after the 1989 earthquake was the War Memorial Veterans Building. A 1996 engineering report described structural weaknesses, including an auditorium ceiling that could collapse in another strong earthquake, but indicated that these conditions were not so severe as to require closing the building immediately. Like all Civic Center buildings, the Veterans Building also needed systems modernization and general repair. Plans for a seismic retrofit and an overall upgrade were developed, and a $122,755,000 bond measure to support the work was prepared. Long-standing tensions with veterans groups over use of the building erupted over the rehabilitation program, and a number of such groups actively opposed the bond issue.[88] Only 55 percent of the voters supported it at the November 5, 2002, election. A decade passed before a new rehabilitation plan would be undertaken.

By 2010, the War Memorial board of trustees had developed a plan to use internally generated funds to rehabilitate the Veterans Building without the need for another bond measure. Architect Tara Lamont was enticed out of retirement to return to city service to oversee the project using the same high standards she had set for the Opera House renovation, and the work began in mid-2013. The allocation of space was negotiated, and the San Francisco Museum of Modern Art, which still controlled the fourth floor, transferred that floor to the San Francisco Opera to develop into a new opera center with performance and rehearsal space, a costume shop and other work areas, and offices. The company raised $21 million to its cover costs.[89] Improvements to the building, including additional dressing rooms behind the Herbst Theatre stage, a gallery for the San Francisco Arts Commission and a café on the first floor, and a renovated bar in the basement made the building more useful. The changes cost $154 million, and the building reopened to wide acclaim on September 21, 2015.[90]

Following the longstanding space-sharing problems between the arts community and the veterans groups, the usual controversies flared up at this time as well. Although the refurbished space on the second floor and half of the third floor contained offices and meeting rooms for veterans groups, several of these groups—not surprisingly, since the focus of the renovations was mostly on the art community's needs—felt that they were not treated properly and filed a lawsuit.[91]

Centennial Celebrations

The Civic Center reached its centennial in 2015. After one hundred years of planning, design, debates, fundraising, and construction to build a world-class City Beautiful Civic Center, San Francisco now had the most complete Civic Center according to its original plans in the United States. It now comprised thirteen monumental public buildings, ten of which had been built or beautifully restored after the 1989 Loma Prieta earthquake at a cost of more than $1.5 billion. Arts and entertainment venues were now so plentiful and popular that on some nights as many as 20,000 people participated in local cultural events. Large residential buildings were being constructed on the historic district's perimeter, beginning to make the Civic Center a twenty-four-hour-a-day neighborhood. Although the center's public areas remained unattractive, if not unsafe, the city had made it clear it was committed to developing new improvement plans. The hundredth anniversary should have been a time for celebration, but the year passed without note. The public's—and many city officials'—lack of understanding about the historical significance of the Civic Center, and the resulting decades of neglect, had taken a toll. The California Historical Society's elaborate year-long centennial commemorating the Panama-Pacific International Exposition was one-dimensional, focusing primarily on the history of the Exposition site. No reference was made to the PPIE's impact on local politics, the key election of James Rolph as mayor, or the Exposition's seminal role in creating the Civic Center. Mayor Lee hosted the United States Conference of Mayors in San Francisco in June, including a grand banquet in City Hall. New LED lighting replacing the old flood lights was installed on the building's exterior. The public was invited to the plaza to see the new lighting and a special light show. A documentary about City Hall was produced for showing subsequently on television. However, this effort was likewise one-dimensional and focused only on the building and not how it was intended to be a crucial part of a planned magnificent Civic Center. It was a public relations event that did not provide any background or knowledge about the broader context. The late *San Francisco Chronicle* columnist Herb Caen's complaints about the lack of a fiftieth anniversary commemoration were still apt a half-century later for the centennial. Indeed, some of the negative attitudes, ignorance, and even disdain toward the Civic Center that were endemic for decades continue to this day.

But there are also exciting efforts underway to help revitalize the Civic Center and combat some of that neglect. In spring 2017, the planning department held a competition for consultant teams to prepare the Civic Center Public Realm Plan. They selected a team head by CMG Landscape Architecture, which began work on July 1, 2017, almost twenty years after the start of the previous planning effort undertaken when Willie Brown was mayor. This effort will cost three times the amount of the previous effort. However, after this very long hiatus from having a comprehensive plan in place to address the Civic Center as a whole, hopefully these new projects will lead to changes that make the area more welcoming in the twenty-first century, and that will inspire the community to become more engaged in learning about and understanding the Civic Center, and ultimately be more excited by its remarkable and unique heritage.

Epilogue

On the evening of April 24, 2018, in the old Civic Auditorium more than a hundred San Franciscans gathered to listen and review the initial report and alternative plans for the public areas of the Civic Center which had been prepared by the consultants CMG Landscape Architects along with city staff as part of the Civic Center Public Realm Plan that had been authorized by Mayor Edwin Lee in 2014. Phil Ginsburg, San Francisco Recreation and Park Department general manager, opened the workshop with rousing remarks emphasizing that the Civic Center is a critical space at the heart of the city, containing the most remarkable collection of monumental municipal buildings of any American city. He called it a place for the city to celebrate, mourn, protest, play, and be entertained as well as an elegant historic place which should be welcoming to all people. He concluded by saying he sensed an energy and interest in the room about the Civic Center which he had never seen.

Nicholas Perry of the city planning staff explained the criteria and guidelines for the Public Realm Plan. Willett Moss of CMG Landscape Architects, the chief consultant, presented three alternative plans for review covering the plaza, Fulton Street, and UN Plaza. He said that they would be discussing these plans with a wide variety of groups during the upcoming months and then prepare a refined single plan. It was a watershed moment in the recent history of the Civic Center, and the excitement for what might result from this Public Realm Plan among the attendees, as Ginsberg noted, was palpable.

The enthusiasm to improve the Civic Center today far exceeds that generated when the last effort to produce a plan to improve the public realm was undertaken. Mayor Brown had aborted that plan before the work was completed in anticipation of possible problems affecting his upcoming reelection. No member of the board of supervisors expressed concern about the fact that the plan would not be completed, nor about the effects it would have on the conditions of the Civic Center more generally. Neither did any civic or preservation group.

Today, however, the situation is reversed. This major planning effort involves highly regarded consultants and participants from all city departments involved with the area. Because it is a broad effort, the mayor does not control the work. Despite this diverse and wide institutional support for the project, still there is much to be done. From the three alternatives presented for the Public Realm Plan, a single plan must be refined, and not just based on design ideas, but in a way that will generate strong public support. Moreover, the environmental review of the plan, which will take one or two years, has to be completed before the board of supervisors can make a decision to adopt the plan. Additionally, the actual cost of implementing the plan could be daunting. During this time, the historic patterns of disinterest and neglect could reoccur.

One of my goals with this book has been to try to head off a return to the same-old ways with the Civic Center, and instead to encourage through a deeper understanding of this site, the historic opportunity that this new planning initiative represents for San Francisco.

Civic center is not a descriptive term but a concept arising from the progressive reform era at the beginning of the twentieth century. It aimed to beautify and improve cities and uplift its people. San Francisco's Civic Center was the outgrowth of Congress granting the city the right to hold the Panama-Pacific International Exposition in 1915. Without it the city's divisive politics would probably have never allowed the Civic Center to happen. The PPIE changed the politics in San Francisco by electing as mayor James Rolph Jr., who pushed through the design and construction of the Civic Center and City Hall and oversaw the fulfillment of the plan for the next twenty years.

For the next eight decades, through periods of great inspiration and despite long periods of inaction, the city has maintained this historic site. It embraced the spirit and goals of John Galen Howard's 1912 plan for the Civic Center by completing it with the current total of thirteen massive buildings. This has been a powerful and enduring achievement.

Indeed, the San Francisco Civic Center represents a historic planning and political success worthy of a reputation much greater than that of a local landmark or simply being included on the National Registry of Historic Places. It should be viewed both locally and around the world as a unique manifestation of a national aesthetic and social movement which can never be replicated but that continues to exist—and plays a profound role—in San Francisco today. It is justly worthy of being nominated as a UNESCO World Heritage Site.

However, before such distinctions for the site can be achieved, the public areas of Civic Center have to be rehabilitated and made welcoming to all people. That is the purpose of the Public Realm Plan—to transform the Civic Center's public areas into a highly functional, attractive, and appealing site for the residents and visitors of San Francisco. The implementation of a major Public Realm Plan would exemplify the same urban design and social goals of the original City Beautiful proponents, architects, and thinkers who launched the movement more than 100 years ago. This plan, first unveiled in 2018, represents a historic opportunity to bring the public around to seeing, appreciating and—above all—*experiencing* the extraordinary value of the area.

My personal involvement for more than three decades with the San Francisco Civic Center has provided me with an opportunity to spend much of my life in the rewarding work of learning and writing about American and San Francisco history, and the significant and enduring legacies of urban planning and design. I have felt a singular satisfaction at seeing the realization of hard-fought improvements that the Civic Center has so dearly needed, as well as from the powerful opportunity to record its history through this book. It is indeed my hope that through these efforts the circle of appreciation and understanding of this great place will spread widely.

ACKNOWLEDGMENTS

I would like to acknowledge people who have encouraged and supported me in my endeavor in making this book happen.

As I mentioned in the preface, my longtime friend, Dr. Kevin Starr, encouraged me to complete this project. I would also like to acknowledge his wife, Sheila Starr, who brought the book to the attention of Justin Race, director of the University of Nevada Press, and helped convince him to consider publishing it.

In the preface, I also mentioned the support I have received from Charles Fracchia, the founding president of the San Francisco Museum and Historical Society. In addition to Charles, the whole organization has been supportive of the book, particularly Lorri Ungaretti, administrative director, who helped me with my articles published in the *Argonaut,* including the task of locating and getting permission to use photographs and other images.

Anne K. Mann and her colleagues at the Institute of Classical Architecture and Art in New York read my drafts and made significant suggestions. They encouraged me to write the first chapter on the origins of civic center and fit San Francisco's Civic Center into the larger picture of urban development at the beginning of the twentieth century.

My good friend William Sullivan, PhD, has been there to guide me while I placed the San Francisco experience among several historical movements and within the larger framework of national trends and developments.

Susan Goldstein, Christina Moretta, and the rest of the staff at the San Francisco Public Library History Center have always been responsive and patient with me while I searched for documents and images, often drilling down to the most detailed level while fulfilling my requests.

Many people read and commented on and made significant contributions to drafts of the book. Witold Rybczynski, emeritus professor of urbanism at the University of Pennsylvania, reviewed and commented on my first chapter. The following read and commented on chapters ten and eleven—Rudy Nothenberg, former chief administrative officer of San Francisco; Judy Wilbur, commissioner of the Asian Art Museum; Steve Coulter, former president of the San Francisco Library Commission; and Patrick Carney, commissioner of the City Hall Preservation Advisory Commission. As peer reviewers for the University of Nevada Press, John King, urban design critic for the *San Francisco Chronicle* and Dr. Vincent Michael, Executive Director of the San Antonio Conservation Society, read and commented on the whole manuscript.

The preparation of the book involved many costs, and the following were generous with contributions to help cover those costs—Tom Horn and the Bob Ross Foundation, Alice and Bill Russell-Shapiro, Tom Christian, Mary Lim, Oz Erickson, and Jay Turnbull.

Race of the University of Nevada Press had confidence in my rather turgid manuscript but felt that it could be improved. He recruited Christopher Lura, an experienced editor, to work with me to take the manuscript apart and rework it to emphasize the major themes, remove extraneous details and add explanatory and connecting material to make the book more accessible to people without a deep understanding of San Francisco. I appreciate the work that Justin and Chris have put into it. I have to conclude by commending my friend, John Bare, photographer extraordinaire, who volunteered to prepare a panoramic photograph of the Civic Center for the book cover and one of me making me look half way human. He succeeded greatly in both respects.

Portions of chapters one and four have been adapted from James W. Haas, "San Francisco and the City Beautiful: A History of the Civic Center," Part 1, *Argonaut* 26, no. 1 (Summer 2016).

Portions of chapters five and six have been adapted from James W. Haas, "San Francisco and the City Beautiful: A History of the Civic Center," Part 2, *Argonaut* 26, no. 2 (Winter 2016).

Portions of chapters seven and nine have been adapted from James W. Haas, "Civic Center in the Post-War Years," *Argonaut* 23, no. 1 (Spring 2012).

NOTES

Preface

1. Joan E. Draper, "The San Francisco Civic Center: Architecture, Planning, and Politics" (PhD dissertation, University of California, Berkeley, 1979).
2. Jeffrey T. Tilman, *Arthur Brown Jr.: Progressive Classicist* (New York: W. W. Norton, 2006).
3. James W. Haas, "Edward Robeson Taylor," part 1, *Argonaut* 18, no. 1 (Spring 2007); James W. Haas, "Edward Robeson Taylor," part 2, *Argonaut* 18, no. 2 (Summer 2007).
4. James W. Haas, "Civic Center in the Post-War Years," *Argonaut* 23, no. 1 (Spring 2012); James W. Haas, "San Francisco and the City Beautiful: A History of the Civic Center," part 1, *Argonaut* 26, no. 1 (Summer 2016); James W. Haas, "San Francisco and the City Beautiful: A History of the Civic Center," part 2, *Argonaut* 26, no. 2 (Winter 2016).

Introduction

1. Henry Hope Reed Jr., *The Golden City* (Garden City, NY: Doubleday, 1959).
2. Joan E. Draper, "The San Francisco Civic Center: Architecture, Planning, and Politics" (PhD dissertation, University of California, Berkeley, 1979), 354–98.
3. Paul Boyer, *Urban Masses and Moral Order in America, 1820–1920* (Cambridge, MA: Harvard University Press, 1978).

Chapter 1: The American Civic Center

1. Joan E. Draper, "The San Francisco Civic Center: Architecture, Planning, and Politics" (PhD dissertation, University of California, Berkeley, 1979), 354–98.
2. William H. Wilson, *The City Beautiful Movement* (Baltimore, MD: Johns Hopkins University Press, 1994), 1.
3. Witold Rybczynski, *A Clearing in the Distance: Frederick Law Olmsted and America in the Nineteenth Century* (New York: Scribner, 1999), 299–305.
4. Thomas S. Hines, *Burnham of Chicago: Architect and Planner*, 2nd ed. (Chicago: University of Chicago Press, 2009), 76–77.
5. Hines, *Burnham of Chicago*, 101.
6. Ibid., 119.
7. Wilson, *City Beautiful Movement*, 64.
8. Ibid., 109.
9. Ibid., 36–53.
10. Jon A. Peterson, *The Birth of City Planning in the United States, 1840–1917* (Baltimore, MD: Johns Hopkins University Press, 2003), 105–6.
11. Ibid., 127–28.
12. Hines, *Burnham of Chicago*, 161.
13. Ibid., 171
14. Charles Mulford Robinson, *Modern Civic Art: Or, The City Made Beautiful* (New York: G. P. Putnam's Sons, 1904), 92.
15. Ibid., 94.
16. Ibid., 82.
17. Draper, "The San Francisco Civic Center," 354–98.
18. Wilson, *City Beautiful Movement*, 202–4.

19. Ibid., 238.
20. Ibid., 242.
21. Ibid., 252.
22. Ibid., 86.
23. Ibid., 87.

Chapter 2: Victorian City Hall and Early City Planning in San Francisco

1. *San Francisco Daily Morning Chronicle*, January 1, 1869, 3.
2. *San Francisco Chronicle*, March 13, 1870, 4.
3. A. T. Spotts, "Report of the Board of New City Hall Commissioners," in *San Francisco Municipal Reports for the Fiscal Year 1888–89* (San Francisco: W. M. Hinton, 1889), 764–98, 767.
4. Stephen A. Otto, "Laver, Augustus," in *Dictionary of Canadian Biography*, vol. 12 (University of Toronto/Université Laval, 2003–), accessed December 5, 2015, http://www.biographi.ca/en/bio/laver_augustus_12E.html.
5. Ibid., 768.
6. Spotts, "Report of the Board of New City Hall Commissioners," 769.
7. *San Francisco Chronicle*, December 31, 1873, 4.
8. Spotts, "Report of the Board of New City Hall Commissioners," 775.
9. Ibid., 777.
10. Ibid., 783.
11. Ibid., 785.
12. *San Francisco Chronicle*, June 6, 1890, 8.
13. *San Francisco Chronicle*, June 8, 1890, 16.
14. *San Francisco Chronicle*, July 1, 1890, 7.
15. *San Francisco Chronicle*, July 23, 1890, 3.
16. "Report of the New City Hall Commissioners," July 1, 1892, *San Francisco Municipal Reports for the Fiscal Year 1891–92* (San Francisco: W. M. Hinton, 1892), 633–37, 633.
17. "Report of the Board of New City Hall Commissioners," July 1, 1894, in *San Francisco Municipal Reports for the Fiscal Year 1893–94* (San Francisco: W. M. Hinton, 1894), 509–513, 512.
18. *San Francisco Chronicle*, November 30, 1895, 9.
19. *San Francisco Chronicle*, July 13, 1897, 16.
20. Basin Research Associates, "San Francisco Main Library Project Archaeological Monitoring and Architectural Documentation of the Site of the Former City Hall Completed in 1897" (San Leandro, CA: 1984), 18.
21. Stephen Tobriner, *Bracing for Disaster Earthquakes: Resistant Architecture and Engineering in San Francisco 1838–1933* (Berkeley: Heyday Books, 2006), 4:76.

Chapter 3: California and the Chicago Exposition

1. *Final Report of the California World's Fair Commission* (Sacramento, CA: 1894), 7–8.
2. Ibid., 9.
3. Dianne Sachko Macleod, *Enchanted Lives, Enchanted Objects: American Women Collectors and the Making of Culture, 1800–1940* (Berkeley: University of California Press, 2008), 108.
4. *San Francisco Call*, July 15, 1893, 8.
5. James P. Walsh and Timothy J. O'Keefe, *Legacy of a Native Son: James Duval Phelan and Villa Montalvo* (Saratoga, CA: Forbes Mill Press, 1993), 58.
6. Jon A. Peterson, *The Birth of City Planning in the United States, 1840–1917* (Baltimore, MD: Johns Hopkins University Press, 2003), 10.
7. Samuel E. Moffett, "Western City of Learning," *Harpers Weekly*, September 11, 1897.
8. *San Francisco Chronicle*, December 4, 1898, 4.
9. Judith Robinson, *The Hearsts: An American Dynasty* (Newark: University of Delaware Press, 1991), 295.

10. Bernard J. S. Cahill, "A Plan to Beautify Market Street," *The California Architect and Building News* 20, no. 10 (October 20, 1899): 110–11.

11. Peterson, *Birth of City Planning*, 114.

12. Thomas S. Hines, *Burnham of Chicago: Architect and Planner*, 2nd ed. (Chicago: University of Chicago Press, 2009), 177.

13. Ibid., 178.

14. Ibid., 179.

15. Ibid., 180.

16. Bernard J. S. Cahill, "Adventurings in the Monumental," *The Architect and Engineer of California and the Pacific Coast* 65, no. 2 (August 1918): 71.

17. Ibid., 74.

18. Daniel H. Burnham and Edward H. Bennett, *Report on a Plan for San Francisco* (City of San Francisco, 1905), 39.

19. *San Francisco Chronicle*, December 17, 1904, 9.

20. Burnham and Bennett, *Report*, 88.

21. Ibid., 181.

22. *San Francisco Chronicle*, September 28, 1905, 9.

23. Hines, *Burnham of Chicago*, 189.

24. *San Francisco Chronicle*, January 17, 1906, 9.

25. *San Francisco Chronicle*, March 4, 1906, 26.

26. Hines, *Burnham of Chicago*, 182–88.

27. Ibid., 347.

28. Several hundred copies of the report were provided to the Association for the Improvement and Adornment of San Francisco and others close to the Burnham plan and then distributed further before the primary stock of the printed reports was delivered to City Hall, which helps explain the numerous original copies in libraries and private collections. Michael Dolgushkin, "Daniel H. Burnham's *Report on a Plan for San Francisco*," *California State Library Foundation Bulletin* no. 92 (2009): 8–12.

Chapter 4: The 1906 Earthquake's Aftermath

1. Stephen Tobriner, *Bracing for Disaster: Earthquake-Resistant Architecture and Engineering in San Francisco, 1838–1933* (Berkeley, CA: Heyday Books, 2006), 173.

2. Ibid., 113–14.

3. Richard Reinhardt, *Four Books, 300 Dollars, and a Dream: An Illustrated History of the First 150 Years of the Mechanics' Institute of San Francisco* (San Francisco: Mechanics' Institute, 2005), 7.

4. Ibid., 41.

5. Ibid., 51.

6. *San Francisco Chronicle*, May 13, 1903, 3.

7. Reinhardt, *Four Books, 300 Dollars and a Dream*, 68.

8. *San Francisco Chronicle*, April 30, 1906, 8.

9. *San Francisco Chronicle*, April 29, 1906, 3.

10. Meeting of the Citizens Committee (Committee of Fifty), April 30, 1906, 5–7.

11. *San Francisco Municipal Reports for the Fiscal Year 1905–6 . . . and Fiscal Year 1906–7* (San Francisco: Neal Publishing, 1908), 769.

12. Mel Scott, *The San Francisco Bay Area: A Metropolis in Perspective*, 2nd ed. (Berkeley: University of California Press, 1985), 113.

13. *San Francisco Chronicle*, May 16, 1906, 8.

14. Scott, *San Francisco Bay Area*, 115.

15. *San Francisco Chronicle*, June 12, 1906, 9.

16. *San Francisco Chronicle*, June 16, 1906, 2.

17. *San Francisco Chronicle*, September 6, 1906, 9.

18. *San Francisco Chronicle*, October 11, 1906, 6.

19. *San Francisco Municipal Reports for the Fiscal Year 1907–8* (San Francisco: Neal Publishing, 1909), 1334–45, esp. 1341–42; *San Francisco Municipal Reports for the Fiscal Year 1909–10* (San Francisco: Neal Publishing, 1911).

20. *San Francisco Chronicle*, April 14, 1909, 9.

21. *San Francisco Chronicle*, April 20, 1909, 5.

22. Scott, *San Francisco Bay Area*, 121.

23. *San Francisco Call*, February 20, 1910, 22.

24. *San Francisco Chronicle*, May 24, 1909, 6.

25. *San Francisco Chronicle*, April 26, 1909, 5.

26. Bernard J. S. Cahill, "Adventurings in the Monumental," *The Architect and Engineer of California and the Pacific Coast* 65, no. 2 (August 1918): 76.

27. Scott, *San Francisco Bay Area*, 122.

28. *San Francisco Chronicle*, October 25, 1910, 6.

Chapter 5: The Panama-Pacific International Exposition

1. *San Francisco Bulletin*, January 4, 1904, 1.

2. Frank Morton Todd, *The Story of the Exposition*, vol. 1 (New York: Published for the Panama-Pacific International Exposition Company by G. P. Putnum's Sons, 1921), 35.

3. *San Francisco Chronicle*, October 6, 1909, 1.

4. *San Francisco Chronicle*, March 15, 1911, 4.

5. *San Francisco Chronicle*, April 16, 1911, 32.

6. *San Francisco Chronicle*, August 12, 1911, 16.

7. *San Francisco Chronicle*, November 16, 1911, 1.

8. *San Francisco Chronicle*, December 8, 1911.

9. *San Francisco Chronicle*, December 13, 1911, 1.

10. *San Francisco Chronicle*, December 29, 1911, 1.

11. *San Francisco Chronicle*, January 6, 1912, 18.

12. *San Francisco Chronicle*, January 9, 1912, 1.

13. *San Francisco Chronicle*, January 11, 1912, 1.

14. *San Francisco Chronicle*, January 16, 1912, 1.

15. Bernard J. S. Cahill to James Rolph Jr., April 18, 1912, Bernard J. S. Cahill Records, Environmental Design Archives, College of Environmental Design, University of California, Berkeley.

Chapter 6: Breaking Ground on the Civic Center

1. *San Francisco Chronicle*, January 30, 1912, 3.

2. Ibid.

3. *San Francisco Chronicle*, January 11, 1912, 1.

4. *San Francisco Chronicle*, February 13, 1912, 1.

5. *San Francisco Chronicle*, February 29, 1912, 4.

6. *San Francisco Chronicle*, March 5, 1912, 9.

7. *San Francisco Chronicle*, March 7, 1912, 8.

8. *San Francisco Chronicle*, March 10, 1912, 38.

9. *San Francisco Chronicle*, March 20, 1912, 7.

10. *San Francisco Chronicle*, March 26, 1912, 18.

11. *San Francisco Chronicle*, March 30, 1912, 2.

12. Ibid.

13. *San Francisco Chronicle*, April 2, 1912, 1.

14. Ibid.

15. *San Francisco Chronicle*, May 29, 1912, 20.

16. *San Francisco Chronicle*, June 28, 1912, 12.

17. *San Francisco Chronicle*, July 2, 1912, 13.

18. Bernard J. S. Cahill, "The San Francisco City Hall Competition—A Criticism," *The Architect and Engineer of California* 29, no. 3 (July 1912): 53–75.

19. Jeffrey T. Tilman, *Arthur Brown Jr.: Progressive Classicist* (New York: W. W. Norton, 2006), 75.

20. *San Francisco Chronicle*, June 22, 1912, 6.

21. Cahill, "San Francisco City Hall Competition," 75–78.

22. *San Francisco Chronicle*, July 3, 1912, 20.

23. Sally Byrne Woodbridge, *John Galen Howard and the University of California: The Design of a Great Public University Campus* (Berkeley: University of California Press, 2002), 123.

24. John Galen Howard, "The Future of Architecture on the Pacific Coast," *The Architect and Engineer of California* 29, no. 1 (May 1912): 40–46.

25. Woodbridge, *John Galen Howard*, 123.

26. *San Francisco Chronicle*, March 28, 1913, 11.

27. Woodbridge, *John Galen Howard*, 127.

28. *San Francisco Chronicle*, December 29, 1912, 28.

29. *San Francisco Chronicle*, June 11, 1913, 13.

30. *San Francisco Chronicle*, March 31, 1928, 17.

31. *San Francisco Chronicle*, February 4, 1913, 18.

32. *San Francisco Chronicle*, June 12, 1913, 1.

33. *San Francisco Chronicle*, November 11, 1913, 4.

34. *San Francisco Chronicle*, November 20, 1913, 8.

35. *San Francisco Chronicle*, November 22, 1913, 1.

36. *San Francisco Bulletin*, November 21, 1913, 1.

37. *San Francisco Bulletin*, November 22, 1913, 3.

38. *San Francisco Chronicle*, February 19, 1914, 6.

39. *San Francisco Chronicle*, November 7, 1912, 6.

40. *San Francisco Chronicle*, April 26, 1914, 31.

41. Bernard J. S. Cahill, "The San Francisco Public Library Competition," *The Architect and Engineer of California* 37, no. 1 (May 1914): 63.

42. *San Francisco Call and Post*, May 15, 1914, 2.

43. *San Francisco Call and Post*, May 19, 1914, 4.

44. *San Francisco Chronicle*, May 13, 1916, 4.

45. *San Francisco Chronicle*, November 17, 1916, 10.

46. *San Francisco Chronicle*, February 25, 1917, 33.

47. *San Francisco Chronicle*, March 1, 1917, 10.

48. *San Francisco Chronicle*, March 9, 1917, 9.

49. Joan E. Draper, "The San Francisco Civic Center: Architecture, Planning, and Politics" (PhD dissertation, University of California, Berkeley, 1979), 226.

50. *San Francisco Chronicle*, March 8, 1917, 9.

51. *San Francisco Chronicle*, June 5, 1917, 16.

52. *San Francisco Chronicle*, August 26, 1914, 13.

53. *San Francisco Chronicle*, May 7, 1914, 13.

54. *San Francisco Chronicle*, November 30, 1913, 42.

55. *San Francisco Chronicle*, March 25, 1915, 18.

56. *San Francisco Chronicle*, January 10, 1915, 29.

57. *San Francisco Chronicle*, August 1, 1915, 19.

58. Draper, "San Francisco Civic Center," 223.

59. *San Francisco Chronicle*, June 11, 1915, 34.

60. *San Francisco Chronicle*, December 29, 1915, 9.
61. *San Francisco Chronicle*, December 31, 1915, 4.
62. *San Francisco Chronicle*, January 1, 1916, 3.
63. *San Francisco Chronicle*, August 30, 1916, 16.
64. *San Francisco Chronicle*, August 3, 1918.

Chapter 7: Between the Wars: Mayor Rolph Forges Ahead

1. *San Francisco Chronicle*, June 12, 1922, B4.
2. *San Francisco Examiner*, April 4, 1922.
3. *San Francisco Chronicle*, May 31, 1922, 4.
4. *San Francisco Chronicle*, November 30, 1913, 42.
5. Edward F. O'Day, ed. "San Francisco Public Schools," *Shapes of Clay* 3, no. 6 (San Francisco: Gladding, McBean and Co., July 1927), 6
6. *San Francisco Chronicle*, September 26, 1916, 5.
7. *San Francisco Examiner*, January 7, 1923.
8. *San Francisco Chronicle*, January 19, 1923, 3.
9. *San Francisco Chronicle*, January 8, 1924, 3.
10. *San Francisco Chronicle*, January 24, 1925, 6.
11. *San Francisco Chronicle*, November 28, 1925, 19.
12. *San Francisco Chronicle*, December 1, 1925, 3.
13. *San Francisco Chronicle*, December 2, 1925.
14. *San Francisco Chronicle*, December 6, 1925, 73.
15. Letter from the Committee on Architecture of the San Francisco Arts Commission to Mayor Elmer E. Robinson, July 7, 1948, author's personal files.
16. *San Francisco Chronicle*, February 27, 1925, 17.
17. *San Francisco Chronicle*, April 16, 1925, 9.
18. *San Francisco Chronicle*, July 16, 1925, 13.
19. *San Francisco Chronicle*, January 4, 1928, 4.
20. *San Francisco Chronicle*, February 27, 1931, 4.
21. *San Francisco Chronicle*, December 6, 1916, 1.
22. *San Francisco Chronicle*, February 25, 1928, 1.
23. Ibid.
24. *San Francisco Chronicle*, September 5, 1929, 18.
25. David Cannadine, *Mellon: An American Life* (New York: Alfred A. Knopf, 2006), 374.
26. *San Francisco Chronicle*, September 20, 1930, 2.
27. *San Francisco Chronicle*, May 16, 1936, 4.

Chapter 8: Between the Wars: Veterans and the Temple of Music

1. *San Francisco Chronicle*, April 16, 1916, 43.
2. *San Francisco Chronicle*, September 11, 1919, 7.
3. *San Francisco Chronicle*, September 13, 1919, 13.
4. Arthur Bloomfield, *The San Francisco Opera: 1922–1978* (Sausalito, CA: Comstock Editions, 1978), 16.
5. *San Francisco Chronicle*, May 19, 1920, 17.
6. Bloomfield, *San Francisco Opera*, 17.
7. Ibid., 18.
8. *San Francisco Chronicle*, May 13, 1922, 11.
9. Jeffrey T. Tilman, *Arthur Brown Jr.: Progressive Classicist* (New York: W. W. Norton, 2006), 100.
10. Leta E. Miller, *Music and Politics in San Francisco: From the 1906 Quake to the Second World War* (Berkeley: University of California Press, 2011), 158–60.
11. Bloomfield, *San Francisco Opera*, 20.

12. Ibid.

13. Ibid., 21.

14. Ibid.

15. *San Francisco Chronicle*, June 2, 1927, 5.

16. *San Francisco Chronicle*, June 9, 1927, 4.

17. Tilman, *Arthur Brown Jr.*, 103.

18. Ibid., 104.

19. Bloomfield, *San Francisco Opera*, 22–23.

20. Tilman, *Arthur Brown Jr.*, 104.

21. Bloomfield, *San Francisco Opera*, 24.

22. *San Francisco Chronicle*, November 2, 1928, 1.

23. *San Francisco Chronicle*, December 8, 1928, 13.

24. *San Francisco Chronicle*, August 26, 1929, 1.

25. *San Francisco Chronicle*, September 17, 1929, 10.

26. Bloomfield, *San Francisco Opera*, 25.

27. *San Francisco Examiner*, October 13, 1929, 3.

28. *San Francisco Examiner*, October 14, 1929, 1.

29. *San Francisco Examiner*, October 15, 1929, 5.

30. *San Francisco Chronicle*, March 4, 1931, 1.

31. Bloomfield, *San Francisco Opera*, 25.

32. *San Francisco Chronicle*, November 12, 1931, 13.

33. Tilman, *Arthur Brown Jr.*, 103.

34. Charles Kendrick, *Memoirs of Charles Kendrick*, ed. David Warren Ryder (San Francisco, 1972), xiv.

Chapter 9: Postwar and Modernism

1. *San Francisco Examiner*, April 12, 1942, 8.

2. Roger W. Lotchin, *The Bad City in the Good War: San Francisco, Los Angeles, Oakland, and San Diego* (Bloomington: Indiana University Press, 2003).

3. Roger W. Lotchin, ed., *The Way We Really Were: The Golden State in the Second Great War* (Urbana and Chicago: University of Illinois Press, 2000).

4. San Francisco Registrar of Voters, ballot booklet for general municipal election of November 2, 1948.

5. *San Francisco Examiner*, February 28, 1952, 40.

6. San Francisco Department of City Planning, *An Introductory Plan for the Civic Center*, June 19, 1953.

7. San Francisco Registrar of Voters, ballot booklet for general municipal election of November 3, 1953.

8. San Francisco Registrar of Voters, ballot booklet for general municipal election of November 2, 1954.

9. Minutes of the San Francisco Forward, Building Subcommittee, May 2, 1954, papers of Mayor Elmer E. Robinson, San Francisco History Center, San Francisco Public Library.

10. San Francisco Registrar of Voters, ballot booklet for general municipal election of November 8, 1955.

11. San Francisco Registrar of Voters, ballot booklets for general municipal elections of November 5, 1957, and November 4, 1958.

12. San Francisco Registrar of Voters, ballot booklet for general municipal election of November 3, 1959.

13. *San Francisco Chronicle*, February 12, 1959, 3.

14. Minutes of the San Francisco Arts Commission, August 3, 1959.

15. *San Francisco Chronicle*, March 1, 1961, 2.

16. *San Francisco Examiner*, September 15, 1961; *San Francisco Chronicle*, September 13, 1961.

17. Minutes of the San Francisco Arts Commission, March 5, 1962.

18. Minutes of the San Francisco Arts Commission, September 10, 1963.

19. Minutes of the San Francisco Arts Commission, July 8, 1964.

20. Minutes of the San Francisco Arts Commission, May 25, 1965.

21. *San Francisco Examiner*, May 26, 1965, 1.

22. *San Francisco Examiner*, May 30, 1965, 6.

23. *San Francisco Examiner*, May 27, 1965, 1.

24. *San Francisco Chronicle*, May 27, 1965, 4.

25. *San Francisco Chronicle*, August 13, 1965, 1.

26. Minutes of the San Francisco Arts Commission, March 2, 1966.

27. *San Francisco Examiner*, May 14, 1966, 21.

28. Minutes of the San Francisco Arts Commission, July 10, 1967.

29. *San Francisco Chronicle*, April 5, 1967, 5.

30. *San Francisco Chronicle*, June 19, 1966, 6.

31. San Francisco Department of City Planning, Mario J. Ciampi and Associates, and John Carl Warnecke and Associates, *Market Street Design Plan–Summary Report*, November 6, 1967. Accessed March 30, 2017, https://archive.org/details/marketstreetdesi6196sanf.

32. *San Francisco Chronicle*, May 26, 1968, 11.

33. *San Francisco Chronicle*, December 22, 1970, 5.

34. *San Francisco Chronicle*, May 8, 1971, 8.

35. *San Francisco Chronicle*, November 2, 1971, 4.

36. Ilene Lelchuk, "U.N. Plaza's Architect to Fight Redesign: Famed Planner Calls S.F. Plan no Answer to Drunks, Homeless," *San Francisco Chronicle*, April 18, 2003, http://www.sfgate.com/bayarea/article/U-N-Plaza-s-architect-to-fight-redesign-Famed-2654628.php.

37. Junior League of San Francisco, *Here Today: San Francisco's Architectural Heritage* (San Francisco: Chronicle Books, 1968).

Chapter 10: Late-Century Expansion

1. *San Francisco Chronicle*, December 13, 1965, 27.

2. *San Francisco Examiner*, August 9, 1973, 3.

3. *San Francisco Examiner*, April 4, 1973, 9.

4. *San Francisco Examiner*, May 2, 1973, 6.

5. *San Francisco Chronicle*, May 8, 1974, 4.

6. *San Francisco Examiner*, August 9, 1974, 22.

7. *San Francisco Chronicle*, November 27, 1974, 2.

8. *San Francisco Chronicle*, December 5, 1974, 6.

9. *San Francisco Examiner*, January 14, 1975, 2.

10. *San Francisco Chronicle*, February 4, 1975, 6.

11. *San Francisco Examiner*, February 3, 1975, 3.

12. *San Francisco Examiner*, July 14, 1975, 3.

13. Pace, Eric. "Edward Bassett, Architect, Is Dead at 77." *New York Times*, September 5, 1999, https://www.nytimes.com/1999/09/05/arts/edward-bassett-architect-is-dead-at-77.html.

14. *San Francisco Chronicle*, September 24, 1976, 11.

15. *San Francisco Chronicle*, January 16, 1978, 8.

16. *San Francisco Examiner*, January 10, 1978, 12.

17. *San Francisco Examiner*, June 14, 1981, 4.

18. *San Francisco Chronicle*, March 23, 1987, 5.

19. Letter from James W. Haas to Mayor Dianne Feinstein, April 10, 1985, author's personal files.

20. Memo from City Librarian John C. Frantz to Public Library Commissioners, May 9, 1985, author's personal files.

21. Wiley, Peter Booth. *A Free Library in This City: The Illustrated History of the San Francisco Public Library* (San Francisco: Weldon Owen, 1996), 196.

22. *San Francisco Chronicle*, August 27, 1986, 23.

23. San Francisco Board of Supervisors Resolution 938-86, October 27, 1986.

24. *The San Francisco Civic Center: A Study in Urban Form, Urban Design Recommendations for San*

Francisco's Civic Center (San Francisco: Urban Design Committee, American Institute of Architects, San Francisco Chapter, 1987), 1–24.

25. Wiley, *Free Library in This City*, 198.
26. *San Francisco Examiner*, October 6, 1987, B1.
27. *San Francisco Chronicle*, December 14, 1987, A6.
28. *San Francisco Chronicle*, December 31, 1987, A18.
29. San Francisco Board of Supervisors Resolution 1125-87, December 21, 1987.

Chapter 11: Recent Decades and the Present Day

1. *San Francisco Chronicle*, October 15, 1988, A2.
2. *San Francisco Chronicle*, October 20, 1988, A6.
3. *San Francisco Chronicle*, November 10, 1988, A15.
4. *San Francisco Chronicle*, February 15, 1989, A6.
5. *San Francisco Chronicle*, June 16, 1989, A3.
6. *San Francisco Chronicle*, October 21, 1989, A14.
7. *San Francisco Chronicle*, May 30, 1990, 2/Z1.
8. *San Francisco Chronicle*, April 9, 1993, A23.
9. Mark Cavagnero (architect, Civic Center Courthouse), in discussion with the author, January 22, 2016.
10. Dorothy Kitt (president, California Heritage Council) to the San Francisco Arts Commission, June 28, 1990, copy in the author's possession.
11. Senator Quentin Kopp to Steven A. Coulter (president, San Francisco Public Library Commission), April 23, 1991, copy in the author's possession.
12. Minutes of the San Francisco Arts Commission, April 29, 1991, 7–8.
13. *San Francisco Examiner*, June 10, 1991, A2.
14. *San Francisco Chronicle*, February 29, 1992, C10.
15. *San Francisco Chronicle*, April 11, 1992, A10.
16. *San Francisco Chronicle*, April 23, 1992, A13.
17. *San Francisco Chronicle*, July 7, 1992, A11.
18. *San Francisco Chronicle*, April 17, 1996, A13.
19. *San Francisco Chronicle*, May 7, 1996, A15.
20. *San Francisco Chronicle*, April 15, 1996, A15.
21. *San Francisco Chronicle*, October 14, 1992, A1.
22. *San Francisco Chronicle*, March 16, 1996, E1.
23. *San Francisco Chronicle*, September 21, 1993, A15.
24. *San Francisco Chronicle*, January 7, 1994, A26.
25. *San Francisco Chronicle*, December 11, 1998, A26.
26. *San Francisco Chronicle*, May 28, 1995, 1Z1.
27. *San Francisco Chronicle*, June 1, 1994, A16.
28. *San Francisco Chronicle*, October 25, 1993, E1.
29. Office of the Registrar of Voters, *San Francisco Voter Information Pamphlet and Sample Ballot*, November 8, 1994, 71, https://sfpl.org/pdf/main/gic/elections/November8_1994short.pdf.
30. Tony Irons, in discussion with the author, June 20, 2015.
31. Mark Cavagnero, in discussion with the author, January 22, 2016.
32. *San Francisco Chronicle*, April 27, 1996, A15.
33. *San Francisco Chronicle*, April 11, 1996, A13.
34. *San Francisco Chronicle*, April 24, 1996, A13.
35. *San Francisco Chronicle*, October 20, 1996, A1.
36. *San Francisco Chronicle*, April 25, 1996, A17.
37. *San Francisco Chronicle*, July 18, 1996, A17.

38. *San Francisco Chronicle*, October 29, 1997, A17.

39. *San Francisco Chronicle*, December 9, 1997, A17.

40. *San Francisco Chronicle*, December 23, 1997, A16.

41. *San Francisco Chronicle*, January 5, 1998, A17.

42. *San Francisco Chronicle*, May 15, 1998, A19.

43. *San Francisco Chronicle*, June 4, 1998, A17.

44. *San Francisco Chronicle*, June 23, 1998, A15.

45. Minutes of the San Francisco City Hall Dome Project Review meeting, January 12, 1998, copy in the author's possession.

46. *San Francisco Chronicle*, February 14, 1998, A15.

47. *San Francisco Chronicle*, February 18, 1998, A11.

48. City and County of San Francisco, *Journal of Proceedings, Board of Supervisors* 33, no. 54 (1938): 2153.

49. *San Francisco Chronicle*, November 13, 1998, A21.

50. *San Francisco Chronicle*, January 6, 1999, A11.

51. *New York Times*, January 2, 1999, A7.

52. *San Francisco Examiner*, December 29, 1998, A3.

53. *San Francisco Chronicle*, January 14, 1999, A15.

54. Willie Brown, *Basic Brown: My Life and Our Times* (New York: Simon and Schuster, 2008), 281.

55. *San Francisco Chronicle*, November 25, 1996, D1.

56. *San Francisco Chronicle*, August 13, 1996, B1.

57. *San Francisco Chronicle*, December 4, 1996, E1.

58. *San Francisco Chronicle*, February 26, 1997, B1.

59. *San Francisco Chronicle*, April 16, 1997, A20.

60. *San Francisco Chronicle*, July 15, 1997, D1.

61. *San Francisco Chronicle*, July 16, 1997, E1.

62. Susan Brandt-Hawley to Emily Sano (director, Asian Art Museum), July 14, 1997, copy in the author's possession.

63. *San Francisco Chronicle*, July 31, 1997, C1.

64. *San Francisco Chronicle*, December 16, 1997, A18.

65. David W. Look (Cultural Resources Team Leader, National Park Service) and Cherilyn Widell (California State Historic Preservation Officer) to Emily Sano, September 8, 1997, copy in the author's possession.

66. James W. Haas (chairman, Civic Pride!) to David W. Look and Cherilyn Widell, September 25, 1997, copy in the author's possession.

67. David W. Look and Cherilyn Widell to the author, October 21, 1997, copy in the author's possession.

68. Joan E. Draper (associate professor, College of Architecture and Planning, University of Colorado) to the author, November 10, 1997, copy in the author's possession.

69. David A. Bahlman (executive director, Foundation for San Francisco's Architectural Heritage) to the author, November 21, 1997, copy in the author's possession.

70. *San Francisco Examiner*, September 3, 1998, 5.

71. *San Francisco Chronicle*, September 4, 1998, A21.

72. *San Francisco Examiner*, December 11, 1998, 3.

73. Senator Dianne Feinstein to Bruce Babbitt (secretary of the interior), November 13, 1998.

74. *San Francisco Chronicle*, January 26, 1999, A18.

75. *San Francisco Chronicle*, February 18, 1999, A17.

76. *San Francisco Chronicle*, May 10, 1999, E2.

77. *San Francisco Chronicle*, June 4, 1999, A18.

78. "Defeat at the Old Main of the Heritage Priesthood," *San Francisco Examiner*, July 29, 1999, 23.

79. *San Francisco Chronicle*, October 1, 1999, A20.

80. *San Francisco Chronicle*, March 16, 2003, 12.

81. *San Francisco Chronicle*, March 17, 2003, D1.

82. *San Francisco Chronicle*, July 7, 2007, A1.

83. *San Francisco Chronicle*, May 10, 2009, B1.

84. Simon Martin-Vegue Winkelstein Moris et al., *A Program for Renovation and Revitalization*, San Francisco Civic Center Historic District Improvement Project, San Francisco Department of Public Works, October 1998, http://civiccentersf.org/wp-content/uploads/1998-SFCC-HDIP-Plan-Document.pdf.

85. *San Francisco Chronicle*, October 10, 2015, C1.

86. *San Francisco Chronicle*, October 10, 1998, A15.

87. *San Francisco Chronicle*, November 1, 2002, A23.

88. *San Francisco Chronicle*, September 16, 2008, E1.

89. *San Francisco Chronicle*, November 18, 2015, D1.

90. *San Francisco Chronicle*, September 17, 2015, D1.

91. *San Francisco Chronicle*, November 2, 2015, C1.

BIBLIOGRAPHY

Appelbaum, Stanley. *The Chicago World's Fair of 1893: A Photographic Record*. New York: Dover Publications, 1980.

Bean, Walton. *Boss Ruef's San Francisco*. Berkeley: University of California Press, 1952.

Bloomfield, Arthur. *The San Francisco Opera, 1922–1978*. Sausalito, CA: Comstock Editions, 1978.

Boyer, Paul. *Urban Masses and Moral Order in America, 1820–1920*: Cambridge, MA: Harvard University Press, 1978.

Brown, Willie. *Basic Brown: My Life and Our Times*. New York: Simon and Schuster, 2008.

Burnham, Daniel H. and Edward Bennett. *Report on a Plan for San Francisco*, edited by Edward F. O'Day. City of San Francisco, 1905.

Cahill, Bernard J. S. "A Plan to Beautify Market Street." *The California Architect and Building News* 20, no. 10 (October 20, 1899): 110–11.

———. "Adventurings in the Monumental," *The Architect and Engineer of California and the Pacific Coast* 65, no. 2 (August 1918): 39–97.

———. "The San Francisco City Hall Competition—A Criticism," *The Architect and Engineer of California* 29, no. 3 (July 1912): 53–78.

Cahill, Bernard J. S. "The San Francisco Public Library Competition," *The Architect and Engineer of California* 37, no. 1 (May 1914): 47-63.

Cannadine, David. *Mellon: An American Life*. New York: Alfred A. Knopf, 2006.

Dolgushkin, Michael. "Daniel H. Burnham's *Report on a Plan for San Francisco*," *California State Library Foundation Bulletin* no. 92 (2009): 8–12.

Draper, Joan E. "The San Francisco Civic Center: Architecture, Planning and Politics." PhD dissertation, University of California, Berkeley, 1979. *Final Report of the California World's Fair Commission*. Sacramento, CA: State Office, 1894.

Hines, Thomas S. *Burnham of Chicago: Architect & Planner*. 2nd edition. Chicago: University of Chicago Press, 2009.

Howard, John Galen. "The Future of Architecture on the Pacific Coast," *The Architect and Engineer of California* 29, no. 1 (May 1912): 40–46.

Issel, William. *For Both Cross and Flag: Catholic Action, Anti-Catholicism and National Security Politics in World War II San Francisco*. Philadelphia: Temple University Press, 2009.

Junior League of San Francisco. *Here Today: San Francisco's Architectural Heritage*. San Francisco: Chronicle Books, 1968.

Kahn, Judd. *Politics and Planning in an American City 1897–1906*. Lincoln, NE: University of Nebraska Press, 1979.

Kendrick, Charles. *Memoirs of Charles Kendrick*, ed. David Warren Ryder. San Francisco: 1972.

Lotchin, Roger W. *The Bad City in the Good War: San Francisco, Los Angeles, Oakland and San Diego*. Bloomington, IN: Indiana University Press, 2003.

———., ed. *The Way We Really Were: The Golden State in the Second Great War*. Urbana, IL and Chicago: University of Illinois Press, 2000.

Macleod, Dianne Sachko. *Enchanted Lives, Enchanted Objects: American Women Collectors and the Making of Culture, 1800–1940*. Berkeley: University of California Press, 2008.

Meeting of the Citizens Committee, April 30, 1906. San Francisco: Committee of Fifty, 1906.

Miller, Leta E. *Music and Politics in San Francisco; From the 1906 Quake to the Second World War*. Berkeley: University of California Press, 2011.

Nickliss, Alexandra M. *Phoebe Apperson Hearst: A Life of Power and Politics.* Lincoln, NE: University of Nebraska Press, 2018.

O'Day, Edward F., ed. "San Francisco Public Schools," *Shapes of Clay* 3, no. 6 (San Francisco: Gladding, McBean and Co., July 1927): 1–6.

Peterson, Jon A. *The Birth of City Planning in the United States 1840–1917.* Baltimore, MD: Johns Hopkins University Press, 2003.

Reed, Henry Hope Jr. *The Golden City.* Garden City, NY: Doubleday, 1959.

Richard, Reinhardt. *Four Books, 300 Dollars, and a Dream: An Illustrated History of the First 150 Years of the Mechanics' Institute of San Francisco.* San Francisco: Mechanics' Institute, 2005.

Robinson, Charles Mulford. *Modern Civic Art: Or the City Made Beautiful.* New York: G. P. Putnam's Sons, 1904.

Robinson, Judith. *The Hearsts: An American Dynasty.* Newark, DE: University of Delaware Press, 1991.

Rybczynski, Witold. *A Clearing in the Distance: Frederick Law Olmsted and America in the Nineteenth Century.* New York: Scribner, 1999.

Rydell, Robert W. *All the World's A Fair: Visions of Empire at American International Expositions 1876–1915.* Chicago: University of Chicago Press, 1987.

Scott, Mel. *The San Francisco Bay Area: A Metropolis in Perspective.* 2nd edition. Berkeley: University of California Press, 1985.

The San Francisco Civic Center: A Study in Urban Form, Urban Design Recommendations for San Francisco's Civic Center. San Francisco: Urban Design Committee, American Institute of Architects, San Francisco Chapter, 1987.

Tilman, Jeffrey T. *Arthur Brown Jr.: Progressive Classicist.* New York: W. W. Norton, 2006.

Tobriner, Stephen. *Bracing for Disaster: Earthquakes-Resistant Architecture and Engineering in San Francisco 1838–1933.* Berkeley: Heyday Books, 2006.

Todd, Frank Morton. *The Story of the Exposition: Volume One.* New York: G.P. Putnam's Sons, 1921.

Walsh, James P. and Timothy O'Keefe. *Legacy of a Native Son: James Duval Phelan & Villa Montalvo.* Saratoga, CA: Forbes Mill Press, 1993.

Wiley, Peter Booth. *A Free Library in This City: The Illustrated History of the San Francisco Public Library.* San Francisco: Weldon Owen, 1996.

Wilson, William H. *The City Beautiful Movement.* Baltimore, MD: Johns Hopkins University Press, 1989.

Woodbridge, Sally B. *John Galen Howard and the University of California: The Design of a Great Public University Campus.* Berkeley: University of California Press, 2002.

INDEX

Page numbers in italics indicate illustrations.

ABOUT THE AUTHOR

A descendant of Joaquin Gruenhagen who arrived in San Francisco in 1850, James W. Haas has lived most of his life in the city. After graduating from Stanford University in 1964 with a degree in history, he served for two years as the assistant director of the National Head Start program in Washington, DC. Graduating from Columbia Law School in 1969, he practiced law in San Francisco for almost forty years relating to planning, real estate, historic preservation, and banking. President Jimmy Carter appointed him in 1978 to the federal Advisory Committee on Historic Preservation on which he served for five years. He was also engaged in civic projects including committees demolishing the Embarcadero Freeway and rewriting the City Charter, improving transportation, and developing the new South Beach neighborhood. His major effort for the past 30 years has been the restoration and completion of the Civic Center starting with the new main library in 1984. Mayor Gavin Newsom appointed him to the City Hall Preservation Advisory Commission. Now retired, he has written about San Francisco including a biography of the long-forgotten Mayor Edward Robeson Taylor which appeared in the San Francisco Museum and Historical Society's journal *The Argonaut* in 2007 and articles on the history of the Civic Center which appeared in *The Argonaut* in 2012, 2015, and 2016.